THE SOVIET–AMERICAN ARMS RACE

*For Dot and Bill,
whose generation paid the price
for wishful thinking.*

'I have yet to see any problem, however complicated, which, when you looked at it the right way, did not become still more complicated.'

Poul Anderson (quoted in Arthur Koestler,
The Ghost in the Machine,
Pan, London, 1970, p.77).

The Soviet–American arms race

COLIN S. GRAY
Hudson Institute,
New York

SAXON HOUSE | LEXINGTON BOOKS

© Colin S. Gray, 1976.
All rights reserved. No part of this publication may be reprodqced, stored in a retrieval system, or transmitted in any form or by any means, electronic, mechanical, photocopying, recording, or otherwise without the prior permission of D. C. Heath Ltd.

Published by
SAXON HOUSE, D. C. Heath Ltd.
Westmead, Farnborough, Hants., England.

Jointly with
LEXINGTON BOOKS, D. C. Heath & Co.
Lexington, Mass., USA.

ISBN 0 347 01125 X
Library of Congress Catalog Card Number 75–28542
Printed in Great Britain by Robert MacLehose and Company Limited
Printers to the University of Glasgow

Computer typeset by Input Typesetting, 4 Valentine Place, London, SE1.

Contents

Preface   vii

1 THE NATURE OF AN ARMS RACE   1

2 ARMS RACE DYNAMICS   12
   Theory for Policy   12
   Foreign Policy Goals   15
   Interstate Action–Reaction Processes   18
   Interservice Action–Reaction Processes   23
   Intraservice Action–Reaction Processes   27
   Bureaucratic Politics   28
   The Character of Political–Social Systems   31
   Electoral Politics   33
   Organisational Momentum   37
   Technological Innovation   39
   Follow-on Imperatives   43
   The Military–Industrial Complex (MIC)   47

3 THE ARMS RACE ADVERSARIES: SYMMETRIES AND
   ASYMMETRIES   58
   An American Adversary?   58
   Defence Politics and the Political System   61
   Ideology, Culture and Historical Tradition   65
   Geopolitics and Foreign Policy Goals   69
   Strategic Doctrine and Strategic Weaponry   75

4 PATTERNS OF INTERACTION?   96
   The Many Faces of Reality   96
   Model 1: *Eigendynamik*   100
   Model 2: Random Response   102
   Model 3: Macro Response   104
   Model 4: Limited Response   110
   Model 5: Differential Response   115
   Model 6: Mechanistic Response   123

5	STRATEGIC POSTURES AND NEW TECHNOLOGIES	128
	Arms Control and Strategic Posture	128
	Technology and the Range of Postural Choice	130
	Assured Destruction	149
	Counterforce	160
	Defensive Emphasis	170
	Evaluating Strategic Postures	174
6	ARMS RACE AND ARMS CONTROL	181
Selected Glossary		189
Index		193

Preface

Most scholars and officials concerned with defence and arms control policies are now convinced that there is an urgent need for the analysis of particular problems to be set in the context of a broad understanding of the nature of the arms race system. The lack of such understanding has been very apparent in the major strategic debates of the past twenty years. Time after time, as this book seeks to demonstrate, predicted 'arms race consequences' have been invoked in defence of a particular position, despite the fact that those introducing the alleged 'consequences' have never stood back to consider Soviet–American strategic interaction chains as an arms race. Simplified logical models of interaction processes have been wielded as weapons in debate, while the real complexity of the arms race system has escaped serious investigation. This book is intended as a contribution to an improved understanding of that system. Much of the discussion is inconclusive; we have a redundancy of arms race explanatory theorems. At the very least, though, this book assembles the diverse elements for improved arms race theory and should help to demonstrate the inadequacy of analyses which ignore, with or without explanation, those elements which are found to be inconvenient.

This is also a book about policy choices. In a systematic, though not policy neutral way, the range of postural choice is considered in the half-light provided by the preceding analysis of the functioning of the arms race system. The Strategic Arms Limitation Talks (SALT) intrude forcibly at this juncture, but this is not a book addressed primarily to arms control questions. My argument is that arms controllability is but one of the criteria for a 'good strategic posture'. Unless it is first decided what does constitute an adequate strategic posture, there can be no robust basis for devising arms control policy. Arms control should serve the needs of defence, not vice versa. In the long run, technically poor arms control agreements damage both political detente processes and military security.

An earlier version of this book was written for and issued by the Rand Corporation.* I would like to thank my friends in and around Rand, and in the United States government, for their assistance in this project. In particular, I am grateful to Dr Thomas Brown, formerly of the Mathematics Department at Rand, for his efforts on my behalf. This book is the

* *The Soviet–American arms race; Interactive patterns and new technologies,* WN–8719–ARPA (Santa Monica: Rand, August 1974).

culmination of many years of research and reflection on arms race phenomena and it owes its shape and some of its detail to the encouragement that I have received over the years from like-minded people. Two friends in particular must be mentioned, Mark B. Schneider of the Energy Research and Development Administration (ERDA), and William R. Van Cleave of the University of Southern California. The contribution of my wife, Valerie, as sceptical reader, jargon-diminisher and typist was indispensable. To her, as always, I owe a profound debt of gratitude. Responsibility for the content of this book is mine alone.

Colin S. Gray
September 1975

1 The Nature of an Arms Race

In increasing numbers, bold arms controllers are setting forth upon quests that will, they hope, terminate with the slaying of the arms race dragon. Alas, pure heart and trusty equations will prove insufficient. There is every reason to believe that the complexities of arms race behaviour will prove as immune to the surgery of determined analysis as are many of the problems of political competition to quick technological 'fixes'. However one elects to caricature the arms race, as dragon or as some analogical sporting activity, it is desirable that the reasons for analytical investigation be made explicit. An insubstantial, though firmly held, notion that somehow arms races are *bad* is not the intellectual baggage that is likely to prove useful for any analysis concerned more to understand behaviour than it is to condemn villainy. Balanced analysis cannot be guided by a simple determination to halt, or even to brake, the arms race. Halting an arms race, like achieving detente or securing short term prospects for 'peace in our time', is usually attainable through policies of diminished military effort and/or political accommodation. Contrary to the implications of much of the contemporary writing on arms control subjects, it is not here presumed that a reified arms race – however it functions – is the principal threat to security. Begging many important questions, the fundamental purpose of this study is to help contribute to the making of better defence policy decisions. Logically at least, Americans are not trapped in a labyrinth of behavioural nexi collectively termed 'the nuclear arms race'. By adopting the strategic preferences of some of the more rigorous of the Mutual Assured Destroyers (or MAD bombers, to slip into the pejorative), the nuclear arms race as a bilateral, interstate phenomenon could be decelerated very rapidly indeed. Unfortunately, as nearly all strategic analysts appreciate (though not all will acknowledge), a thorough-going self-denial by the United States of nuclear arms race activity could well have insecurity consequences that would be profoundly unwelcome.

Defence policy prescription, and even the understanding of possible interstate strategic interaction chains, have been hindered by the popularity of the term 'arms race'. To proceed inductively, popular contemporary commentators, diplomatic historians, and arms control analysts assert that there has been a series of arms races from the 1840s to the present day – the phenomenon being generally regarded as one of the less attractive, yet distinctive, features of industrial civilisation. As C. B. Joynt has suggested, it is far from self-evident that the arms race track of interstate conflict may be laid exclusively at the door of the factory system, of the fact 'that States were more consciously aware of the dependence of their arms policy on the policies of other states or the pre-eminence of forces-in-being over territory as an element in national power'.[1] To what do commentators refer when they employ the language of arms race? Unhelpfully, it might just be possible to argue that the term 'arms race' simply beckons the unworldly scholarly pedant and that it is really a term beyond useful definition. In company with, for example, detente, national interest, and similar emotive symbols, arms race is ineradicable from the language of politics.

In policy terms, this study is concerned with exploring the range of strategic postural choices that the United States must face in the mid to late 1970s, identifying the attendant technologies and the arms control possibilities and difficulties in the light of the preceding exploration of arms race processes. In order to do this, a great deal of ground must first be cleared. To a considerable extent, people need to unlearn much of the arms race 'truth' that has been generated by the arms control community over the past fifteen years. This is written without prejudice to the strategic preferences of any individual or group. It so happens, that the bow-wave of popular arms race generalisation has tended to be created by those who have struggled to inhibit the multifarious programmes designed (or at least rationalised) to limit damage. This author is not an assiduous damage limiter; he is more a political container, but he does find the variants on a mutual assured destruction (MAD) theme to be both morally repugnant and profoundly impolitic. Arms race analysis is not here being employed for the attempted demolition of assured destruction (or even of minimum deterrent) arguments. With a more advanced state of arms race understanding, all parties to strategic doctrinal contention should be able to use better arms race arguments, while the resulting defence policy of doctrinal engagement (recognising that policy is not the product only of ideas good, bad or indifferent) should rest upon and engender fewer illusions. The Manichean views of some of the more uncompromising damage limiters are every bit as simplistic and careless as are the opinions of their doctrinal polar adversaries.

Although it is usual to talk of specific arms races, run between distinctive self- and other-conscious adversaries, and in particular classes of weaponry over an identifiable span of years,[2] it is useful to appreciate the limitations of this mode of thinking. It is appropriate to observe that the 'arms race' suggests the following: an abnormal quality to interstate defence interactions (unusual effort and fear, for example); a finite course (even a marathon has a finite length); and heightened danger (that has both promoted the race and been amplified by it). Given a high measure of analytical sensitivity to these features of a race, it would seem reasonable to refer to a Soviet–American nuclear arms race as an affront to notions of *normal* interstate relations. However, such an attitude may well exaggerate the abnormality of Soviet–American strategic relations. Indeed, it may be held that the arms race behaviour of a Great Power differs from the *normal* defence policy behaviour of a Great Power only in that it is 'more of the same'. Furthermore, it is far from self-evident that in this case quantity induces any very marked change in quality.

So-called arms races should not be viewed as pathological conditions to be exorcised by careful analysis. Rather they should be seen as the inescapable products of an international system that is sustained by political conflict as well as co-operation between its members. Once an arms race has 'taken off' into apparently self-sustained technological growth, it is all too easy not to appreciate the political rivalries that fundamentally move the state actors. Soviet–American military competition has not been catalysed and vitally sustained by, and for the benefit of, national security managers who enjoy playing the game of nations. [3] Whatever the small change of bureaucratic politics may have been over the development of particular weapon systems, the Soviet Union has posed and will continue to pose an inalienable threat to Central and Western Europe. The shadow of Soviet military power, if unmatched in the West, is very likely to produce the 'Finlandisation' or 'GDRisation' of all of Europe. The 'threat from the East' has certainly been exaggerated at times, but Cold War revisionism has neglected the basic nature of international politics. Conflict over the future of Europe was inevitable after World War II.

Ideological distaste may play a part in catalysing the political conflict that breathes life into an arms race, but capability analysis is more important. The character of the Soviet regime certainly served to amplify Soviet–American political conflict, but there is every reason to presume that political conflicts and arms races would have followed World War II, regardless of the nature of the Russian political system. The Soviet Union was just too powerful in the European sub-continent.

This somewhat Gothic model of world politics has been presented both to make explicit the framework of assumptions of the author, and to cast some doubts upon the well-intentioned hyperbole of many members of the arms control establishment. For net security producers, a condition identifiable as one of arms race is very much a case of business as usual. In providing definitions of 'arms race', authors tend to state as *a priori* truths some of those things that still need to be proved. Bearing this danger in mind, I favour the following definition:

... there should be two or more parties perceiving themselves to be in an adversary relationship, who are increasing or improving their armaments at a *rapid* rate and structuring their respective military postures with a *general* attention to the past, current, and anticipated military and political behavior of the other parties.[4]

This definition is intended as a minimal statement only. In every race some apparent instances will be found of very specific responses to very specific identified actions (or anticipated actions) on the part of the arms race rival. The definition draws attention to the political relationship between the adversaries and eschews any judgement on the specific nature (a) of the military interactions or (b) of the arms race goals of the racing states. Two very general fallacies attend arms race analysis: they are the nominative and the non-exclusive categories (otherwise known as distinctions without a difference). Once a process has been identified and given a name, in this case, 'arms race', it is reasonable to presume that there is substance behind the name. In much the same way, familiarity has produced the definite article in front of detente. If it has a name, it must exist. Similarly, to turn to the related fallacy, to conceive of arms race is to conceive of non-arms race. Surely so many commentators and historians could not refer to a distinct category of protracted international events known as arms races, unless there were some fairly unambiguous criteria for distinguishing between the relevant events and non-events?

If the history of war teaches anything, it is that the ideas that produce particular force structures and particular conceptions of military use are quite as important as the quantity and quality of forces. Arms race behaviour thus embraces a wide range of activities that may be monitored by the analyst. Those arms race analysts addicted to the contemplation of the cruder measurements of military activity (for example, budgets, weapon system numbers, deliverable warheads and equivalent megatonnage or EMT[5] seem destined to ignore much of the more salient arms race action. As Albert Wohlstetter has demonstrated, the taking of weapons and monetary pulse rates could well lead an analyst to the uncomfortable conclusion that there is no strategic arms race at all.[6] The less restrained members of the arms control movement (or interest) are wont to cite the escalating costs of weaponry, the futile spiralling of action and reaction, and the growing dangers to mankind that attend this 'mad momentum'.[7] This is no straw target: if anything the arms race imagery (or metaphor) has here been understated. Eight points serve to cast doubt upon such imagery.

First, spending by the United States on strategic forces has shown a marked decline from its high point in FY 1959. It has been estimated that approximately one-fifth of the defence budget is spent on strategic forces.[8]

In absolute terms the sum is high (one estimate of investment and operating costs in FY 1973 was close to $17 billion), but one is talking here of 1.4 per cent of the United States' GNP. If by the strategic (or nuclear) arms race one means only strategic forces, it is difficult to see how – regardless of one's ideological cast – the allocation of 1.4 per cent of GNP is squared with assertions of runaway arms race expenditure. Furthermore, it is worth recalling that this figure of $17 billion provides little indication of the scale of strategic investment; rather it points to the particular competitive disabilities of the United States, namely, inflation and very high personnel costs.

Second, statistical neatness is confounded by the fact that the United States, in common with other racing agents of the past, does not pursue the strategic arms race with an all-encompassing dedication. Not all of her defence expenditure is to be attributed to arms race rationales. Nonetheless, the Soviet–American strategic balance far transcends any simple competition in one or even a handful of dominant weapons (in different environments). The most prominent indices of who is up and who is relatively down are certainly such crude items as numbers of intercontinental ballistic missiles (ICBMs), submarine–launched ballistic missiles (SLBMs), manned bombers, deliverable warheads, or gross megatonnage, EMT and the like. However, in this arms race the total military posture is potentially politically significant in Superpower relations.

Third, the United States is currently spending very close to 5 per cent of her GNP on defence (the estimate for FY 1976). At the height of World War II the figure was close to 40 per cent. This is not to suggest either that too much or too little is currently being spent. It is simply to suggest that the financial facts give the lie to those who see the United States as an armed society wherein defence spending is out of control. Bearing in mind the connotations of the term 'race', the United States is not really trying – at least in obvious financial terms.

Fourth, there has been no simple action–reaction mechanism or 'spiral' fuelling the strategic arms race.[9] Each side has certainly been sensitive to the programmes of the other, which is to say that there are *prima facie* grounds for exploring the Soviet–American relationship to see if it qualifies for characterisation as an arms race. On the other hand, each side has tended to do that which best accorded with its own strategic beliefs and with the interests of its bureaucratic power constellations. For good reasons, the 'other side' more often than not has appeared, for example, as a very *American* opponent. In the absence of evidence to the contrary, one naturally tends to presume that the adversary behaves according to a familiar strategic logic.

Fifth, an assault on the action–reaction postulate (and some of the claimed evidence for the operation of a tight action–reaction chain, for example, relating to MIRV) has come to serve the policy prescriptive interests of nearly all major bodies of opinion seeking to influence national security affairs. The pendulum against action–reaction has now swung too far.

Sixth, the arms race 'spiral' metaphor returns us to Herbert York's proposition alleging that the United States has suffered a diminution in security as the arms race has condinued.[10] This is beginning to be a justifiable proposition, but not on grounds that Herbert York would find acceptable. Rather could one argue that the United States is now approaching a period wherein, according to certain prominent indices of relative capability, she will be quite unambiguously behind the Soviet Union. Anyone who is familiar with the Rand vulnerability studies of the 1950s – whatever the *political* viability of their assumptions may have been[11] – could scarcely fail to appreciate that the Superpowers moved out of the shadows of serious and well-justified first strike fears with the advent of the SLBM and the second generation ICBM.

Seventh, spending on strategic forces today is contributing not to diminishing American security, but to the maintenance of a strategic context within which Soviet leaders may fairly be expected to exercise the utmost political caution.

Finally, considerable violence is done to understanding when analysts and commentators uncritically endorse Robert McNamara's notion of a 'mad momentum' to the strategic arms race. As with most of the alarmist expressions that attend arms race commentary, there is some truth to it. However, the past quarter century has been littered with the blueprints and even prototypes of weapon systems that the United States did not deploy. For reasons of strategic doctrine, adversary inactivity, budgetary constraints, and technological objection, many 'favourite sons' have failed to graduate to deployment. Really, there is a surfeit of sufficient general explanations of the life cycles of the individual weapons. Sensible quests for the internal dynamic (or *Eigendynamik*) of arms race behaviour have tended to fall foul of the redundant causality trap. For example, multiple independently targetable re-entry vehicle (MIRV) technology can be shown to be the product of strictly domestic processes and reasoning – with the Soviet Union playing only a useful legitimising role. However, it does happen to be a fact that multiple re-entry vehicle (MRV), MIRV and now manoeuvreable re-entry vehicle (MARV) technologies solved certain *strategic* problems for their principle proponents.

Quantitative dissection of the course of a 'candidate arms race' is important, but it does risk running aground on such factors as the non-arms race related expenditure of the participants, the unavailability of reliable defence expenditure statistics for many states, and the dimensions of arms race behaviour that involve very low (or no) defence expenditure. Soviet writers have always maintained that an important aspect of strategic superiority is superiority of doctrine. Western aspirations for the education of ignorant Soviet strategists would seem to have been fundamentally ill-judged. The doctrinal and planning dimensions of arms race activity are well-illustrated by reference to Secretary of Defence Schlesinger's announcements of changes in, and below the level of, the Single Integrated Operations Plan (SIOP). The 'effort' and 'demonstrable results of effort' graphs that arms race analysts like to employ, showing resources expended and weapons deployed, would entirely neglect a good part of a development such as this. In Secretary Schlesinger's words:

> The requirements in terms of weaponry remain fully to be investigated. But as a first-brush treatment of the issue, there is no necessity for substantial additional weaponry. What we need to have is improvements in doctrine and plans, and improvements in command and control, associated with the implementation of any of those options.[12]

If my theorem is correct, namely, that arms race behaviour (for Great Powers, at least) differs from normal defence behaviour in intensity and not in kind, it should follow that investigators of arms race phenomena are studying the regular warp and woof of international politics, rather than some atypical condition. Bearing in mind the longevity of arms control and disarmament concerns — from 1817 very intermittently, from 1899 intermittently and from 1958 continuously and in reoriented form,[13] it is incredible that a question such as that posed here is not easily answered. What is different about an arms race? If one were to imagine a political context wherein the current Superpowers were still suspicious of each other, in best and regular (i.e. normal) Great Power fashion, but wherein the arms race had ceased, how would this context differ from the present one? On pure cabability grounds alone, each would have to regard the other as being the outstanding international danger. The Chinese could not kill 200 million Soviet or American citizens in half an hour. In developing their strategic plans, preparing budgets, and defending the bureaucratic resultant before sceptical politicans, officials would be bound to make extensive reference to Soviet capabilities. For the only two first class Superpowers to cease to view each other as political rivals and as a source of military threats, there would have to be either a basic change in the structure of world politics, or an overwhelming danger to both of them simultaneously (Super-plus Power China, or an extra-terrestrial danger).

The contemporary Superpower arms race condition is imposed by the structure of the international hierarchy. The Powers are, necessarily, political rivals, yet there are few media for their political competition that would not pose unacceptable risks. Competitive alliance acquisition could provide a substitute for domestic arms production in prestige terms, but not in terms of militarily decisive (or even very useful) capabilities gained. Furthermore, as both Superpowers know, allies, clients, wards, or dependants constrain as well as liberate. The international political odium that increasingly attaches to imposed foreign security connections, along with their control problems, enters the debit column. In short, there is no very obvious substitute for arms race activity.

The use of the arms race analogy inclines many people to believe that the strategic relationship between the Superpowers cannot endure. A race, being an abnormal episode in international life, must terminate in one of the more usual ways in which arms races do end (war, resolution of political differences, victory, and so on). It is worth recalling that England and France are widely held to have been locked into a naval race for forty-six of the years between 1840 and 1904, yet did not fight. From time to time, political and military anxieties, and/or technological advances, generated a fiercer pace to the military preparations of one or both sides, but it can be misleading to refer to specific time-bounded periods of arms racing. Popular usage notwithstanding, arms races of the kind appropriate to many of the more lurid understandings of the term (frenetic activity, each side out for superiority, etc.) really occur only in wartime. Such an idea destroys the tidy conceptual categories into which we may try to force international political data. As Samuel Huntington has stated, in talking of arms races one is talking of matters of degree.[14] The indices and signals of arms race intensity will vary from year to year. Indeed the gestation process for a strategic weapons system (or a new technology) can be so long — anywhere from five to fifteen years (depending on the choice of identification of the point in time of project initiation) — that it must be conceived, developed, and even deployed in substantial ignorance of its strategic and political environments.

Many of the more obvious peaks and troughs of prominent arms race activity relate not to contemporary determined arms race intent, but rather to the stage of the weapons (or even of the force posture) cycle attained. A substantial increase in expenditure for strategic forces may reflect not a new determination to be first in the competition, but rather the fact that, following a successful development programme, very large sums have to be provided for the procurement of the systems in question.

Conceptually, there is no difficulty in outlining the principal features of a clear and unambiguous context wherein there would be no Superpower arms race. Strategic indifference is usefully precise, but obviously impossible. Neither the Soviet Union nor the United States could ever be indifferent to the military preparations of the other. But one can postulate realistically, if not too hopefully, a context wherein each party exercised a far greater self-restraint in strategic force development, procurement, and improvement programmes than currently is the case. For example, as several analysts have suggested, the Soviet Union could have elected not to provide MIRVed replacements for its SS–9s and SS–11s, as a means of facilitating MIRV controls in SALT II.[15] The initiation of SS–17 and SS–19 deployment in 1975, as replacements for the SS–11, illustrates the thesis that the Soviet Union is not moved by arguments for restraint. Under the terms of SALT I, some arms race moves are prohibited – but everything else is permitted (the Soviet Union does not endorse the notion that there is a *spirit* as opposed to a *letter* of a treaty or agreement).

There are excellent reasons for believing that the Soviet Union would be interested in strategic self-restraint only for reasons of resource constraint or tactical diplomatic advantage. Soviet leaders and writers on strategy do not appear to share the Western arms controller's view of the nuclear arms race as an interaction sequence that should be approached as though it were a technical problem mix. Greater affluence at home means a less well-disciplined society, while strategic forces lend to the Soviet Union a growing diplomatic weight abroad. Soviet leaders expect political conflict with the United States: their enormous investment in ICBMs and SLBMs is investment in a diplomatic instrument. Their probable political aspirations may be thwarted (for the demotion of the United States on the international hierarchy, for the effective containment of the China problem, and for the domination, not conquest, of Western Europe and the Middle East), but the evidence thus far available to them is surely ambivalent at worst and encouraging at best. In the wake of SALT I (and SALT II – if the Vladivostok accords are to be the basis of a treaty), Soviet leaders probably hope that Americans will learn to live with certain specific inferiorities. After all, the Soviet Union lived in the shadow of a strategically preponderant United States for over twenty years. The list of indices in which the United States lags behind may be expected to expand over the years ahead.

The strategic arms race is an expression of interstate political conflict. (It is also about the distribution of influence domestically, but this is of a second order of importance.) The only prospect for the termination of the race would be if the United States were to choose to leave the field altogether.

Notes

[1] C. B. Joynt, 'Arms Races and the Problem of Equilibrium', in *The*

Yearbook of World Affairs, 1964 (Stevens and Sons, London 1964), p. 25.

[2] I have outlined a scheme for the comparative analysis of arms races in my article 'The Arms Race Phenomenon', *World Politics,* vol. 24, no. 1 (October 1971), pp. 45–57.

[3] This elitist theory of the arms race has been propounded by Richard J. Barnet; see 'The Game of Nations', *Harper's Magazine,* vol. 243, no. 1458 (November 1971), pp. 53–9; *Intervention and Revolution: The United States in the Third World* (New American Library, New York 1968), pp. 23–36; *The Economy of Death* (Atheneum, New York 1969), pp. 78–101.

[4] Gray, 'The Arms Race Phenomenon', p. 40.

[5] EMT measures the surface destructive potential of a nuclear warhead. The EMT figure for a total and variegated nuclear arsenal is calculable by means of the relationship $EMT = NY^{\frac{2}{3}}$, where N is the number of warheads of yield Y; the lethal radius in terms of blast is proportional to the $\frac{1}{3}$ power of the yield and the area is proportional to the square of this radius. See Ian Bellany, 'The Essential Arithmetic of Deterrence', *RUSI Journal,* vol. 118, no. 4 (March 1973), pp. 28–34.

[6] Albert Wohlstetter, *Legends of the Arms Race,* USSI Report 75–1 (United States Strategic Institute, Washington, D.C. 1975).

[7] 'Mad momentum' was a term popularised by the Secretary of Defense, Robert McNamara, in his address to the United Press International Editors and Publishers in San Francisco on 18 September 1967 (see 'McNamara Explanation of "Thin" Missile Defence System', *The Washington Post,* 19 September 1967, p. A. 10).

[8] Alton H. Quanbeck and Barry M. Blechman, *Strategic Forces: Issues for the Mid-Seventies* (The Brookings Institution, Washington, D.C. 1973), pp. vii, 60, 66.

[9] This is the subject of Chapter 4.

[10] Herbert York, *Race to Oblivion. A Participant's View of the Arms Race* (Clarion, New York 1971), p. 228. It is true that the number of Soviet warheads that could be delivered to American targets has risen very sharply as the arms race has continued. However, this is a very unsatisfactory basis for claiming that the security of the United States has diminished as an approximate function of arms race velocity. Security relates not merely to numbers of weapons, but to the likelihood that they will be used and to the perceptions of individual Americans regarding that likelihood.

[11] This is a reference to, and slight expansion on the claim by Bernard Brodie that the economic training of many leading American strategists has fostered an insensitivity to political considerations (*War and Politics* (Macmillan, New York 1973), p. 475, note 48).

[12] News Conference, 24 January 1974, p. 9 (mimeo).

[13] 1817 was the date of one of the most succesful of all arms control agreements, the Rush–Bagot Treaty limiting naval armaments on the Great Lakes. 1899 was the year of the first peace conference at The Hague.

[14] Samuel Huntington, 'Arms Races: Prerequisites and Results', in Carl J. Friedrich and Seymour E. Harris (eds), *Public Policy, 1958* (Graduate School of Public Administration, Harvard University, Cambridge, Mass. 1958), p. 43.

[15] For example, see Herbert Scoville, Jr, 'MIRV Control is Still Possible', *Survival,* vol. 16, no. 2 (March/April 1974), pp. 54–9; and Lawrence L. Whetten, 'Soviet Interests and MIRV Control', *Survival,* vol. 16, no. 2 (March/April 1974), pp. 59–63.

2 Arms Race Dynamics

Theory for policy

Testing, re-formulating, and re-testing hypotheses may one day be a prominent feature of arms race analysis, but at this juncture one can do little more than clear the ground, appraise all the more plausible possiblities systematically, indicate tentative conclusions, and stress the explanatory value of synthesis. It is now appreciated quite widely that the near single causal explanations of arms race dynamics that held sway in different arms control circles in the 1960s were grossly oversimplified. Specifically, the mainstream of arms controllers gave every appearance of adhering to the view that a traceable process of interstate action and anticipatory over-reaction drove the arms race.[1] On the Left, economic causation raised its head yet again. In many variations, on one theme of argument, the arms race was held really to be about the economic and institutional health of an amorphous military-industrial complex (MIC).[2] Arms race phenomena have provided a rich hunting ground for polemicists and ideologists.

The most basic questions seem never to have been asked by analysts in search of reasonable answers to pressing policy problems. There is no authoritative definition of 'arms race': very few analysts seem to have been sufficiently intrigued to ask precisely what it was. References to the arms race consequences of ABM, or MIRV, or SALT I bedeck the literature. Credulous legislators and journalists should be disturbed to learn that supporting the phrase 'arms race consequences' is no impressive array of social scientific or diplomatic historical studies. So partial in their selection of arms race truths are the mainstream arms control writers that it is difficult to believe that their intuition has been much disciplined.

Following fifteen none too successful years of arms control experience (and particularly the SALT experience), nine years marked by the ascendancy of assured destruction doctrine, and a rising chorus of cogent criticism, there is a slow, but growing, appreciation that much of the revealed wisdom on strategic doctrine, arms control doctrine, arms race doctrine, and the nature of the adversary, has been at worst wrong and at best oversimplified. Muddying the pure water of the arms control creed, John Newhouse has indicated the complexity of arms race processes:

> The arms race is not impelled by technology alone, nor by technology in

tandem with the notorious action–reaction cycle. Both these forces are partially shaped and balanced by politics, by the relations between the powers, by the attitudes and policies of political leaders who may or may not actively seek to improve these relations, for whatever purpose.[3]

Quite so. However, it is desirable that analysts seek a greater precision than that deemed adequate for his purposes by Newhouse. For one of the purposes of this study, that is, the identification of possible 'arms race consequences' of current and future American postural choices (or their absence), the factors likely to be operating on the Soviet decision makers are matters of more than academic interest. It may be frustrating for an official wanting to know what the likely Soviet response (if any) would be to, say, the Trident II SLBM to be told that (a) the arms race is complex (which he already knows), and that (b) analytically, there are eleven principal arms race fuelling agents (since he probably expects his hired policy analysts to distinguish between the more and the less important). Parsimony is desirable if one is seeking to emphasise that which is clearly dominant analytically. In the field of arms race analysis there has, however, been a surfeit of parsimony. The current state of the arms race analytical art permits only the assembling of building blocks for theoretical advance. The state of our knowledge at present has been succinctly described thus: 'We just do not have an adequate explanatory model for the Soviet–American arms race.'[4]

In policy terms, it is most important that policy makers and their close advisers be protected from facile arms race theorising. Self-confident assertions of Soviet proneness to reaction, or the lack thereof, rest to an undue degree upon the projection of Western logical models on Soviet strategists, policy makers and defence bureaucracies. The dangers inherent in the projection of self upon others have already been well expounded by Matthew Gallagher and Karl Spielmann.[5]

The mirror image fallacy has been well-exposed. Unfortunately, it seems to have been widely understood to apply almost exclusively to the family of action–reaction models, but it may be just as fallacious to impute generalised (from the American experience) bureaucratic behaviour, or generalised foreign policy reasoning, to another political culture as it is to impute familiar strategic doctrine and, really, an essentially Western strategic engineering approach to strategic questions to that culture. On the other hand, intellectual fashion should not swing too far in the opposite direction. To recognise the possible dangers of mirror image assumptions is not to require that an idiosyncratic anti-model be asserted in their place. However impenetrable to Western gaze Soviet decision processes or strategic motives are, the fact remains that arms race business must and will be conducted. Soviet behaviour, deeds and works are open to Western interpretation.

In seeking to answer the question 'What drives an arms race?' the following list of considerations merits close attention and provides the framework for the remainder of this chapter:

1. Foreign policy goals.
2. Interstate action–reaction processes.
3. Inter-armed service action–reaction processes.
4. Intra-armed service action–reaction processes.
5. Bureaucratic politics.
6. The character of political–social systems.
7. Electoral politics.
8. Organisational momentum.
9. Technological innovation.
10. Following-on imperatives.
11. The Military–Industrial Complex.

These are not mutually exclusive, but they may be presented as if they were. For example, rational strategic reaction decisions may always be 'bureaucratised' by an analyst who sees in the bureaucratic politics paradigm the essential scalpel for analytical surgery. Such an analyst may well confuse necessary for sufficient explanations. After all, every defence decision may be 'explained' in terms of which bureaucratic actors did what, and so on. Similary, every defence decision may be explained in the mode of strategic interaction. One should add that typically, in official presentations, all defence decisions of possible arms race relevance are so explained.[6] The Joint Chiefs of Staff (JCS) would not publicly defend a new submarine system on the grounds that 'the Navy wanted it.' Showing a decent respect for the susceptibilities of taxpayers and the political guardians of taxpayers, the JCS would expound the strategic virtues of the said system. Some forms of argument are legitimate and others are not.

Presuming open-mindedness on the part of arms controllers, which may be presuming too much, the signal virtues in the presentation of a 'marketing list' of the type listed above are that the partial nature of some favourite explanatory sons may be exposed, and that it may be appreciated that a particular decision (e.g. to deploy the Sentinel, ABM system, or to accept the principle of common aggregate ceilings in SALT II) could be explained in a number of different ways. For reasons of community affiliation, intellectual conviction and ideological predisposition (and these three are really inseparable), an individual may still prefer to point his angry pen at barons from Boeing and their ilk, but at the same time he should be compelled to prepare his case rather more carefully than hitherto.

Foreign policy goals

Braving the wrath of those addicted either to conspiratorial or to 'push of great forces' lines of reasoning, it is here asserted that politicians and senior officials determine major arms race moves. Hence it may fairly be observed that to the principal individual human arms race actors, strategic arms are seen as instruments of diplomacy. Similarly, arms control negotiations are seen to be political and not technical processes. American arms race/arms control behaviour has not always accorded with this political perspective, but it is still a fair generalisation. Whether or not strategic arms should be so regarded is quite another question. Arms race behaviour by an identified rival is taken as an index of political will – through not usually as an index of precise political intention. The United States would seem to have lost her past enthusiasm for the retention of a competitive edge, for whatever advantages such an edge might yield. However, having lived since 1917 in the shadow of superior military power abroad, the Soviet Union, understandably enough, is showing scant enthusiasm for the depoliticisation of strategic weaponry.

There would seem to be a near constant conflict coefficient which has resulted in the thwarting of two opposed lines of arms control reasoning. Stated succinctly, the armament tension dilemma so beloved of arms controllers in years past [7] is a conceptual irrelevance. Given the nature, past histories, and conflicting interests of the current Superpowers, it may fairly confidently be asserted that international conditions are unlikely to be improved much either by an 'arms first' or by a 'tension first' approach.

The familiar arms control aspiration of effecting a technical end-run around political difficulties is now firmly discredited. The path to substantial processes of detente does not lie through SALT or Mutual (and Balanced) Force Reductions (M(B)FR). Experts have recognised belatedly what men in the street – unhindered by trained incapacity – appreciate intuitively; namely, that states that distrust each other very seriously are not likely to effect agreements that place any important constraints upon their freedom of defence policy action. Unfortunately, the reverse proposition has been assumed to be true. Many Western analysts reasoned that since political discord thwarted that hoped for progress in arms control that would, in its turn, promote political confidence, it should be true that progress in arms control would be possible once the politics had been 'put right'. Unfortunately, the United States is contending with a Superpower that sees no incompatibility between the atmospheric conditions of detente and a most vigorous programme of strategic force improvement. To Soviet leaders, energetic arms racing reflects (a) the conviction that the index of relative strategic power is very relevant to prestige and diplomatic weight, (b) the determination that the balance of forces shall continue to be seen to move in the Soviet direction; and (c) the fact that detente progress is certain to stop far short of the resolution of political differences with the United States (an ideological impossibility). In other words, detente will not proceed to the point of take-off, whereafter arms control or questions of relative strategic balance will be subjects of indifference. If anything, the SALT I and Vladivostok agreements, married to Soviet analysis of the domestic mood in the United States, must serve to encourage Soviet leaders to press on with their arms race activities.

The 'tension first' paradigm is undoubtedly correct. However, its acceptance may easily mislead unless one is prepared to grant the strong possibility that the synergistic combination of mild detente and very limited measures of arms control is likely to fail to 'go critical'. This would seem to be the condition of the Superpower relationship today. Increased political confidence between Moscow and Washington (whatever the tactical and strategic calculations) made SALT I possible. SALT I symbolised detente, but its asymmetries (allied in the minds of observers to other contemporary Soviet activities – for example, in the Middle East) have provoked dissent within the United States that now imperils the very detente that produced SALT I. The contentious domestic material attendant upon arms control negotiations and agreements was a subject much under-represented in the now classical arms control literature of the period 1960–63.

Significant measures of arms control are most unlikely because the Superpower and indeed the European detentes have nowhere to go. Those who hope that progress in detente will reach a point of 'take-off', whereafter substantial measures of arms control will either be irrelevant[8] or very easy to accomplish, choose to ignore the constraints on the prospects for detente. These constraints include the permanence of Soviet control in Eastern Europe; the impossibility of any substantial liberalisation of Soviet society (certainly not to the point where Soviet foreign policy need be justified to any considerable, sceptical, non-official domestic constituency); the prudent mutual suspicions that must inform the policy making in any two states that share such a lonely pinnacle of influence.

These comments must not be allowed to mislead. The argument here is not that detente is entirely a snare and a delusion. What is claimed is that it is most unlikely that current or foreseeable progress in detente will serve either to put the arms race into reverse or even to moderate the pace of arms race activity to any very marked degree.[9] Indeed, the level of effort expended thus far on strategic forces, and even on defence generally, in the United States in the 1970s, suggests that the extant condition is one of arms 'walk'.

Impatient arms control enthusiasts have registered their dissatisfaction with the arms control accomplishments both of SALT I and of the Vladivostok agreements. According to the 'tension first' proposition, detente should have brought forth an arms control lion, not a mouse. Recorded history did not begin in 1945. Barry Steiner has shown that the naval races between Britain and France and Russia from 1884 to 1904 and between Britain and Germany in the years 1898 to 1912 were apparently immune to phases of improved political relations.[10] It is tempting to argue that the momentum behind military programmes in an arms race context is always substantial. Ships are under construction, or silos have been dug, so that any dampening effect of detente processes in year N is unlikely to be discernible in diminished military effort until N+ 1 or 2. Alternatively, it could be suggested that in an arms race political leadership loses a significant measure of control over the military establishment. The 'interest' in substantial and continuing defence programmes will be so powerful that the political leadership cannot fine tune its arms race activity. The military managers of the race will have forged powerful alliances with legislators, industry and the mass media and the burden of detente proof will rest upon the political leadership.

There is some merit in the above arguments, but nowhere near as much as their proponents believe. It is, of course, a fact that rapid gear changing in the pace of military effort is very expensive and is certain to promote sharp controversy. The fact that the arms race rumbles on during periods of detente should be attributed not so much to the difficulties of political interdiction as to the appreciation that detente is far removed from a resolution of the political issues that fuel arms competition.

The political framework for detailed arms racing activity is provided by the appreciation that competition with the Soviet Union is unavoidable. This obvious fact is the *sine qua non* for understanding the nuclear arms race (or indeed any arms race); to ignore it, as many arms controllers seem bent upon doing, is to perform *Hamlet* without the Prince. The 'armament tension dilemma' and similar social scientific formulations quite miss the point that the arms race is, at the highest and least specific level, about political conflict. To engage in arms racing does not necessarily mean that major war is anticipated in the very near future. Some wars are preceded by arms races and others are not. It is true that armaments may combine synergistically with political issues so as to exacerbate a political conflict, but it is also true that limited, technical measures of arms control will make little contribution to international order unless they reflect changed and/or converging political wills. As SALT I ratified the progress in Soviet–American detente and rested (from the Soviet point of view) upon the confidence engendered by the Superpowers' efforts to bring about a nuclear non-proliferation treaty (NPT), so the Washington Naval Arms Limitation Treaty of 1922 rested upon the *de facto* granting of a free hand to Japan in the Western Pacific.

It is not easy to demonstrate the foreign policy utility of being ahead in strategic arms. Indeed, there is a school of theorists who claim that different states of strategic arms imbalance have been largely irrelevant to the foreign policy behaviour of the Superpowers.[11] Suffice it to say that the Soviet leadership, at least since the fall of Khrushchev, has deemed it essential to attain a position of undeniable parity, and preferably parity-plus. Similarly, although fashions in doctrine and terminology have changed, every postwar American administration, including the present one, with Schlesinger's references to the need for essential strategic equivalence, has insisted on maintaining strategic forces that would not look grossly inferior to those of the Soviet Union. These simple remarks do, of course, slide over matters of the utmost complexity. For example, parity or effective parity is more an arms control rallying cry than it is a useful analytical tool. And what does 'essential equivalence' mean, in detail, when comparing two asymmetrical force mixes, guided by different doctrines and serving different political goals?

The suggestion here is that foreign policy goals catalyse and sustain an arms race. They legitimise the games played by bureaucrats, the money spent by weapons laboratories, and the promotional efforts of corporations and armed services. The importance of making quite explicit this fundamental incentive to arms racing is to suggest the inherent limitations of the other driving factors put forward. Well-intentioned arms control endeavours to interdict putative interstate action-(over) reaction chains, or to restructure defence bureaucracies, may moderate the pace of competition, and may certainly accomplish some financial retrenchment, but they will not halt the arms race. As long as foreign policy makers see an adversary abroad who poses a political and military threat, and who cannot be thwarted by the acquisition of balance-turning allies (almost) alone, then arms race activity will continue to seem a prudent response. Analyses of MICs or of bureaucratic games will yield knowledge of some of the important detail of arms race behaviour, but it will only be detail.

The above should not be seen as a complacent dismissal of the evidence of unnecessary systems being funded, or being funded prematurely. Rather it should be seen as an attempt to distinguish first order from second order questions.

Interstate action–reaction processes

There are three families of action–reaction models, relating to interstate, interservice and intraservice relations. Although the first variety asserts a system dominance, whereas the other two assert a subsystem dominance, all three presume a narrow strategic rationality.

When phrased permissively, there is little in the action–reaction proposition with which a reasonable man could disagree. For purposes of, *inter alia,* deterrence, defence, diplomatic weight and reputation, two states are racing in armaments. Each watches the behaviour of the other very closely and may be expected to react to programmes, deployments, or signals of foreign policy intention that could rebound to its relative disadvantage. Thus phrased, one has really done little more than to restate the fundamental condition for an arms race. Philip Guedalla's comment on the 'discovery' of the concept of sea power springs to mind: 'but if Mahan discovered nothing in particular, he discovered it very well.'[12] Resting on no very apparent analysis, Robert McNamara resorted to a very mechanistic action–reaction argument in the context of his announcement of the decision to deploy the primarily anti-Chinese Sentinel ABM system.[13] The introduction of this argument and its subsequent employment reinforces the suspicion that action–reaction has all too often been used as conceptual ammunition intended to lend some analytical ballast to arguments hostile to the deployment of new weapon systems. If it is true that arms race actions necessarily trigger rational reactions that negate the value of the spurring actions, then clearly both parties are wasting money and proliferating military hardware to their mutual disadvantage. Two caveats were often ignored. First even if an action–reaction mechanism does fuel the arms race, it does not follow that arms control interdiction of such a mechanism need lead either to a termination of the race or to an improvement in the security condition of the United States. The fuel of action-reaction is (to the extent that this paradigm is useful) ultimately injected into the Soviet–American strategic system because these two states are sensibly distrustful of each other – reflecting their conflicting interests. Second, one cannot rule out, *a priori,* the possibility of inaction–reaction, or of action-inaction (non–) sequences[14]. As some American arms controllers were ready to argue in 1965 and 1966, nothing would so discourage Soviet (and American) ABM plans as much as the United States' MIRV programmes.[15]

An important reason why even in 1975 one finds that the most basic arms race questions have been accorded scarcely a passing analytical glance is that arms race analysis has been captured and manipulated by policy advocates. It is interesting to observe the thoroughgoing rejection of simple action–reaction models that has been recorded over the past several years. With policy advocates having shifted gears, it could be that all contending parties are now ready to consider the viability of a middle ground, even though such ground is certain to lend less obvious policy support. The most uncompromising statement of the action–reaction mechanism was made by Robert McNamara in the following terms:

> What is essential to understand is that the Soviet Union and the United States mutually influence one another's strategic plans. Whatever be their intentions, whatever be our intentions, actions – or even realistically potential actions – on either side relating to the build-up of nuclear forces, be they either offensive or defensive weapons, necessarily trigger reactions on the other side. It is precisely this action–reaction phenomenon that fuels an arms race.[16]

In a celebrated article in *Scientific American,* George Rathjens purported to demonstrate how the action–reaction mechanism had functioned in the 1960s.[17] Although very many arms controllers, legislators and journalists came to accept action–reaction as Holy Writ, a trickle of social scientists and area specialists have undermined confidence in the metaphor.

Fundamentally, the action–reaction hypothesis required that one regard the arms race adversaries as single rational strategic men, united in adherence to common strategic conceptions. No one has ever actually stated action–reaction in terms as stark as this, but a little reflection does reveal that the assumptions of the proclaimed mechanism require a quite unacceptable measure of suppression of evidence of diversity. Furthermore, action–reaction has all the hallmarks of the mechanistic and overly technical approach to strategy and to arms control that has limited the work of much of American strategic thought. The arms race, so this paradigm could be held to suggest, is driven not by political ambition, not by the thrust and counterthrust of two parties seeking to gain or even deny political advantage but rather by strategic threats to strategic requirements. Action by one or both parties threatens stability – defined apolitically as a condition characterised by the security of mutual assured destruction capabilities – and the inevitable reactions are intended to restore stability. If it can be shown that the two racers do not share a common strategic ideology, and if one is less than certain that strategic ideology is of very much significance for the making of procurement decisions, then much of the predictive promise of action–reaction is negated.

Action–reaction can accommodate a fairly wide variety of complicating suggestions. Most of the leading arms controllers have enjoyed close, if intermittent, relations with government, and are aware that rational strategic men attend university seminars; they do not act as states in international politics. Once the salience of the domestic institutions and coalitions that eventually bring forth strategic programmes has been granted, and once the length of the weapon system gestation period has been fully appreciated, it is none too radical a step for an analyst to conclude that the domestic details of the arms race should not be seen as supportive of action–reaction arguments, but rather as subversive of the principal theses that stem from an action–reaction world view. Citing the Soviet threat comes to be seen as part ritual utterance – the legitimate language of weapon system advocacy – and part essential support. Strategic rationales may come and go, but ABM and the MIRV go on forever.

The notion of two arms racers playing rational strategic games has suffered a fatal dose of criticism. In general terms it has run foul of the domestication of strategic and international political analysis. Now one finds that for very different reasons nearly all the principal contenders in the arms debate are eager to stress the domestic processes of each racing agent.

Damage limiters are pleased to damn action–reaction, because autarkic arms race models suggest that one might well succeed in deploying those weapon systems that minimum deterrers consider provocative, without provoking offsetting deployments abroad. If no confidence is to be placed in assertions that the deployment of, for example, more accurate re-entry vehicles *must* provoke offsetting Soviet reactions, then clearly the task of the hard-target counterforce salesman is facilitated.

Minimum deterrers of various political hues are pleased to be able to point accusing fingers at domestic defence bureaucracies, at villainous missile makers and the like. The arms race is often portrayed as a convenient figment of over-active strategic imaginations, which is partially true in a formal sense, but misleading in that while the *real* contests (in both Superpowers) are between strategic maximalists and strategic minimalists, interstate competition is no illusion – it exists. The threat to American security stems not from timetables of aggression drawn up in the Kremlin, but from the domestic weapons culture. What is needed to halt the strategic arms race is not the consummation of the Vladivostok accords in a SALT II treaty that is almost meaningless as a measure of arms control: it is some drastic reform at home, where arms control could well begin and end.

The degree to which action–reaction has been discredited as comprising *the* driving force for the arms race is well illustrated in the recent writings of George Rathjens, one of its early and more wholehearted populisers. Rathjens writes cautiously, almost defensively; for example:

> To the extent that the 'action–reaction' explanation of the arms race has validity as a rationale for the ABM treaty, it would also seem to apply to an ASW treaty.[18]

And

> ... much of the analytical literature and testimony in the past, including

some of our own, has suffered from having treated the nations involved as unitary actors whose behavior it is assumed is, or in any case *ought* to be, governed by 'rational' considerations of national interest. (Emphasis as in the original.)[19]

Attracted by the machinations of apparently often self-serving domestic interests, some analysts have gone too far in their rejection of action–reaction logic. Provided it is remembered that the arms race adversary is capable of reacting in a variety of complex and often obscure ways, the notion need not impede arms race understanding, nor need it lend authority to spurious special interest arguments. States may react in both the anticipatory and the sequential modes. As John S. Foster has argued, the task of a responsible research and development community is to anticipate what an intelligent and well-funded adversary might choose to do in the future.[20] If an idea appeals to American technologists, it is reasonable to presume that the idea will both occur and be attractive to their Soviet counterparts also. One signal danger in this rational anticipation phenomenon is that a research trail is being blazed for a technologically less advanced adversary. Sequential or true reactions as a mode of defensive arms race activity suffer from the limitation that the United States is competing with a very closed society. To await firm evidence of Soviet system development action would be to accept a technological lead time disadvantage in excess of five years.

Much utility could be added to the generalities that attend action–reaction terminology if more serious attention were paid to the actual behaviour, inferable doctrine, and (often) inferred political processes of the adversary. McNamara, Rathjens, and the arms control community of the late 1960s may have been correct in asserting the existence of an action–reaction mechanism; where they failed to do justice to their subject was in their neglect of the obvious point that American actions would catalyse *Soviet* reactions. Furthermore, it is an advance to recognise that, in the context of this study, we are discussing American and Soviet strategic men, carrying into policy action the postulates and recommendations of the American or Soviet arms control community, rather than rational strategic men writ large. It is a further advance to recognise that Soviet, as well as American, arms race behaviour is the result of doctrinal contention and bureaucratic and personal disputes, and that reactions may be severely time-lagged and even almost unrecognisable as specific responses.

Interservice action–reaction processes

As with the interstate action–reaction hypothesis, so the inter-service action–reaction hypothesis comes in various subtle shades. The forms that such action–reaction may assume may be summarised as follows: defence–offence or offence-defence *offsetting* reactive processes; parallel (imitative) competition, (i.e. offence–offence); and 'separate development' competition.

All action–reaction models relate to the question 'How does the nuclear arms race work?' and not to the question, 'Why is the arms race being run at all?' Within the political framework discussed above, there is ample evidence to suggest that the precise course set by each racing state has more to do with calculations and struggles of an *intra* – as opposed to an *inter*state character. Taking first the more obviously strategically rational action–reaction theme, a great deal of the information one would like to possess about the interstate adversary is simply unavailable – or at least unavailable in time. In a very real sense every arms racing state must give the appearance of running a technological arms race with itself. Moreover, history bequeathes to the present an internally competitive bureaucratic structure. Each dimension of United States' (and the Soviet Union's) arms racing endeavour is the responsibility of a particular armed service. In the war surrogate of an arms race, the proximate enemy is not the Soviet Union, it is the Office of the Secretary of Defense (OSD), the Office of Management and Budget, the Army, etc.

The Soviet threat is salient in that it (a) legitimises arms race expenditure; (b) somewhat vaguely disciplines US arms race activity; and (c) vitally influences the climate of opinion that dictates the degree of budgetary permissiveness that permeates the Administration and Congress. But the threat provides no very obvious yardstick, unambiguously requiring either more or less arms race effort, or suggesting beyond reasonable doubt what direction US racing efforts ought to take.

Implicit in the tight interstate action–reaction model is the notion that each action indicates, inherently, an appropriate reaction. Hence rational strategic responses are the stuff of which arms races are made. This is very far from the whole truth. In the first place, the intelligence community may exhibit very sharp internal disagreements as to the character of the threat. (For example, could the Tallinn Line air defence system be upgraded to possess a major ABM capability? Does the Soviet medium range bomber force constitute a threat to North America?) Intelligence estimates are an important part of the currency of inter-service strife. Secondly, even if the scale and character of the threat is generally agreed upon in technical terms (for example, it may not be disputed that the Soviet Union has deployed 313 'heavy' ICBMs which could, granted favourable assumptions, eliminate most of the Minuteman/Titan force) men of good will and equal competence may honestly disagree as to what, if anything, should be done in response. Incomplete information, doctrinal diversity, and different institutional interests serve to guarantee that the monitoring and multiple appreciations of the threat are most unlikely to promote a near-automatic consensus as to how (if at all) particular elements of the threat should be countered.

Therefore, a sweeping arms race overview that portrayed the strategic poles of action and crisp, offsetting reaction would clearly miss most of the arms race action. Political leaders and very senior officials do not inhabit a world populated only by military strategic problems. Even if the strategically rational and correct reaction to an arms race action is identified with high confidence (as officials believed to be the case over the dilatory and spasmodic Soviet ABM deployment programme), the strategic need for the *correct* strategic response may be far less pressing than strategically extra-rational factors. In practice, it is extremely unlikely that major weapon system decisions are based on only one ground. MIRV and a very limited ABM system, the two technology streams that have attracted particular arms control attention in recent years, have been deployed because they solved some very different problems for effective coalitions within the United States government. The various single causal rationales for their deployment that have been offered are analytically insufficient.[21]

Legitimised by the political conflict that sustains the arms race, armed services and offices within them are required to defend their cherished programmes in the language of strategy rather than organisational aggrandisement. The fact remains that the threat to naval or air force interests is not, in any very immediate sense, provided by malevolent Russians; rather it is provided by malevolent civilian budget officers and weapon system project officers in the other services who are competing for scarce funds. The paragraphs that follow therefore explore the three principal forms of interservice action—reaction phenomena.

First, there is the classic offsetting or bypassing competition between offence and defence. Despite satellite photographic and infra-red reconnaissance, and despite electronic surveillance and probing and radar telemetric monitoring in peacetime, most Western weapon systems can only be tested against other Western weapon systems. The operational worth of Soviet military technologies is necessarily appraised, in good part, in terms of what is known of their Western counterparts. The principal source of the analytical ammunition deployed to frustrate the legitimate ambitions of the United States Army's ABM interest was not extant or even directly projected

Soviet penetration technologies: it was the penetration technologies conceived by the United States Air Force and the Advanced Research Projects Agency (ARPA). Folly is not here imputed. It is certainly not foolish to assume that what the United States expects to be able to do tomorrow, the Soviet Union should be capable of accomplishing the day after tomorrow. The point is that an army ABM team was essentially racing against an air force penetration team. Victory in such a contest need go not to whoever is right, but rather to whoever is able to marshall the larger number of battalions. To be technically *right* is certainly helpful, as MIRV proponents discovered, in that potential and actual opposition is thereby pre-emptively deprived of its most effective form of argument. But strategic development interaction between services provides only the raw material for defence politics. To have a system that works, and works well, is one thing; to sell it to one's own service, to the JCS, to the OSD, to the White House, and then to the Congress, is something else.

Second, there may be parallel competiton, in which two or more services are seeking development and deployment approval for weapon systems that are very similar in strategic or tactical function. Distinctive one environment oriented armed services accord well with tradition, and indeed with most military missions, but there are tasks and capabilities that transcend the obvious jurisdiction of any one service. To fulfil adequately even core missions, each armed service must encroach into marginal mission territory. Thus one finds, for example, that the US armed forces have, in effect, four air forces, though admittedly of very different orientations. Moreover, many Western Europeans and Russians would hold that all three American armed services maintain missile forces that could be termed strategic (counting the Army's 450-mile range Pershing missile).

Interservice competition has accelerated the pace of US arms racing endeavours, since to lose a particular race is to suffer a very immediate organisational loss. It is true that parallel research and development efforts are wasteful in that financial, material, and human resources are expended on more projects than will be funded for procurement. However, such competition provides a hedge against the failure of any one or more of the technological tracks being followed. Such competitions were a particular feature of the mid-1950s, given the somewhat permissive weapon systems management philosophy adhered to by Secretaries of Defense Wilson and McElroy.[22]

The strategic deterrent mission has offered to all services (though principally to the Navy and Air Force) a large and institutionally lucrative area that had no historic claimant. Both the Air Force and the Navy had to adapt to uncongenial technologies. For a considerable period following any successful war, each armed service tends to be run by those leaders who had command over the dominant (or at least most prestigious) weapon of that service. Hence the Air Force has been run by bomber generals, the Navy by carrier admirals, and the Army by airborne generals. The conceptual lead time problem certainly impaired the pace at which the Navy and the Air Force pushed for ballistic missile and nuclear submarine development. Polaris patrols are a far cry from the tradition of Midway and Leyte. Similarly, sentimental attachment to the B–25 and B–29 is hardly conducive to enthusiasm for silo-squatting beneath wheat fields in Montana.

Enthusiastic or not, armed services will search for justifications to be where they understand the money (and/or the prestige) to be. Just as all services strove to get on the strategic deterrent, or at the least the nuclear, bandwagon in the mid-1950s, so each service strove to maximise its counter-insurgency image in the early and mid-1960s. Strategic rationales for redundant capabilities can always be devised. Hedging against a greater than expected threat and complicating the other side's strategic planning open the door to the ingenious service salesman. Prestige and political considerations can help determine the programme of an armed service. For example, contrary to the wishes of its Special Projects Office, the Navy insisted that stellar inertial navigation be developed for the improvement of the accuracy of the Poseidon SLBM. The principal reason for this insistence was to deprive the Air Force of sole responsibility for counterforce strikes. Responsibility shared is prestige (and possibly budgets) diminished.

Third, a different kind of arms race process is a competition of 'separate development'. Trade offs are not conceptually legitimate between all programmes. Naval spokesmen might argue (braving the kind of uniformed melée that strengthens the hands of civilians) that because the Trident submarine will fulfil all conceivable deterrent, though not damage limiting, functions, the manned bomber force and the Minuteman/Titan force can safely be phased out. Regardless of the strategic merits and demerits of this argument, it is a strategically legitimate point of view. One is discussing like and like. On the other hand, eras of budgetary parsimony ensure that every interest in every service must *sell* its product as well as it is able.

Each service is selling products that are, in some measure, incapable of comparison. It is very unclear to what extent the hard-selling of dissimilar products accelerates the arms race. Since budgetary ceilings and congressional goals for budget cutting tend to be somewhat arbitrary, it is most probable that the street market aspect of programme purveying results (a) only in some marginal transfer of funds, and (b) in the generation of considerable heat and ill-will. Nonetheless, strident endeavours to sell carrier task forces, tactical aviation, air defence, and so on, do contribute to the generation of the anxiety that supports the legitimacy of an arms race.

Intraservice action–reaction processes

Complementary to the theme that interservice rivalry drives the arms race is the observation that much of the fine detail as well as some of the hard–selling of particular programmes is determined and catalysed by intraservice interactions. Each service would seem to be racing against itself.

This national intraservice dynamic can be overstressed. It is true that American equipment is generally tested against American equipment, or against allied equipment that bears some of the hall-marks of American thinking. However, it should not be forgotten that some American and Soviet equipment has undergone field testing in South East Asia and in the Middle East over the past decade. Intraservice competition is certainly explicable in terms of the bureaucratic politics paradigm. However, as cited earlier, it also reflects strategic necessity. There is nothing absurd about American arms programmes being re-directed as a result of interactions between opposing American or allied military capabilities. So long as force remains the ultimate argument of diplomacy, it is the duty of armed forces to provide maximum effectiveness at minimum cost. Those arms controllers who discern absurdity in the tail-chasing of American research and development have been noticeably silent on the question of non-utopian alternatives.

Necessarily, B–52s seek to penetrate the NORAD system, while British and American submarines are hunted by NATO anti-submarine warfare forces. To conclude from this that the United States is running an arms race with itself would be a *non sequitur*. Like it or not, the Soviet Union and the United States are potential military adversaries. Hence, sensibly, what lessons there are to be learnt from the October War of 1973 will be learnt. Many defence problems cannot confidently be resolved simply by pushing forward the state of the art. The problem of the vulnerability of aircraft to the SAM–6 and SAM–7 requires very careful appraisal of the operational characteristics of those systems.

The technological races between, say, tank and anti-tank technologies, or air defence and aircraft penetration technologies are run both as a legitimate enterprise supportive of desirable arms race activity, and as an enterprise necessary to sustain the bureaucratic health of the promoting organisations. Motives are mixed. A dedicated defence scientist will be delighted to have contributed to the success of a project designed to provide the navy with a follow-on missile to the Polaris A–3; strategic conviction and personal interest being in harmony, he will undoubtedly subscribe to the notion that the security of the United States will thus be enhanced. At the same time, technological success could well mean bureaucratic success. In other words, job security, promotion, funding largesse, some internal redistribution of prestige, and so on, will all be advanced.

It is tempting to subscribe to the notion that the arms race adversary is a bureaucratic friend who serves to justify the real business of the military bureaucrat. That real business is to build bigger and better aircraft, submarines or tanks. Since one is pushing hard against a large number of technological frontiers precise detail of the Soviet threat is as unnecessary as it is probably unobtainable. With the real and very proximate enemies being those bureaus within the same armed service (and some in other services) that threaten to increase their share of the service (or general defence) budget, analytical contests are conducted within the familiar and widely acceptable framework of tried and trusted American doctrinal assumptions. This refers to the fact that many US arms control and defence policies seem to have required, in order to be effective in action, that the adversary negotiate and/or fight according to American rules. One significant cost of a possibly irreducible measure of domestic competition is that the distinctive features of the interstate adversary may be under-recognised.

Bureaucratic politics

In recent years the bureaucratic politics paradigm has been advanced as a tool for the thorough-going reinterpretation of foreign and defence policies. The rise in scholarly attention of this approach is attributable to the following factors: the experience of many academics as 'insiders' in the 1960s; the in-tray eye-view of foreign and defence policies thus experienced that prompted the desire to reframe the common explanatory hypotheses that have been the stock in trade of academia and the *lingua franca* of officials[23]; a widespread dissastisfaction with US policies towards the outside world, many of the errors which are understood to stem from domestic structural weaknesses; and the appearance of a major work that has served as a near-sacred text, namely, Graham Allison's *Essence of Decision*.[24] Summarised and re-phrased: the retailers of bureaucratic politics argue that an undue number of studies of foreign and defence policies ignore most of the real action – which occurs at home. It is easy to find flaws in the bureaucratic politics paradigm. One could cite its ethnocentrism, its essential triviality, its anti-democratic implications, its limited explanatory value and its impossible demands for detail from closed societies. However, it is more sensible to be generous. Although scholars such as Graham Allison and Morton Halperin have stated explicitly and forcefully that which every competent scholar (not to mention official) already knew,[25] the worth of their missionary activity is readily to be appreciated in the new course taken by much of the strategic, international relations, and even diplomatic historical literature, as well as by university teaching.

The arms race is managed and driven by officials who occupy particular positions of authority within national bureaucratic structures. American or Soviet arms race actions or reactions are the negotiated or legislated resultants of domestic contention. Too often, so it is claimed, strategists and foreign policy analysts have written of the affairs of state as though they were directed by one rational strategic man, operating on the basis of a *'single, national strategic calculus'* (emphasis as in the original).[26] The shorthand language of international relations encourages easy dismissal of domestic complexities. All writers and speakers (myself included) find it convenient to refer to 'Soviet action', 'American policy', or to the fact that 'the Soviet Union has decided to do X'.

The bureaucratic politics paradigm is not intended merely to flesh out the rather ascetic explanation of state behaviour that is provided by rational actor analysis; it is also hoped that prediction may be improved. For example, if the Soviet Union is not to be regarded as a rational strategic man, reasoning in a manner analogous to an archetypal Western arms controller, one's confident predictions of particular arms race sequences begin to lose their authority. As the national arms race decision processes are appreciated to be extremely messy, partly untraceable and, in the case of the arms race rival, almost wholly unknown, bold predictions of Soviet reaction proneness look very thin indeed.

Used with reservations, the bureaucratic politics paradigm can do nothing but good. It leads the analyst to regions of arms race activity that contain the explanation of what is otherwise often quite inexplicable policy behaviour. However, powerful logical models have a tendency to captivate and to capture the less wary. Offering proof of the existence of a law of the instrument, scholars armed with a bureaucratic political scalpel are likely to unearth much trivia and to downgrade the significance of strategic, doctrinal, and interstate action—reaction considerations.

Any model casts both light and shadow. This is as true of the bureaucratic politics paradigm as of any other. Cautiously employed, the bureaucratic politics model sensitises the analyst to the fact that most defence decisions are not the product of one purposive authority, but rather of the pushes and pulls of competing individuals and agencies. Even in those cases where the President may be said to have decided, it is reasonable to presume that his 'decision' is taken in cognisance of the balance of opinions within the defence bureaucracy, of congressional and electoral considerations, and of regional and/or nationwide economic factors.

Bureaucratic politics emphasised that an arms race is not run by two unitary camps, nor does each camp determine its arms race moves solely as a result of strategic debate. The stock in trade of the scholar is ideas. Hence he tends to overemphasise the salience in policy making, and to real world problems, of better as opposed to worse ideas. In bureaucratic politics, ideas (and their advocates) are the servants of organisational interests. Every interest succeeds in finding a doctrinal creed that provides legitimate rationales for the men, machines and money necessary for the health of its guardian organisation. Some of the more obvious dangers that attend bureaucratic political analysis of the strategic arms race must be specified.

First, American bureaucracy is not Soviet bureaucracy. In place of a mirror image rational (American) strategic man in Moscow, one might erect a no less illusory mirror image (American) bureaucracy in Moscow. As Gallagher and Spielmann [27] and Uri Ra'anan have demonstrated, extreme caution is necessary when predictions are made concerning the results of bureaucratic games played in a very alien political culture. Ra'anan's analysis of the 'feudal' nature of political power in Moscow should serve to give pause to any analyst rash enough to presume a generality of bureaucratic procedures and behaviour.[28]

Second, if one is interested to discover how and why the Superpowers have behaved as they have in the arms race, a bureaucratic political perspective will yield (a) insufficient information on the Soviet Union, and (b) more information about American weapon programmes than one really wishes or needs to know. More and more trees will be discovered, but the shape of the woods may well be lost. A necessary scholarly art is the ability to remain ignorant of trivial details (though, admittedly, criteria for triviality are not easy to establish).

Third, as yet it is far from certain whether or not bureaucratic politics will yield conclusions superior in policy utility to those derived from strategic analysis. After all, to an important degree capabilities do speak for themselves. It is more likely than not that a team of bureaucratic political analysts, funded on a foundation grant for three years or more, granted inconceivable and unprecedented access to Soviet files and personnel, and charged to discover the details of the internal processes that have resulted in a major programme of strategic forces improvement, would conclude by writing a report that supported what we already know (or strongly suspect, by inference from capabilities and declarations). Fourth, in an arms race each racing state must cope with the actual behaviour of the other. The details of who supported the arguments of the Strategic Rocket Forces' spokesmen and why, is far less significant than the fact that the Soviet Union will very soon have a large force of SS–19s deployed. Finally, political interdiction arguments are important, but are probably chimerical. If the arms race defence decision action is at home, then arms control action must be directed at the domestic processes that produce negotiated policy results. Unfortunately, as yet it would seem that the Western Kremlinological community is profoundly ignorant of who takes what defence decisions, and in what fora. Signals and even indices of arms race self-restraint could well be provided in aid and comfort of 'allies' in the Soviet Union. But any miscalculation, or just mistiming, in the West of the internal Soviet balance of forces could result in the signals and indices being seized upon by Soviet maximalists as evidence of diminishing political will in the United States.

Bureaucratic politics open the door on many crucial details of programme vicissitudes, shifting rationales, and political coalitions. As a critique of the more simple action–reaction models it is quite devastating. However, great care must be exercised in determining just what the paradigm does and does not explain. As a 'warts and all' perspective, it can show why brand X rather than brand Y was deployed. In its focus upon the interests of individuals and organisations it does tend to lead the scholar away from strategic reasoning. Such reasoning is, by implication at least, presented as being instrumental to the achievement of the goals of national sub-units. In focussing on the bureaucracy, it tends to see foreign adversaries as necessary threats. For example, Perry McCoy Smith has shown how the USAAF scanned the horizon for a post war enemy — and naturally lighted upon the Soviet Union.[29] The understanding of the arms race as serious interstate business, run for good and sufficient reasons, does not fare well in the context of such analysis. In short, this perspective distorts as well as illuminates, as do other perspectives.

The character of political/social systems

As with most arms race arguments, theorems focussing upon domestic societies and political systems come in both strong and weak forms. In its strong form, the character of the political/social systems perspective yields a proposition such as 'an arms race is driven by the social and political necessities of domestic societies'. The catalysing and sustaining agents for a military competition are not, so it goes, interstate conflict, nor the fears and anxieties that drive an action–reaction mechanism, nor the games played by bureaucrats; they are rather the fears, anxieties and aspirations of a whole society.

A more elitist formulation of the argument would hold that 'the ruling class', 'the power elite', 'the national security managers', or whatever, generates and sustains interstate military competition in order to foster domestic social and political stability. The fears, alarms and satisfactions that necessarily attend an arms race wonderfully concentrate the public mind in 'healthy' ways. Patriotic feeling is encouraged, national solidarity and identification is enhanced, authority – political, military, economic and social – should be strengthened in the face of foreign danger. V. R. Berghahn has made a persuasive case to the effect that the leaders of Imperial Germany saw their naval challenge to Great Britain after 1898 as much, if not more, in the context of domestic stability, as they did in the context of enhancing their international leverage *vis-à-vis* Great Britain (and France and Russia).[30]

This form of argument is very common indeed. Noting the apparent utility of arms racing to a society, it is easy to introduce the thought that if an arms race had not existed, then surely it, or a surrogate, would have had to be invented. At which point the notion almost suggests itself that perhaps many arms races were invented for domestic reasons. This argument proceeds to the effect that the conventional *Realpolitik* explanation of foreign and defence policy behaviour (interests clash, the use of force is legitimate, etc.) comprises little more than a conflict ideology.[31] Thus the arms race is seen as an instrument of general social control. The best exposition of this theme is to be found in George Orwell's *1984*. Political, economic, military and social leaders the world over are thus in alliance against their peoples.

This kind of argument may seem to follow from crude structural–functional models. If structures have functions (which is a truth of only limited utility), it should follow that the structure of Soviet–American strategic relations can be explained in terms of the functions performed for each domestic society. From the base assumption that interstate conflict is the invention of an elite, providing an ideology for vigorous arming, one can proceed to uncover a most impressive array of domestic functions served by an arms race. It is commonplace to suggest that a foreign threat and a very high level of military spending are vital conditions for Soviet rule. Respect for authority and social and political discipline would erode rapidly if Soviet leaders no longer called for (and sought to enforce) the utmost vigilance and great consumer sacrifices. In the Soviet case, at least, there is much to recommend the view that conflict is an essential ingredient in the official ideology.

Variations may be played on the above theme. It could be argued that military competition is only superficially the province of officials, political spokesmen and corporation executives (and shareholders): the real dynamo is a pathological public mood. Scholars as different in approach as Michael Howard and Anatol Rapoport have given some support to the epidemiological view of an arms race: that a whole population is infected with a war psychosis.[32] To cure the arms race condition, in response to this theorem, it is necessary to re-educate the relevant publics and to immunise them against war moods.

In its weak form, the character of the political/social system perspective does not go so far as to assert that during the course of their histories particular societies assume a military competitive character in order to alleviate internal tensions. Instead, it is suggested only that an arms race is not a superficial activity that may be conducted by bureaucrats and politicians in a manner largely unaffected by the political system within the rules of which they are operating, or by the mores and character of the social system upon which the political system is superimposed. The weak form of this perspective is important in that it reminds analysts that the bureaucratic politics paradigm – or, indeed, similar models – may seduce them into ignoring the distinctive features of the state and society on behalf of which officials are acting.

The importance of the character of this perspective is well illustrated in Jonathan Steinberg's study of the naval policy of Imperial Germany.

> An arms race is, after all, an immense social, political, legal and economic process. Its influences penetrated every corner of the societies involved, and its attendant manifestations are simply too complex to fit the standard categories of historical analysis. Even if the subject of study is only one of the participants in such a race, as is the case here, the number of elements in that nation's social, cultural, economic and religious traditions which significantly affect the course of the arms race is very large.[33]

Overenthusiastic acceptance of the validity of Steinberg's argument could lead the analyst into a morass of domestic trivia from which he is unlikely to emerge with any worthwhile conclusions. If everything is relevant to arms race dynamics, then the subject matter becomes impenetrable to the scholar. Commonsense suggests not that arms race enquiry requires a total analysis of the social and political contexts of arms expenditure, but rather that deep social and political forces (and norms and structures) could help to explain the movements of the principal human arms race actors.

Electoral politics

No commentator has suggested that the American side of the Soviet–American arms race is driven exclusively by electoral considerations. However, appropriate arms race behaviour has been an issue in every presidential election since 1956. It may also be alleged that arms race behaviour, both military and political, has occasionally been tailored to the perceived needs of friendly candidates in mid-term congressonal elections. Electoral politics is generally conceded to be one among many spurs (and, in principle, also a potential brake) to arms racing.

Electoral political factors have a bad name among arms control analysts for the following reasons: strategic complexity fares ill on the hustings; strategic oversimplification seems to accord the party arguing for more, an inherent advantage in the context of public sloganeering; in all significant respects, the raising of defence as an electoral political issue would seem to have resulted in accelerated arms race efforts. Until very recently it has been widely understood that there were no votes to be obtained by arguments for the slackening of the pace of defence programmes. The apparent reason why 'neglecting national security' issues have very often failed to take off to the advantage of the challenging party would seem simply to be that the public was not persuaded that national security was being slighted. It was not because the public was unresponsive to the theme. For example, in 1964 and in 1968 the Republican candidates raised the cry of 'The Republic in danger!'

Barry Goldwater's arguments over the alleged inaccuracy and unreliability of American missiles were a little arcane for most voters, while his demand that pre-delegated authority for the use of nuclear weapons be devolved upon lower echelons of the military was, again, a somewhat technical topic and unattractive to the electorate. In 1968, Richard Nixon's raising of a 'security gap' issue, and his announced determination to restore unquestionable American strategic superiority, may have contributed to the late rally for Hubert Humphrey. The Democratic reply was swift in coming and (at least apparently) crushingly persuasive.

In principle, at least, there is scant reason to decry the impact of electoral political considerations on arms race behaviour. After all, politicians should be responsive to the wishes of their constituents. On the other hand, it is a fact that the electorate as a whole is unschooled in the finer points of nuclear theology. In short, strategy making for the hustings yields the advantage to the man who has the clearest and simplest argument that touches deep chords in his audience. The general public does not read the annual posture statement, nor specialised articles, nor can one presume that the occasional articles on SALT in the daily press are at all widely read and comprehended. Officials and Congressmen could well find themselves in very deep political trouble indeed were the electorate as a whole ever to comprehend the grisly logic of mutual assured destruction, for example. One suspects that very many astrategic Americans would be very unhappy were they to appreciate that their country's arms control establishment regards it as desirable that they be hostages in perpetuity to Soviet nuclear retaliation.

The appreciation that political incumbents were potentially vulnerable to charges of an arms race 'gap' character has driven President after President to hedge against the possibility of a 'gap' campaign sticking. Having campaigned on the platform of 'I will be more attentive to the genuine needs of defence than will the other candidate', Presidents can find it difficult to reverse themselves at short notice. The arms race acceleration moves ordered by President Kennedy in 1961 reflected, in part, a genuine uncertainty over the state of Soviet programmes (U–2s had not flown since May 1960), and in part an intention to provide military indices to the Soviet Union of the political will of the new Administration. But the moves also reflected the fact that Kennedy had ridden to office on the issue of the missile gap. Robert McNamara's embarassing admission in February 1961 that 'today the Russians probably have no more intercontinental ballistic missiles than the United States'[34] was hastily *clarified* by Press Secretary Pierre Salinger, who asserted that it would be 'premature' to presume that no missile gap existed. Having argued in a 'more for defence' mode, with Congress and the country expecting and desiring major budgetary amendments upwards, it is politically impossible to say, in effect, 'despite the waging of an honest campaign, we now find that our claims and arguments were wildly exaggerated'.

There is evidence to suggest that President Johnson decided to overrule Robert McNamara on Sentinel ABM deployment as a result of his discerning the first serious stirring of Republican electoral noises on the subject.[35] As always, a bevy of rational strategic arguments were to hand and were duly involved, in defence of Sentinel deployment. An important domestic political virtue of the MIRV programmes has been the conceptual leverage that they were believed to be likely to wield in a debate over ABM deployment. Paradoxically, in the light of later developments, the arms control establishment was strongly pro-MIRV in the mid–1960s. .Furthermore, MIRV had no stronger proponent than Robert McNamara.

The electoral political advantage of MIRV has shifted in recent years from being a card demonstrating the folly of ABM to being cited as evidence of a limited and balancing degree of American superiority. Domestic opponents of SALT I were confronted with extant, if eventually vulnerable, statistics showing the American lead in numbers of deliverable warheads. Given the 'numbers game' aspect of domestic strategic debate, Robert McNamara fixed on deliverable warheads as being the most accurate indicator of the relative standing of the strategic forces of the arms race rivals.[36] Yet again, selective strategic analysis was invoked in aid of political needs. This is not to argue that McNamara was wrong, only that the quantitative analyses upon which he laid particular stress did not tell the whole story. The number of deliverable warheads is certainly a very important index of strategic power, but – particularly when appraised in the context of low throw–weight potential – it may suggest a false benchmark of adequacy. A large, though temporary, lead in deliverable warheads should assure the destruction of the adversary, but it may be of little value for less apocalyptic strategies of a counterforce nature.

Those who wish to pursue a prolonged career in politics need to recognise that politics is about winning elections, as well as about moral principles, safeguarding the general interest of the nation and so on. Politically ambitious men, representing districts wherein a considerable defence constituency resides, have a very strong motive to register a pro-defence voting record. Armed services and weapon system prime contractors appreciate political reality and make some endeavour to spread defence business around so that the column of partially dependent Congressmen is as large as possible, consistent with reasonable industrial competence. There is nothing surprising, shocking or even very heinous in the above facts. Critics of *de facto* functional alliances between Congressmen, industry and the armed services need to appreciate that, within some limits of strategic and ethical judgement, political representatives are charged with contributing to the well-being of their constituents and that there is scant evidence of congressional dissimulation on defence issues. Interest and strategic belief tend happily to coincide.

Despite the fact of the possible vulnerability of Congressmen to the political effects in their districts and states of sharp downturns in defence spending, it does not follow that the arms race must therefore rumble on indefinitely. The defence constituency is not of overwhelming significance in all districts and states.[37] Moreover, congressional defence debates of recent years have shown that many more individual politicians than might be expected are prepared to vote according to their conscience and their understanding of the strategic issues.

It is uncertain to what degree a President would be vulnerable in 1976 to a charge of neglect of the national security. It is tempting to claim that the public debates over ABM, MIRV (to a much lesser extent) and SALT have resulted in a much more strategically literate electorate. This ought to be the case, but it probably is not. Nonetheless, it is perhaps not unduly rash to argue that the vulnerability of Gerald Ford on defence issues will depend on the inherent worth of the challenger's arguments and the ease with which these are publicly comprehended. More or less flexibility in strategic targeting or the worth of relative EMT assessments are not the stuff of which a hard-hitting campaign is made. The kind of charges that might have substantial political appeal, and which would be extremely difficult to answer, would include such propositions as 'the Russians are cheating on the terms of SALT I', and 'SALT II is a very bad bargain for the United States'.

Organisational momentum

Organisational momentum is to be understood as enjoying symbiotic relationships with bureaucratic politics, with technological innovation and with MIC strains of explanation. The literature of political science is permeated with the understandable notions that *decisions* are of particular importance and that the course of policy may be traced by reference to a sequence of decision points. The decision making approach to foreign policy occupies a fairly hallowed place in the kitbag of scholarly tools of analysis. Scholars tend naturally to be attracted to events or interaction sequences that seem to stand out from their surrounding landscapes on the grounds of dramatic quality, unusual consequences, financial cost implications and believed risks. Books, articles and newspaper reports tend not to be written on such a subject as 'weapon research as usual at the Los Alamos laboratories', yet the tendency to focus attention on issues such as 'the decision to deploy Sentinel' and the like does bias understanding of the inertial factors that constantly bring forth issues requiring decision.

Organisational momentum refers to the vast and ongoing activity that constitutes business as usual. The overwhelming majority of arms race details are managed by continuing institutions geared to carry on a certain level of endeavour according to well-established routines. The arms racing bureaucracies constitute departments, agencies, bureaus and offices that draw their life from (and define their existence in terms of) particular arms race missions and duties or, more specifically, from particular classes of weapon systems. For example, National Intelligence Estimates (NIEs) may fluctuate in their threat assessments, but the Special Projects Office (SPO) of the Department of the Navy is in the business of developing, procuring, deploying and servicing ever more sophisticated nuclear powered ballistic missile-firing submarine (SSBN) platforms for SLBMs.

As long as there are weapons laboratories, research and development organisations in the armed services and in the OSD, weapon using organisations, weapon producing corporations and money available for research, development, testing and evaluation, new weapon ideas are going to be forthcoming. By the time a new defence technology attracts public attention as being of some arms race significance, at which time the non-official arms control community may join battle with the research and development community and with the prospective military organisation, that technology will probably have close to a decade of research and development history behind it. The extent and determination of the constituency or coalition that is forged to promote a particular technology will grow as the project gradually approaches the point where major development (leading to procurement) decisions must be taken. This is not to argue that defence technologies cannot be stopped. The research and development community produces an ever-changing menu of technological options, a number of which will either never find their way into the hands of a military user formation, or will be employed for precise purposes that are very different from those originally intended.

Many arms race moves are more akin to phenomena illustrative of Elizabeth Young's 'ripening plum' syndrome than they are to direct arms race interaction decisions.[38] Arms racing organisations, responding to no very specific military threat, constantly pressure their political masters to permit their products to be purchased. If there is no dramatic alteration in the climate of opinion that sets the rough boundary for defence expenditures, the level of effort of each segment of the arms racing bureaucracy will tend to change only very gradually over time. For many good reasons, budgetary allocations to defence bureaucracies tend to vary only very slightly from year to year. The best guide to the level of next year's budget is the level of this year's budget. Feast and famine cycles in financial allocation for defence upset that certainty which should facilitate the smooth progress of programmes. Fluctuations in defence expenditure requests of much more than 5 per cent per annum that are not clearly the product of inflation or of, say, a rise in military pay invite sharp public questioning. Acceptance capital is already in the bank for a defence budget that looks very much like a previous allocation mix.

Given the benefits of continuity, given the limitations on officials' time, given certain unpleasant consequences of reopening old issues that have already been settled by a negotiated compromise, it is hardly surprising that an administration does not indulge its intellectual curiosity in an annual zero-based budgetary review exercise. Most of the items in the defence budget are there because they, or their close relations, were there last year. Therefore, beyond the few very prominent budgetary items that are the subjects of contention on the more obvious of arms race grounds, there exists the vast bulk of arms race related and supporting activities that constitute, in practical political terms, legitimate business as usual. Subject to higher discretion, the intelligence community cranks out irregular, but frequent, threat analyses, while the armed services, often in alliance with the Office of the Director of Defense Research and Engineering, will come forth with more 'effective', and certainly more costly weapon ideas. As President Eisenhower expressed it in 1953, the defence policy of the United States must be geared to the 'long haul'.[39] 'Arms race as usual' activities are legitimised by a settled pattern of expectations. The Department of Defense and each major organisation within it knows, with a high degree of confidence, what its fair share of the federal budget ought to be. This fair share is expected to be allocated, just as the size of the margin likely to be cut by Congress is also identifiable in advance. Ritual budget-cutting invites the inflation of estimates.

Upsets and near upsets can occur. For example, the passion raised in the Senate in 1969 in opposition to the ABM certainly exceeded the expected level. Also, step level jumps do, very occasionally, occur in the level of obligational authority approved for defence. For international political competitive reasons, the settled expectations of the Department of Defence were pleasantly shattered by the rearmament drive launched on the occasion of (but not by any means totally as a result of, or for the conduct of) the war in Korea. The settled expectations of the late 1950s were upset by the accession of an administration that revised military doctrine, that redefined the intensity and scope of the political threats to the United States and her allies and that had domestic political obligations that had to be honoured.

In summation, the more dramatic arms race decisions rest on the basis of the regular ongoing activity of large organisations whose duty it is to nag constantly at military technological frontiers. Innovation is routinised.

Technological innovation

A special case within the general ambit of organisational momentum is the momentum or inertia of technological improvement. An influential and in many respects, persuasive school of arms race analysts holds that the strategic arms race really comprises a whole family of offence–defence and defence–offence races within each arms racing country. The principal stimulus to innovation comes, in this view, not from *evidence* of military developments abroad, but rather from the inquisitiveness and creative genuis to be found within the respective research and development communities.

Given that one is generally acknowledged to be engaged in what is termed an arms race, patriotic duty, career prospects, scientific duty, and (often) strategic commonsense all suggest that one follow whither technological ideas beckon. The interstate adversary can always be invoked to dignify and provide some rationale for a research programme that scientists wish to carry out anyway. With lead times being so long for new military technologies, and with the available evidence of the detail of Soviet research programmes (in their early stages, at least) being so unsatisfactory practically any interesting lines of military research may be justified on the grounds that one must anticipate future needs. To avoid technological ambush in the arms race many years hence, it is only sensible to fqnd a very wide range of research activities.

Necessarily, the scientists and technologists on each side are 'racing' to diminish their own ignorance (the enemy is not Soviet technology; it is the physical unknowns that attract scientific attention) and to counter (offset or bypass) the technologies of their own side. Even if the general character of the military programmes of the other side is familiar, precise operating characteristics (reliability, vulnerability to X-ray bombardment, etc.) must be inferred and inferred not merely from general principles, but from what is known of the performance parameters of the similar systems of one's own side.

This notion of the bilateral momenta of parallel technologies has seduced many analysts and legislators into identifying the routinisation of technological innovation as being the greatest single culprit responsible for the arms race rumbling on. Such authorities as Herbert York[40] and Jerome Wiesner[41] (and to some degree, almost the entire non- and semi-official arms control communities) are up to a point correct beyond question in their contentions. The crucial question is what do they think they are explaining?

Highly motivated, technically competent and adequately funded teams of research scientists will inevitably produce an endless series of bright new (or refined) weapon ideas. Furthermore, the existence of what General R. C. Richardson has termed 'conceptual lead time' must also be recognised.[42] A research and development community will conceive of new technological feats that might be performed long before strategic theorists have established the desirability of their performance. Technical ideas that are today only in the earliest stages of the research and development cycle will be operationally relevant to the strategic environment of the mid- to late 1980s and on into the 1990s. Who has a crystal ball that will illuminate, in 1976, the precise strategic needs of US or Soviet defence policy in 1988 or 1995?

As with all good arguments, the proposition that technology tends to precede doctrine can be taken too far. The relationship between technology and doctrine is by no means a settled one. On occasions, men of strategic vision have pressed for the adoption of strategic doctrines that would rest for their operational success on the performance of technologies as yet uninvented or at least, grossly inadequate. Under the guidance of Lord Trenchard, the Royal Air Force subscribed to an official credo of strategic bombardment long before a strategic bomber worthy of the name had been built. Official doctrine, to the extent that one internally consistent strategic creed is ever a reality, should not be seen solely as a dependent variable, to be shifted as the weapons laboratories indicate that new tasks can be performed. The strategic beliefs of senior officials and of politicians are not unimportant as a factor encouraging or discouraging lines of technical enquiry.

Whatever its strategic beliefs, no American administration has been or is likely to be able to suppress totally research and some development activity along strategically undesired lines of technical enquiry. Strategic doctrinal emphases will come and go, but the vast and variegated military establishment (and its industrial allies) continues to cover the entire spectrum of doctrinal interests. Three points are important here. First, the quantity of defence–related research in the United States is so great that very detailed central control of what is and what is not being investigated is as impossible as it would be undesirable. Second, the defence ideology (not employed here in a pejorative sense) of the United States specifies that, regardless of the strategic doctrinal preferences of today, a very broad research base is prudent. Hence scientists must be permitted to investigate phenomena that are of no immediate policy interest (or which are believed to contain undesirable 'provocative' features). The needs of tomorrow are not confidently predictable today. Therefore research teams are to be viewed as national assets to be dispersed only if absolutely necessary. Third, bureaucratic (and more generally, defence) politics tie the hands of senior officials and political leaders. The favourite technological sons of the air force or the army may be rejected, but opposition is appeased by the continuation of funding for research and development. This tactic preserves research teams as national assets, keeps hope alive (and opposition muted) in the organisational and industrial parents and demonstrates the prudence of arms race managerial performance. Thus, in practice, it is possible to say of an ABM system or of a follow-on manned strategic bomber, 'not in the next fiscal year'. Only very occasionally is it possible for an administration to say, 'never, for this or for similar technologies'.

The delaying or compensating tactic of funding continued research and some development effort is not of indefinite utility. Eventually, as was the case with the Nike-X ABM system in 1966–67, the point is reached where bureaucratic proponents argue persuasively that further research and development alone is unprofitable, and that what is needed now is field of operating experience. The technological plums will thus be alleged to have ripened.

Contrary to the implications of a fairly extreme interpretation of the bureaucratic politics paradigm, the settled strategic beliefs of political authority vitally affect the content and tactics of bureaucratic behaviour. For example, the United States Army has waxed and waned in its official enthusiasm for limited nuclear war in rough accordance with the doctrinal winds blowing from the White House through the Office of the Secretary of Defense. As a whole, the Army prefers to plan for major conventional war. More forces are likely to be funded and military officers are far more confident that they understand such combat. However, some of the weapons laboratories and a small minority within the Army, have continued to press for improvements in tactical nuclear capabilities. Despite the official anti-tactical nuclear weapons emphasis, throughout the 1960s and early 1970s something akin to a technological ambush was laid for the official anti-nuclear doctrine for ground combat. In brief, a whole family of very low yield fission and fission–fusion weapons has been or could now be developed, which, if married to precision guidance technologies, could be held to undermine many of the arguments long employed in defence of a conventional emphasis posture.

Imminent in the new tactical nuclear technologies is the doctrinal–operational possibility of very early and very heavy nuclear use for maximum battlefield effect. However, the political opposition in the United States and in NATO–Europe to greater reliance on tactical nuclear weapons (TNWs), in combination with hostile official doctrines, seems almost certain to frustrate the policy possibilities of the new generation of TNWs. Therefore, as a high confidence generalisation, one cannot assert that doctrine follows technology. Nonetheless, there are many instances where this has been the case. It could be asserted that doctrine follows policy which follows technology. Even with strong political and strategic leadership, the defence policy of the United States is a coat of many colours. The dominant theme may be generalities pertaining to assured destruction, flexible response, limited strategic options, realistic deterrents, and similar slogans, but lurking within the Department will be strong pockets of doctrinal dissent.

Whatever may be the official strategic rationales for funds expended, military bureaucracies are constantly preparing themselves for war. Strong arms control advocates, following their creed, are aware of the fact that strategic forces sufficient beyond doubt for a range of deterrent needs must be provided, while at the same time the armed services must be discouraged from designing and deploying weapons systems (or weapon system 'improvements') that might seem to yield a war-fighting edge of military significance. But there is simply no way in which many cumulative marginal or substantial improvements in performance can be prevented. By way of illustration, the following statement by Jack Ruina is instructive: 'On the issue of guidance accuracy, there is no way to get hold of it, it is a laboratory development, and there is no way to stop progress in that field'.[43] Naturally enough, weapon system user organisations are performance, as opposed to cost, oriented. Today it is taken for granted that succeeding generations of, say, manned aircraft or missiles will be not merely replacements; they will constitute inevitable modernisation. New systems are deployed not because the old ones have become too unreliable to use but because, to some significant degree, they are better and they are available. No iron laws of the procurement cycle are here advanced. The fact is merely recorded that new weapons cannot be sold before the end of the operational life of the systems that they replace unless they offer advantages of performance. Our culture adheres to the ideology of technical progress. This year's model is expected to contain improvements over last year's, and the improvements are likely to be deemed more important than are the attendant costs. A qualitative arms race is the inevitable product of interaction between interstate conflict and the scientific revolution. Vast and fairly constant investment in research and development ensures the routinisation of military invention, the guarantee that the flow of 'product improvements' is unlikely to cease or even to diminish very markedly. Necessarily, an arms race between Great Industrial–Scientific Powers must betray bilateral momenta of the processes and products of technological innovation.

Appraised in isolation, an undue appreciation of the onward rush of technological innovation could seduce the analyst into the adoption of a very apolitical and fatalistic perspective on the arms race. Instead, new technical ideas or even emerging technical capabilities should be seen, along with strategic threat assessments, as being a most important unit in the currency of bureaucratic political contention. Some ripening plums fall rather than are picked.

Follow-on imperatives

James Kurth has suggested that there are four principal theories that may be invoked in explanation of American strategic weapons procurement. These are 'the strategic, the bureaucratic, the democratic and the economic'.[44] In combination, the bureaucratic and economic explanations yield reasoning in one of the MIC moulds that are on the market.

The distinctive contribution of Kurth's writings has been to re-package and highlight a hypothesis that has been familiar for many years; namely, that the armed services endeavour to maintain a fairly steady flow of work for the eight major defence production lines in the US. There are many specific objections and questions that may be raised in connection with Kurth's data base. Useful, if somewhat harsh, critiques have already been offered by others.[45] In pursuit of the chimera of the best, some of Kurth's critics would seem to have neglected to place a proper value upon the good.

Appraising the record of the allocation of major aerospace development and production contracts, Kurth establishes beyond reasonable doubt that the business needs of the major production lines would seem to have been an important factor in the selection of contractors and in the timing of the awards of contracts. Particularly when abstracted in summary tabular form,

Kurth's theory merits very serious consideration from those analysts who are wont to suppress the messy details of domestic arms race processes in order to present the strategic rationales for particular arms race moves in full clarity.[46]

Kurth's perspective stops short of the eclectic approach advocated in this study. However, he does find that in the case of some strategic systems, for example, the F–111, MIRV, ABM, B–1 and even Trident, the bureaucratic, democratic (my 'electoral politics' factor) and even, somewhat grudgingly, the strategic explanation, do in varying measure have some merit.

Despite the evidence of very detailed case studies that is presented in Kurth's analyses, it is difficult to escape the conviction that intellectual sleight-of-hand has been perpetrated. A very similar point has been made above in connection with the bureaucratic politics paradigm. Two perspectives of limited value exist; yet each can be employed so as to provide superficially *sufficient* explanations of many arms race actions and reactions.

Every strategic idea that is adopted and absorbed into what is termed defence policy must have a bureaucratic history. No strategic idea is organisation neutral. From a systemic arms race perspective, bureaucratic political analysis should yield a truth that is far less important than the no less valid strategic, lagged and ambiguous truth in action–reaction. If the prime concern is with the rise and fall in relative state fortunes, and the dangers thereto attendant, rather than with mastering, largely for its own sake, the fascinating detail of policy making, some measure of indifference to bureaucratic political histories can well be justified. If the Kremlinological art really were to permit more than inspired speculation over the detail of Soviet defence decision making processes, the result could be unfortunate. One single virtue of our confronting a largely 'black boxed' Soviet arms racing bureaucracy is that we must, of necessity, be concerned only with behaviour, or the resultant. Some lifting of the veil of secrecy would no doubt result in the vociferous Western arms control school being manipulated by the 'evidence' revealed of Soviet internal debate and struggle. In brief, signal orchestration for the manipulation of credulous Western arms controllers should be expected to increase.

The above is no plea for continued ignorance. Clearly American ignorance of Soviet defence programme intentions has, on occasions, prompted operationalisation of 'worst (plausible) case' hypotheses and of Robert McNamara's greater than expected threat (as a formal force planning instrument). There are grounds for doubting whether far greater knowledge of the ins and outs of policy making in Moscow would much improve the American arms race performance. For well over two decades the Soviet Union has been racing against one of the most open political structures in the world. The record of Soviet arms race performance, considered over a quarter of a century, does not suggest in and of itself that over-much profit has accrued to them as a consequence of their being able to chart the course of the internal defence policy debates in the United States. Those optimists who reject this argument as being unduly pessimistic are recommended to read Richard Neustadt's book, *Alliance Politics*, and to draw their own conclusions.[47]

As an explanatory theorem, the follow-on imperative is useful in that it suggests some constraints on the autonomy enjoyed by the players of bureaucratic political games. Weapon system development and production contracts may be let not merely as a consequence of bureaucratic victory but also as a consequence of impending and clearly foreseeable corporate need. This need will leave some scope for bureaucratic contention, but its scope will have a very definite perimeter.

As with bureaucratic politics, one wonders whether those attracted to follow-on arguments are not really engaged in a fundamental statement of the obvious and in an exercise in trivialisation. The Soviet–American arms race does help serve the function of contributing to social integration in the Soviet Union. Is one therefore to conclude that the Soviet Union races in order to reduce the socially fissionable material that is contained within Soviet society? Of course not. 'Follow-on', as with a number of other economic theories of strategic weapon development and procurement, is disturbingly similar in logical genus to the Soviet negative example given above. This is not to deny that Kurth's argument has merit. The difficulty is to know quite what he is explaining.

Kurth very sensibly qualifies his argument in order to cover himself against the charge that he has neglected strategic, electoral, political and bureaucratic phenomena and to grant some merit to the considerable evidence that serves to cast doubt upon the worth of his arguments.[48] However, these facts remain: Kurth uses the word 'imperative'; the follow-on notion (and its close relative, 'bail-out') is central to his analysis; and he *could* be making very extensive claims for its explanatory power (in my opinion, Kurth seems to lack the courage of his model).

Kurth could be held to be offering his readers a well-packaged bundle of commonplace truths. To expand slightly on his refrain, the following is a sequential itemisation of the more salient features of his argument:

1 Major production lines for very sophisticated strategic systems are few in number (eight, so Kurth maintains).
2 These production lines are viewed by government as being vitally important national resources.

3   Each production line maintains very close contact with its principal source of military orders. (Mary Kaldor, among others, has made the point that much of what passes for bureaucratic political squabbling is really only the more public end of industrial rivalries.)[49]

4   The government deems it prudent on strategic, economic and electoral grounds to see that each major production line is maintained in operation (the separate military bureaucracies and sub-bureaucracies naturally share this judgement).

5   To a significant degree, the producer creates the (specific) demand for his own product. In general terms, of course, the Air Force, for example, does not need to be persuaded of the virtues of a follow-on air superiority fighter, etc. The production line knows what its consumer wants.

6   Limited funds, competition for defence dollars, technological innovation and a dynamic threat ensure that weapon generations and even step level jumps or knight's moves to new technologies, will occur at frequent intervals. In other words, because of costs, (as well as superior performance and partially substituting systems) weapon types that were once purchased in thousands will now be purchased only in hundreds.

7   The exponential trend in weapon system costs has meant that there are far fewer major weapons programmes to be funded and that each major contract for development and/or for production will be worth far more than its predecessors.

8   Therefore, to stay in business each major production line needs a major contract at fairly regular intervals.

9   To an important degree, prime contractors select themselves. Expertise in particular technologies is distributed unevenly.

10   To the extent possible, contracts go to the more competent of the economically needful corporations. However, every major production line can rest assured that it will be provided with enough work.

11   In the event that a corporation should find itself in serious trouble, it is certain (provided it is one of the big eight) that a timely contract, or, if all else fails, undisguised financial support, will be awarded.

What has Kurth uncovered or illuminated that could be of significance to the understanding of arms race dynamics? Redundant causation besets the argument. Every one of his weapon system case histories is explicable in its course by reference to other theories of weapons procurement.[50] This does not mean that Kurth is wrong, only that his explanatory hypotheses lack the power of exclusivity or even near-exclusivity. They are weak explanations, as are all arms race theories that have an explanatory centerpiece and do not make any very serious forays along alternative tracks. From Kurth's analyses,[51] given an understanding of total arms race activity, could any of the following statements reasonably be held to follow?:

1   Major weapons are developed and procured in order to sustain the economic health of major corporations (in other words, the arms race is a make-work enterprise) – Not true.
2   Major weapon systems are developed and procured beyond the needs suggested by strategic, electoral, and bureaucratic considerations – Probably not. This is very much a matter of judgement. Reflection on the strategic worth of Kurth's population of weapon systems, as appreciated at the time, does not yield any very obvious candidates for the make-work column.
3   The timing of major contract awards reflects corporate need rather than any 'logic' of the arms race – Perhaps. Though to a degree subversive of the possible worth of the theory, timing is a function of electoral political consideration (strategic rather than economic in character), budget cycle schedules, arms control bargaining reasoning and the hardy perennial of technology being ripe.
4   Major contracts have occasionally been awarded on the basis of economic need rather than optimum industrial–scientific capacity – True, but it does not follow that major contracts have been awarded to the incompetent.
5   Major contracts have been awarded of a technological character unnecessary for the fulfilment of US defence objectives and de-stabilising (by conventional MAD criteria) of the arms race, solely as a consequence of the need to fit the contract to the needful contractor – Not true. Analysts may disapprove of accurate MIRVs or of ABM defence, but there is no evidence in the public record that suggests such a subordination of defence policy.

On the basis of the above reasoning, the follow-on imperative should be regarded as a necessary partial truth. The above analysis should not be interpreted as evidence of indifference to cost overruns, managerial malpractice, etc. The sole concern here has been to appraise follow-on arguments in the context of arms race considerations.

The military–industrial complex (MIC)

The concept of the MIC, like bureaucratic politics and the momentum of technological innovation, reflects a necessary and somewhat limited truth about an arms race. All too often, the proponents of MIC arguments are less than specific over the writ of their explanatory claims. Presented with a vast morass of facts concerning military–industrial (and often congressional) interdependencies, we are somehow presumed to be able to draw the right conclusions. Bold propositions that would link raw evidence to conclusions (by and large already arrived at by intuition/ideology) tend to be noticeable by their absence. Again the question arises, what do MIC theories purport to explain? Regarding MIC (and related scandal theory arguments) I find myself in close agreement with Bernard Brodie. All too often the basic intellectual posture of the theorist is of the 'it stands to reason' variety.[52] MIC writings today are clearly in the tradition of the 'merchants of death' literature of the interwar years.[53] Employing a form of reasoning that has recurred on the same subject forty-five years later, Salvador de Madariaga advanced the commonsense proposition that the responsibility for international conflict, arms races and wars must be laid at the door of the men who profit most from those conditions: it stands to reason. In de Madariaga's words:

> Let us print it in capitals for it is blatant, open and obvious, in fact it is a platitude: ARMAMENT FIRMS ARE INTERESTED IN FOSTERING A STATE OF AFFAIRS WHICH WILL INCREASE THE DEMAND FOR ARMAMENTS.[54]

In language scarcely less strident, angry denunciations of the villainy of military–industrial interests have been a major growth industry of recent years. Of what does the theory consist? While there is no single MIC theory, there is a unified body of assumptions from which very few MIC theorists would dissent.[55] The following constitutes the core of the MIC theme:

1 Interstate conflict, foreign policy goals, strategic threats, etc. constitute a conflict ideology which legitimises the energetic pursuit of their interests by those domestic institutions and groups which must defend their activities by reference to foreign dangers.

2 Whether the interstate conflict ideology is an example of genuine false consciousness or whether it was designed and has been manufactured as a Big Lie is a matter for debate. Whether corporate vice presidents in the aerospace business really believe in the 'Soviet threat' is of no importance to an understanding of the dynamics of the MIC.

3 Once catalysed (there are some causal difficulties here that theorists have simply ignored), an arms race promotes the snow-balling growth of two (or more) MICs. The domestic defence interest becomes enormous in size and in complexity. The core of the MIC is the armed services and dependent industries. But dependence works two ways. Organised around particular weapon system types, the services and some of their sub-divisions vitally need, for their sense of self-importance, respect, budgetary and personnel career prospects, etc., the endless flow of new product ideas that industrial allies wish to sell them.

4   Despite its popular acronym, the MIC is understood to have licensed chapters in Congress, among journalists, in academia, in the labour unions and among the ranks of senior civilian executive officials. Whatever issues may divide the separate components of the MIC, they are all united in a common dependence upon the international political conflict that catalysed, sustains and rationalises the arms race.
5   The MIC comprises a loose coalition of complementary interests; it is not an organised conspiracy. By any criterion the generically pro-defence (MIC) interest is extremely powerful and indeed is not constrained seriously by any countervailing power.
6   In reality, the MIC constitutes a conspiracy against the general public. The effective, *de facto,* horizontal and vertical integration that expresses the central truth about the MIC means that weapon system supply and strategic demand have fused.
7   The MIC controls its domestic environment by the exercise of positive and negative sanctions (economic and political), and by spreading and sustaining that interstate conflict ideology whose wide acceptance is required if public approval is to be gained.
8   A similar MIC exists in the Soviet Union. Each MIC needs the other.
9   A very sharp decline in interstate conflict plus a consequent easing of the 'mad momentum' of the arms race would be disastrous for all segments of the MIC. Industry would lack contracts, military career prospects would dim, the bureaucratic fiefdoms of the national security system would be subject to rapid erosion, academic consultants would lack employment, etc. In short, the costs of peace would be high.
10   The threat of detente usually poses no insuperable problems. Such arguments as 'negotiate from strength', 'intentions can change very rapidly', 'military strength, not weakness, induces the respect abroad that engenders policies of detente', all serve to insulate the level of ongoing arms racing effort from the more serious possible depredations that could result from a condition of detente.

What can the above points be held to have explained? If an MIC endeavours to secure its own perpetuation, how did it arise in the first place? Is one to presume that there was once an acute military danger from abroad (1950–52?), but that the MIC, once brought forth, took off into self-sustained growth and hence needed a constant threat from abroad as a formal legitimising agent? Moreover, does the existence of an American MIC ensure that there will be a threat from abroad? Putative adversaries will presumably appraise an American MIC with alarm. Once born, the MIC abroad may be trusted to provide ample raw material for the threat assessment arm of the

American MIC – in other words, the intelligence community.

Does the mere existence of an MIC offer proof enough that there is villainy afoot? Is it not a fact that detailed analyses of the inter-dependencies that link legislators to officials to military officers to corporate executives and so on, are really offering nothing more than a description of the domestic arms race condition? In and out of itself, the evidence of the scale of the domestic defence interest and of the working arrangements that bind its separate parts implies nothing in particular concerning the dynamics of arms racing. When two Superpowers race in armaments over a period of many years, the defence interest or MIC is naturally going to comprise a cast of millions (including men in uniform and industrial workers) – so what? I believe that conflict of interests between separate security communities is an enduring feature of international (tribal, city, etc.) relations. Whether or not particular conflicts are catalysed by communities that seek relief in foreign adventure from domestic troubles, it is very obvious that all conflicts (as opposed to war – which raises other questions) offer some benefits to particular domestic groups. MIC theorists believe that they are doing more than just describing the domestic power constellation attending an arms race. They would have us believe that the MIC sustains and directs the arms race (and interstate conflict more generally) for its own advantage. Thus, if there were no MIC, there would be no arms race. Unfortunately, this proposition cannot be tested, because all arms races must be managed and fed by the activities of MICs. It should now be clear that MIC reasoning suffers acutely and fatally from the condition known as conceptual circularity.

If MIC theorists do not intend to argue that there is something improper about MIC activities, it is difficult to see why the concept has attracted so much attention. The term 'complex' allows an analyst to avoid hard questions about structures and boundary. 'Complex' lacks precise meaning. It suggests a dense thicket of interrelated things, but it suggests no particular form or purpose. At best, the concept of an MIC should be seen as a suggestive fiction: suggestive in that it serves to emphasise the quantity and diversity of the attentive publics for the participants in defence policy making (or defence politics); a fiction in that the MIC as such is not a unified player in the domestic games of defence politics. All candidate components of the MIC may agree that more rather than less should be spent on defence, but (a) the overall size of the defence budget is determined by many factors (e.g. domestic opinion, habit, momentum, etc.). and (b) each separate interest within the MIC is eager to acquire more funds for itself and also to deny undue financial success to competing interests. Defence budget allocation decisions may redistribute influence within the MIC. In other words, a great deal of the competitive activity indulged in by armed services and their sub-divisions and by major corporations, is intended to counteract the influence-potential of similar activity undertaken by rival organisations.

The fact that all individual human members of the MIC, whatever their specific policy disagreements may be, share a common set of broad assumptions concerning potential foreign dangers proves nothing at all. If the MIC is represented as being more of an attitude-set (a state of mind) than a cluster of interests, it could well be that a combination of self-selection processes and the romance-stripping effect of responsibility produce or encourage a common set of attitudes. A central tenet of the bureaucratic politics paradigm is that 'where you stand depends on where you sit.'[56] Understood as Allison intended it, this axiom expresses the truth that individuals define institutional (and even some personal) postures with the closest attention being paid to institutional interests. Reinterpreted and raised to a higher level of consideration, the axiom could be held to imply that responsibility wonderfully concentrates the mind and tends to narrow the bounds of perceived policy freedom. Attitudes and opinions that, to a radical disarmer, seem archetypal of an MIC-dominated mentality, may reflect nothing more sinister than the fact that the individual under scrutiny has a form of employment that requires that he take seriously some of the unpleasant possibilities that lurk in the international environment.

Undecided in MIC literature generally is the precise nature of the relationship between the M and the I. Given that the MIC is a pejorative concept, is one side more to blame than the other, or should one really conceive of the two sides as being one for all practical purposes? It is my impression that industrial, as opposed to military, villainy is seen to be the more damaging feature of MIC activity. The military, however wrongheaded in the eyes of MIC theorists, is at least credited with having some redeeming features. Soldiers do bear physical risks and they do have statutory roles to play in the making and the execution of defence policy.

Redeeming features are difficult to identify with respect to the corporate giants who (a) allegedly reap excessive profits from the production of items that the country does not need; (b) to a significant degree create the demand for their own products; and (c) via the symbiotic ties that they enjoy with particular segments of the military bureaucracy transfer their rivalries to the region of bureaucratic politics. There is something to be said for these and related points – but not much.

Many commentators seem to believe that aerospace corporations inhabit a world structured by Kurth's follow-on and bail out imperatives and by cost-plus-fixed-fee (CPFF) contracts (i.e., the corporation cannot fail to make a substantial profit: if fee is a fixed percentage of cost, the higher the cost, the higher the fee). The world is not quite this simple. To cite but the major examples, commentators thoroughly persuaded of the cosiness of the military contracting world would do well to contemplate the experiences of General Dynamics with the F-111, Lockheed (Georgia) with the C-5A and Grumman with the F-14. Furthermore, at the other end of the scale, the world of the small-scale military sub-contractor is one of the least secure in industry.

Much of the MIC literature is really of the indiscriminate data and anecdote collecting variety. A great deal of attention has been paid to the phenomena of the movements of retiring senior military officers into defence industry and of civilians between the Department of Defense and industrial posts.[57] The purpose of this analysis is less than clear. As Bernard Brodie argues persuasively, men who retire tend to lose all influence within their former service.[58] This is more than argument by intuition. Malpractice or ethically dubious activities and deals have not been uncovered in this area. Like much of the investigation that has sought to lift the veil from the international arms traffic, MIC analysis has been characterised by much meaningless statistical collection. To provide good answers, one must first have posed good questions.

Contrary, perhaps, to the impression given above, I am not hostile to MIC theorising. In principle, possible MIC-related hypotheses could be of the most profound importance for the understanding of arms race dynamics. Unfortunately, the important questions have yet to be posed, let alone answered. From an arms race perspective, the following are the more significant questions to be asked of MIC data: What is the character of the power of the MIC? What evidence is there to suggest that foreign (security) policy has been unduly influenced by corporate/military bureaucratic needs? What evidence is there to suggest that industrial–congressional pressure has caused an administration to purchase major weapon systems for which it saw no strategic requirement?

To be generous, one can but note that alleged MIC domination of American foreign and defence policies has yet to be substantiated. The absurdity of much of the MIC literature is easily demonstrated by reference to the Korean and Vietnam wars. The MIC, as it is widely understood today, scarcely existed in June 1950, and if the MIC manipulated the United States into the war in Vietnam, it must be far more incompetent than is usually granted.

MIC theorists, along with many arms controllers, quite unjustifiably project an American-style MIC onto the Soviet Union. In the words of Gallagher and Spielmann:

> ... the question has been here considered whether the phenomena described in this country as the 'military–industrial complex' represents

a model that can be accurately applied to the interpretation of the Soviet scene. As it happens, the findings on this score are negative.[59]

Whatever the validity may be of the as yet largely unformulated propositions concerning the baleful influence of the MIC on American arms racing endeavours, a quite different model would be needed for the probing of Soviet phenomena. It is difficult to resist the suggestion that MIC theorists have been fatally blinkered by ideology. Knowing in his heart that the MIC is evil, the typical MIC theorist has felt himself to be under no particular obligation to demonstrate the precise nature of the evil-doing. The facts do not speak for themselves.

The eleven factors discussed in this chapter comprise much of the raw material that must be shaped into any theory of arms race dynamics. Accepting the danger of possibly succumbing to the taxonomic fallacy, the above discussion has sought to demonstrate the required scope of satisfactory arms race explanation. To present a list of eleven complementary factors invites the charge of indecision, or of adhering to the maxim 'when in doubt cite everything'. Doubt there certainly is as to which particular mix of explanatory factors produced arms race actions X or Y. However, there is no doubt that arms race analysts must not choose between the explanatory factors here discussed. There is no single correct explanation. Looking over the long history of, for example, MIRV development and deployment – from conception to an initial operating capability took twelve years (1958–70) – one is struck by the fact that nine or ten exclusive and sufficient explanations for the success of the programmes could be expounded, and all would be at least partially correct.

Notes

[1] Michael Nacht has sought to deny the validity of this claim, but the written and spoken record of the late 1960s is against him. See 'The Delicate Balance of Error', *Foreign Policy,* no. 19 (Summer 1975), p. 173.

[2] For a brief, but telling, critique see Brodie, *War and Politics,* pp. 290–6.

[3] John Newhouse, *Cold Dawn: The Story of SALT* (Holt, Rinehart and Winston, New York 1973), p. 268.

[4] Johan J. Holst, 'Comparative' U.S. and Soviet Deployments, Doctrines, and Arms Limitation', in Morton A. Kaplan (ed.), *SALT: Problems and Prospects* (General Learning Press, Morristown, N. J. 1973), p. 68.

[5] See Matthew Gallagher and Karl Spielmann, *Soviet Decision-Making for Defense: A Critique of U.S. Perspectives on the Arms Race* (Praeger, New York 1972), particularly Chapter 1.

[6] See Graham Allison, *Essence of Decision: Explaining the Cuban Missile Crisis* (Little Brown, Boston 1971), pp. 4–5, 10–38.

[7] A standard and much-celebrated treatment of this is J. David Singer, 'Threat-Perception and the Armament-Tension Dilemma', *Journal of Conflict Resolution,* vol. 11, no. 1 (March 1958), pp. 90–105.

[8] A version of this argument has been propounded in George H. Quester, 'Will Deterrence "Just Fade Away"?' (paper prepared for the Aspen Arms Control Summer Study, 1973).

[9] See Colin S. Gray, 'The Racing "Syndrome" and the Strategic Balance' (paper given at the Stiftung Wissenschaft und Politik, Ebenhausen, West Germany, 1 May, 1975).

[10] Barry Steiner, *Arms Race, Diplomacy and Recurring Behaviour: Lessons from Two Cases,* SAGE Professional Paper in International Studies, vol. 2, no. 02–013 (SAGE, Beverly Hills, Calif. 1973); and 'Arms Race Processes and Hazards' unpublished Ph.D. dissertation (Faculty of Political Science, Columbia University, New York 1970).

[11] For a prominent and well-argued example of this view see Walter Slocombe, *The Political Implications of Strategic Parity,* Adelphi Papers, no. 77 (Institute for Strategic Studies, London May 1971). For a cryptic, but useful, survey of positions see Quanbeck and Blechman, *Strategic Forces: Issues for the Mid-Seventies,* pp. 9–10.

[12] Philip Guedalla, *Men of War* (Hodder and Stoughton, London, p. 47.

[13] McNamara, 18 September 1967.

[14] See Chapter 4.

[15] See Ted Greenwood, *Qualitative Improvements in Offensive Strategic Arms: The case of MIRV,* C/73–7 (Center for International Studies, MIT, Cambridge, Mass. August 1973), pp. 188–201.

[16] McNamara, 18 September 1967.

[17] George Rathjens, 'The Dynamics of the Arms Race', *Scientific American,* vol. 220, no. 4 (April 1969), pp. 15–25.

[18] George Rathjens, 'ASW, Arms Control and the Sea-Based Deterrent', in Kosta Tsipis et al. (eds)., *The Future of the Sea-Based Deterrent,* (MIT Press, Cambridge, Mass. 1973), p. 125.

[19] George W. Rathjens, Abram Chayes and J. P. Ruina, *Nucelar Arms Control Agreements: Process and Impact* (Carnegie Endowment for International Peace, Washington D.C. 1974), p. 1.

[20] John S. Foster, in US Congress, Senate Committee on Armed Services, Preparedness Investigating Subcommittee, *Status of US Strategic Power,*

Hearings, Part I, 90th Congress, 2nd session (US Government Printing Office, Washington, D.C. 1968), p.49.

[21] For example, technological determinism may be sampled in Ralph Lapp, *Arms Beyond Doubt: The Tyranny of Weapons Technology* (Cowles, New York 1970), p. 178.

[22] See Colin S. Gray, 'The Defence Policy of the Eisenhower Administrations, 1953–1961', unpublished D.Phil. dissertation (Rhodes House Library, Oxford University, Oxford 1970), Chapter 10.

[23] A superb study in this genre is Graham T. Allison, 'Questions About the Arms Race: Who's Racing Whom? A Bureaucratic Perspective', in Robert L. Pfaltzgraff, Jr (ed.), *Contrasting Approaches to Strategic Arms Control* (Lexington Books, Lexington, Mass. 1974), pp. 31–72.

[24] Allison, *Essence of Decision.*

[25] See Morton H. Halperin, 'Why Bureaucrats Play Games', *Foreign Policy,* no. 2 (Spring 1971), pp. 70–90; Graham T. Allison and Morton H. Halperin, 'Bureaucratic Politics: A Paradigm and Some Policy Implications', in Raymond Tanter and Richard H. Ullman, (eds), *Theory and Policy in International Relations* (Princeton University Press, Princeton 1972), pp. 40–79; and Morton H. Halperin, *Bureaucratic Politics and Foreign Policy* (Brookings Institution, Washington, D.C. 1974).

[26] Allison, 'Questions About the Arms Race . . .', p. 60. In its prescriptive mode, strategic theory cannot accommodate bureaucratic 'games'. Strategic theory indicates what a rational strategist ought to do in order to ensure the best of the worst (to indicate the minimax proposition of game theory).

[27] Gallagher and Spielmann, *Soviet Decision-Making for Defense.*

[28] Uri Ra'anan, 'The USSR and the Middle East: Some Reflections on the Soviet Decision-Making Process', *Orbis,* vol. 17, no. 3 (Autumn 1973), pp. 946–77.

[29] Perry McCoy Smith, *The Air Force Plans for Peace, 1943–1945* (Johns Hopkins Press, Baltimore 1970), pp. 52–3, 68–9, 113.

[30] V. R. Berghahn, *Germany and the Approach of War in 1914* (Macmillan, London 1973).

[31] A very useful presentation of this thesis (as a scholarly task and *not* as an exercise in advocacy) is Steven Rosen, 'Testing the Theory of the Military–Industrial Complex', in Rosen (ed.), *Testing the Theory of the Military–Industrial Complex* (Lexington Books, Lexington, Mass. 1973), pp. 2–3.

[32] Michael Howard, *Studies in War and Peace,* (Temple Smith, London 1970), pp. 102–5; Anatol Rapoport, *Fights, Games and Debates* (University of Michigan Press, Ann Arbor, Mich. 1960), Chapter 3.

[33] Jonathan Steinberg, *Yesterday's Deterrent: Tirpitz and the Birth of the*

German Battle Fleet (MacDonald, London 1965), p. 28.

[34] *Time*, 17 February 1961, p. 12.

[35] See Morton H. Halperin, 'The Decision to Deploy the ABM: Bureaucratic and Domestic Politics in the Johnson Administration', *World Politics*, vol. 25, no. 1 (October 1972), pp. 62–95. A slightly more strategic interpretation of the decision is to be found in Edward R. Jayne II, *The ABM Debate: Strategic Defense and National Security*, C/69-12 (Center for International Studies, MIT, Cambridge, Mass. 1969), particularly pp. 372–3.

[36] See McNamara, 18 September 1967.

[37] See Bruce M. Russett, *What Price Vigilance? The Burdens of National Defense* (Yale University Press, New Haven, Conn. 1970); and James R. Anderson, 'The Balance of Military Payments Among States and Regions', in Seymour Melman (ed.), *The War Economy of the United States: Readings in Military Industry and Economy* (St Martin's, New York 1971), pp. 137–47.

[38] Elizabeth Young, *A Farewell to Arms Control?* (Penguin, London 1972), p. 195, note 51.

[39] See Gray, The Defence Policy of the Eisenhower Administrations, 1953–1961, Chapter 4.

[40] See Herbert York, *Race to Oblivion;* and his testimony to the US Congress, Senate Committee on Foreign Relations, Subcommittee on Arms Control, International Law and Organization, *Arms Control Implications of Current Defense Budget, Hearings*, 92nd Congress, 1st session (US Government Printing Office, Washington D.C. 1971), pp. 92–9.

[41] Jerome Wiesner, 'The Cold War is Dead, But the Arms Race Rumbles On', *Bulletin of the Atomic Scientists*, vol. 23, no. 6 (June 1967), pp. 6–9. Dr Wiesner has also expressed this view elsewhere, for example, in Donald G. Brennan, (ed.), *Arms Control, Disarmament and National Security* (Braziller, New York 1961), p. 14.

[42] General R. C. Richardson, 'Can NATO Fashion a New Strategy?' *Orbis*, vol 17, no. 2 (Summer 1973), pp. 427–8.

[43] J. P. Ruina, in US Congress, Senate Committee on Foreign Relations, Subcommittee on International Organization and Disarmament Affairs, *Strategic and Foreign Policy Implications of ABM Systems, Hearings, Part 3*, 91st Congress, 1st session. (US Government Printing Office, Washington, D.C. 1969), p.672.

[44] James Kurth, 'Aerospace Production Lines and American Defense Spending', in Rosen (ed.), *Testing the Theory of the Military–Complex*, p. 135.

[45] For example, Arnold Kanter and Stuart J. Thorson, 'The Weapons Procurement Process: Choosing Among Competing Theories', in Rosen, ibid., pp. 157–96; and Edward P. Levine, 'Methodological Problems in

Research on the Military–Industrial Complex', ibid., pp. 294, 296, 300–1.
[46] Kurth, 'Aerospace Production Lines . . .', pp. 140–3.
[47] Richard Neustadt, *Alliance Politics* (Columbia University Press, New York 1970).
[48] 'Aerospace Production Lines . . .', particularly pp. 137, 144–52.
[49] Mary Kaldor, 'The U.S. Arms Industry', unpublished mimeograph, March 1973, pp. 3–4, 7.
[50] For example, Kurth claims that the scale of the Polaris programme is explicable in terms of bureaucratic politics ('Aerospace Production Lines . . .' pp. 146–9). This is true, but also misleading. Harvey Sapolsky has shown that the number of Polaris submarines was set at forty-one because that was the number that would permit the SSBN force to cover the entire Soviet target list *on its own*. There was bureaucratic and political reasoning behind this fact, but there was also a very clear strategic rationale (*The Polaris System Development: Bureaucratic and Programmatic Success in Government* [Harvard University Press, Cambridge, Mass. 1972], pp. 160–1).
[51] Other examples of Kurth's work on the follow-on theme are 'A Widening Gyre: The Logic of American Weapons Procurement', *Public Policy*, vol. 19, no. 3 (Summer 1971), pp. 373–404; and 'Why We Buy The Weapons We Do', *Foreign Policy*, no. 11 (Summer 1973), pp. 35–56.
[52] Brodie, *War and Politics*, p. 290.
[53] One major difference between interwar and contemporary 'merchants of death'/MIC writings is that the role of the military was not emphasised in the earlier period. A useful, brief comparative analysis is Robert R. Ferrell, 'The Merchants of Death, Then and Now', *Journal of International Affairs*, vol. 26, no. 1 (1972), pp. 29–39.
[54] Salvador de Madariaga, *Disarmament* (Coward–McCann, New York 1929), p. 11.
[53] For a sympathetic synthesis of MIC propositions and assumptions see Rosen, 'Testing the Theory of the Military–Industrial Complex', particularly pp. 23–5.
[56] Allison, *Essence of Decision*, p. 176.
[57] For a brief sample of the popular MIC literature on this phenomenon see Richard F. Kaufmann, *The War Profiteers* (Anchor, New York 1972), pp. 81–7; and Barnet, *The Economy of Death*, pp. 101–12.
[58] Brodie, *War and Politics*, p. 291.
[59] Gallagher and Spielmann, *Soviet Decision-Making for Defense*, p. 76.

3 The arms race adversaries: symmetries and asymmetries

An American adversary?

In Chapter 2, familiar and not so familiar United States-oriented factors were presented and appraised. Wherever appropriate, qualifications were inserted to the effect that each racing state was driven by a unique mix of fuelling agents. The critics of simplified interstate action–reaction models have now demonstrated beyond reasonable doubt that such models enjoy only marginal relevance to an understanding of arms race dynamics. To cite the most obvious example, the missile build-up by the United States between 1961 and 1967 may well have inclined Soviet leaders to endorse a missile build-up of their own which far exceeded the size that might have contented them had the US programme been of more modest proportions. Even this fairly non-controversial example raises many questions. Aside from the issue of the determination of the ultimate or cut-off size of the two forces, were not largely sequential quantitative missile build-ups the inevitable product of technological innovation, bureaucratic interest and strategic commonsense? Neither side could rest content with a force of first generation ICBMs. Furthermore, each side is strongly motivated to explore technologies known to be under investigation by the other, if only to discover what there is to discover in such technologies, and hence to be prepared to undertake imitative or offsetting programmes if necessary. Pertaining to 'if necessary' is the thought that perceived technological necessity does not drive the two arms race adversaries with comparable force. The fair measure of autonomy and political coalition possibilities that incline American theorists to the view that technology drives the arms race are not operative to a similar degree in the Soviet Union.

The purpose of this chapter is to demonstrate that the state sub-systems of the arms race cannot be usefully 'blackboxed'.[1] Proposed thus, it is unlikely that any analyst would disagree. However, there is no straw target here. Pervading the arms control literature are five strongly-held convictions. First, Soviet–American internal differences are real and many, but they are not of great importance for an understanding of arms race dynamics. Both sides have large military establishments, weapons laboratories, economic constraints, an arms control 'interest' and an MIC. In short, the functional equivalents of most of the actors discernible on the Washington scene may be located in Moscow.

Second, granted divergences of political lture, political–administrative practices, and institutional forms, modern technology carries its own logic for arms programmes. The strategic doctrines that link technology to policy know no political boundaries. Language (or strategic jargon) may differ from country to country, but a hard-target killing re-entry vehicle has the same meaning in any language. Third, the more obvious apparent differences in doctrine and the undeniable differences in weaponry reflect no two distinct political/strategic cultures but rather the fact that the Soviet Union is behind the United States. In the words of Roman Kolkowicz:

> Soviet strategic doctrine and capabilities appear to have lagged behind those of the United States by about five years ..., modern defense technology determines to a large extent the kind of strategic doctrines and policies that will be adopted by the super-powers. Thus, technology seems to have a levelling effect which subsumes political, ideological and social differences in various political systems.[2]

Fourth, the time-lag that still separates the Superpowers, the tendency to equality that is a feature of a qualitative arms race, assisted by judicious measures of arms control and by American strategic educational endeavour, will result in a very substantial measure of strategic convergence. In short, there may be some hyperbole in fundamentally American-style mirror-imaged notions of the arms race adversary, but time and technology both point to a growing convergence. Secure in his sense of America's analytical superiority, Newhouse writes as follows:

> Acceptance of this severe and novel doctrine (MAD) illustrates the growing sophistication of Soviet thinking nd some willingness to break with fixed attitudes, including the old Russian habit of equating security with territorial defense. And it points up the American interest in raising the Russian learning curve – in creating a dialogue that will encourage, however gradually, a convergence of American and Russian thinking about stable deterrence.[3]

Fifth, strategic arms are really a technical problem to be solved by the skilful application of appropriate arms control doctrine. The Russians seem to appreciate this. After all, this was what SALT was really all about (wasn't it?). But there are still some neanderthalic strategic thinkers in business who see strategic arms as having some diplomatic utility. The principal danger of strategic armaments is the danger that they pose to all mankind through the risks of accident, miscalculation or (in Dror's terminology) 'crazy state' behaviour.[4] There is no real danger of strategic weapons being employed directly or indirectly for coercive ends. Hence the common task at SALT, and in parallel unilateral efforts domestically, is to stabilise the arms race.

It is my contention that the above selected opinions and others of their genus are fundamentally in error. The variety of arms race phenomena is here being forced into a technical, apolitical, American Procrustean mould. Exaggeration is to be avoided, though it can be useful when differences of perspective should be sharpened for their comparison. There are some similarities between the Superpowers – above all else they share a mutual ascination. It is not here implied that each Superpower has blithely 'done its own strategic thing' in its own idiosyncratic way. Each is constrained by the knowledge that an arms race is, among other more salient things, a preparation for war. Nuclear Potemkin villages, if not unmasked by satellite reconnaissance, might serve for deterrence, but they must promote unease among military men who are acutely aware of their responsibilities in war. In principle, each side is prepared to be 'educated' by the other, in that a good idea, if it suits, will be accepted. Furthermore, since the United States has tended to be the arms race leader, it is only reasonable to expect that the Soviet defence community would learn rather more from their American counterpart than vice versa. However, there are boundaries to strategic intellectual absorption: boundaries set by ideology, technology and the strength of domestic strategic preferences (and their bureaucratic champions).

To cite but one example, the first generation Soviet SSBN that was at all comparable to the Polaris boats, (the Yankee class) was fitted with sixteen SLBM tubes, while, two generations on, the new longer Delta class boats could also carry sixteen SLBMs. The Soviet Union experimented with twelve launch tubes on the first Delta class boats, but is now returning to the higher number. This is stretching coincidence a little too far.

For the purpose of improving our ability to predict the likely arms race consequences of the pursuit of different technologies, it is important that the major asymmetries between the arms racing adversaries be fully appreciated. Much of what follows in this chapter is familiar and acceptable to a wide range of opinions, but its implications are often neglected because it is downgraded in importance by the operation of tacit arms race theories. An individual may note the probable facts of asymmetry, yet still fail to draw the conclusion that, at the most basic level, the arms race is about different things to the two sides. If an analyst is convinced that both sides are striving honestly to freeze the arms race on a plateau that is deemed to be inherently stable, it is difficult to know what would constitute convincing evidence to the contrary. There is sufficient momentum behind the research and development programmes of the United States for almost any Soviet programme to be rationalised as a prudential and, in political terms, defensive reaction.

The beginning of wisdom is the recognition of ignorance. In general terms, the asymmetries between the United States and Soviet Union as state racing agents are clear enough. To be avoided is the temptation to fill in the missing details of Soviet domestic practice with available information concerning 'the American way'. Similarly, as Gallagher and Spielmann (*inter alia*) have argued, simplified logical models are no substitute for detailed knowledge.[5] Furthermore, Western logical models, derived from Western phenomena, are particularly inappropriate. Bureaucratic and technological models of arms race behaviour are grossly inadequate even for the exploration of American behaviour; so how much less satisfactory should we expect them to be for countries with very different political systems? The discussion that follows is segmented into the following categories: defence politics and the political system; ideology, culture and historical tradition; geopolitics and foreign policy goals; and strategic doctrine and strategic weaponry.

Defence politics and the political system

Analysts tend to find what they are looking for. If one sets out firmly convinced that hidden behind the veil of Soviet secrecy there lies a pluralistic policy making system, different only in detail from that familiar in the United States, then clearly one is likely to discern exactly that. Hawks, doves and special interests may all be identified. Unfortunately for our understanding, whatever the logic of bureaucratic politics ought to be, there is very good reason to believe that the rules that govern Soviet defence politics are fundamentally different from those that operate in Washington.

The implications of asymmetry are very serious for the comprehension of arms race dynamics. The compound inertial processes (organisational, technological) that many arms controllers perceive as pushing the arms race ever onwards, operate to a different degree in the Soviet Union. The notion that a political executive is effectively the captive of domestic forces that have large stakes in the arms race may need drastic modification if it is to be applied to the Soviet experience. There are indeed very powerful forces impelling the Soviet arms race effort, but they are (in part) different forces from those widely believed to drive American endeavour.

The most obvious distinction between the Soviet and American contexts is the absence of substantial electoral political constraints on official Soviet behaviour. This is not to say that a Soviet leader is not vulnerable to the charge that he has neglected the national defence – as Khrushchev discovered – but it does mean that provided the leadership can carry its senior party comrades with it and can avoid seriously antagonising the marshals, the domestic politics of defence decision making have been attended to. Unlike those with a need to know in Moscow, the general public is kept in ignorance of the details of strategic weaponry, of the state of the strategic balance and certainly of the technical, political and financial issues that surround any particular, major strategic decision. In other words, with respect to defence at least, the Soviet Union is a command political system.

The above is beyond dispute. Where many Western analysts would divide is over the question of the distribution of power within and between the parallel bureaucracies of party and government. Western arms controllers are naturally and understandably inclined to look for friends and allies within the Soviet structure of authority. Franklyn Griffiths, among others, has argued that the best hope for arms control is for the arms control interest on each side to 'interdict' the policy making processes of the other in a positive manner.[6] This aspiration is soundly based as a general theme, but in practice it is confronted by several barriers. First, our policy making map of the Soviet bureaucratic landscape contains some very ill-explored regions. Second, even if friends and allies can be identified, there is reason to suspect that their freedom of action in no important way parallels that of their superficial equivalents in the United States.

To be more specific, the Soviet political system is not merely one of the central command and control variety; the Soviet bureaucratic structure would also seem to be governed far more by central direction than is the case in the United States. The reasons are not hard to find. Detailed policy truth, inspired by the correct application of Marxism—Leninism, must stem from the party's leaders. The circularity in Soviet thought is important here. The Communist Party of the Soviet Union rules because it has the correct ideology. A particular cabal or group of leaders enjoy that position because they are the authoritative interpreters of the sacred texts. The ideology cannot be wrong, therefore policy failure is the fault of the the leader who read the runestones incorrectly.

Beyond the ideological metaphysics of the right to command obedience, it must be appreciated that what might be termed the command model of political authority has behind it nearly six decades of operational practice. Communication chains in Soviet government tend to be vertical rather than lateral. Central authority in the United States government is limited by such constraining factors as the capacity of the President, the ability of subordinate bureaucracies to forge coalitions among themselves and with elements in Congress and in the country at large and the considerable latitude allowed officials to pursue their separate interests beyond detailed central observation.

The contrast with the Soviet Union could hardly be more sharp. The energy and ability of individual Soviet leaders is relevant to the way in which the system functions, but with implications foreign o those that would follow in Washington. Inept and/or lethargic leadership in the Soviet Union is unprotected by constitutional niceties. Such a leader, in these more liberal days, is likely to find himself banished to write his memoirs. The political jungle aspects of the Soviet succession context naturally encourage tough, vigilant and energetic leadership. Also, it places a premium on close political control and on the support of one's position by means of an extensive system of political patronage. Personal fealty claims serve to limit (and direct) the ambitions of dependent officials and the scope of lateral 'bureaucratic politicking'.

While personal loyalties and an ethos of obedience to a politically infallible central authority are important factors making for a bureaucracy whose autonomy is very severely constrained, there are also more formal methods. Specifically, the activities of officials are monitored by the parallel bureaucracy of the CPSU, while obedience and strict adherence to one set of rules and procedures is encouraged by the climate of mild fear and anxiety promoted by the ubiquitous vigilance of the KGB.

The above may overstate the case, but only slightly. The point is to emphasise that far more decisions are made at the topmost level of political authority in the Soviet Union than in the United States.[7] Soviet bureaucracy is far more compartmentalised than is the case in Washington. The kind of bureaucratic games orchestrated (for example) by Morton Halperin in 1968 in support of SALT would be quite unthinkable in the Soviet context.[8] Soviet civilian officials lack the knowledge and the mandate to intervene in military matters. Illustrating this point with reference to the Soviet SALT delegation, Newhouse writes:

> Later in the same round, Colonel-General Ogarkov, then listed as the second-ranking member of the Soviet delegation, took aside a US delegate and said there was no reason why the Americans should disclose their knowledge of Russian military matters to civilian members of his delegation. Such information, said Ogarkov, is strictly the affair of the military.[9]

The extent to which the Soviet military establishment influences major defence policy decisions has long been a bone of contention among Western analysts. Certainly, it would seem to be the case that the Soviet defence establishment — unlike much Western practice a totally uniformed establishment even at its most senior level — is relatively more powerful than its American counterpart.[10] It is presumed by most Western analysts that the Soviet armed forces played critical, if undramatic, roles in the succession crises of 1953—55 and again in not opposing the ousting of Khrushchev in 1964. It is tempting to argue that the price paid by the post-1964 collective leadership included a measure of budgetary largesse and civilian non-intereference in matters of professional military concern. Examining the Soviet Union in 1975, it is possible to argue that Brezhnev had to pay a substantial price in order to secure military acquiescence with the terms of SALT I and the Vladivostok accords. It is reasonable to presume that there is something in this argument, but there is also good reason to believe that the argument is to be employed with extreme caution. Evidence is lacking in support of the notion that a very moderate detente-oriented leadership has been compelled to pursue arms racing options and even political semi-adventures abroad as a result of military and hard-line party pressure.

Without denying the inevitability of disputes over detail and policy emphasis, where are the facts that suggest serious divergences of opinion between civilian and military leaders? The comprehensive Soviet military build-up in the 1960s and early 1970s reflected both international political commonsense and traditional Soviet combined arms military doctrine. Having lived dangerously through Khrushchev's political adventuring, all prudent and responsible Russian officials, it seems sensible to presume, were in agreement that in the military area, and particularly in the strategic nuclear field, the Soviet Union was in need of more arms. Similarly, it seems unlikely that the debate over intervention in Czechoslovakia was a polarised one between the military and civilians. The dangers inherent in Dubcek's weak leadership must have been obvious to all. The four new ICBM systems and new classes of SSBNs that have been discovered by American national technical means of verification following the signing of SALT I may constitute a compensation package (such as was apparently agreed to in the United States with the JCS, duly dignified as certain 'assurances', etc.),[11] but, much more likely, they may reflect the political judgement that to press hard in weaponry pays political dividends.

Similarly, what is one to make of the Soviet role in the October War of 1973? Brezhnev's firm personal endorsement of a policy of detente was widely believed to have precluded Soviet support for such a venture as crossing the Suez Canal. However, Brezhnev's brand of detente was widely misunderstood by wishful thinkers in the West.

It is not my intention to present a picture of harmony and of an absence of bureaucratic or budgetary strife in the Soviet Union. Differences of opinion and attitude are discernible, in part reflecting institutional interests, in part personal affiliation (as with Khrushchev's ties to the 'Stalingrad' as opposed to the 'Stavka' group of Soviet marshals). The principal difficulty is to know what to make of the discordant noises that are monitored in the West. Seeking to impose some order on the field, in his study of Soviet strategic elites Roman Kolkowicz distinguishes between the following: the conservatives, the technocrats, the rationalists (a synthesis of the two previous views) and the Americanologists.[12]

This last elite, centred on the Institute of World Economy and International Affairs and on the Institute of the USA, has attracted particular attention in the West in recent years. Individuals from these institutions are well knowj to Western arms controllers; they write in a sophisticated and knowledgeable way of Western policies and debates and to an important degree, it is presumed that these men are a conduit for Western ideas to the Soviet leadership. Under the guise of criticising American strategic policies, or of praising the detente-oriented efforts of 'sober-moderate' circles in the West, much indirect criticism of domestic hardliners may legitimately be made. Here, at long last, should be a civilian centre of strategic expertise, licensed to engage in discreet bureaucratic combat with less enlightened military and party opinions and interests. The Director of the Institute of the USA, Georgi Arbatov, has certainly received political promotion, and he is known to be a trusted associate of Brezhnev, but it is far from clear what influence, if any, he and his apparently more moderately opinioned colleagues have on Soviet defence policy.

Whatever signals of bureaucratic contention are received, it is well to remember the constraining influence of the Soviet political culture and of the tightly disciplined structure of Soviet government. Western arms race analysts tend to have their own favourite Soviet military writers or, indeed, Soviet civilian strategic writers. By means of selective quotation from selected Soviet writers, Soviet adherence to almost any strategic doctrine can be demonstrated, ranging from assured destruction plus insurance to total first strike counterforce.

Ideology, culture and historical tradition

I do not believe that the nuclear arms race is driven by two interlocking and irresponsible research and development communities. Rather it is political conflict that gave birth to and has sustained the race. The political sources of conflict may certainly be specified in terms of wartime agreements believed to have been broken, territorial malpractices duly noted and the like. However, it is also relevant to observe that the posibilities for the progress of detente and for the braking of the arms race, even over the long term, are severely constrained by the way in which Soviet leaders approach the world — domestic and foreign.

Soviet citizens are reared on an ideology of conflict. War may not be inevitable, but capitalist powers are irreconcilable enemies of socialism. In best Darwinian fashion, Soviet leaders adhere to the proposition that life is a constant struggle and that only the fittest survive. Ideology has usefully predesignated who is the fittest, of course. When Soviet leaders bargain abroad, they are expected to return with demonstrable advantages gained.

Conflict and struggle may assume many forms and be conducted through many media. Unlike the world view adhered to by many American arms control experts, the Soviet world view does not deny the political utility of strategic nuclear power. Such power is in part a hedge against the possibility of war, but it is seen even more as an instrument of political pressure, as an index of political weight and as a symbol of political status. As Johan Holst, William Van Cleave and others have indicated, international conflict is not eschewed when the Soviet Union enters into protracted arms control negotiations.[13] Given equal negotiating competence (which in SALT I and II, as so often before, manifestly has not been the case), the party that is stronger should achieve a negotiated outcome that truly reflects its predominance. Concessions are interpreted as a sign of weakness. Intelligent and dedicated bargainers are supposed to sell their bargaining chips, not give them away. Similarly, each party is presumed to know what its interests are. Hence the American penchant for advancing, in rapid succession, a variety of alternative agreement packages invites not a reciprocal flexibility, but rather confusion and a determination to press even harder to see if more advantageous packages will be produced.[14]

Normal political relations between the two Superpowers do not mean what many analysts would seem to believe. One is not merely considering the relations of two joint pre-eminent powers betweej whom mutual suspicion should be expected, regardless of the character of their political systems. One is also considering future relations with a power whose leaders are imbued with the notion that conflict is inevitable and even desirable.

For reasons of historical memory (e.g., Pearl Harbour) and military–technological bias, American strategists have, understandably enough, been obsessed with the least likely strategic scenario – an intercontinental surprise attack. This fixation is easily defensible: it is the worst plausible case and the risk-taking propensities of others are unknowable. The fact remains that with the Soviet Union one is racing with a power whose leaders sincerely believe in the eventual triumph of their system. Strategic adventurism, indeed any form of adventurism, would be a heinous crime. Similarly, one is racing with a power whose leaders take a very broad view of the factors relevant to interstate competition. American analysts may believe that a set of strategic hedging programmes will induce self-restraint on the part of Soviet leaders, but those Soviet leaders are likely to be more impressed by the prospective state of that permanently operating factor from Stalin's time known as 'the stability of the rear'. Americanologists in Moscow are not loath to identify the forces in American society that are opposed to expensive and allegedly dangerous arms race behaviour.[15]

Soviet ideology and historical experience exert an influence hostile to heavy reliance on fairly narrow technological factors for policy success. Strong historical forces, contradictions within and between societies, not military–technical derelopments, are supposed to promote political change. This broad and often apparently amorphous concern with the political, which is given a very wide meaning, is particularly unfortunate in the context of an arms race with the United States. American strategic studies, in contrast to the rough Soviet analogue, have highlighted the problems and opportunities posed by technological change. The entire record (theoretical and practical) of the Western arms control movement is really a testament to the limited utility of attempting end-runs around political difficulties. Perhaps the most explicit statement of the fundamental assumption that underpins much of American strategic ideology has been provided by Roman Kolkowicz.

> The development of technology has proceeded in the autonomous and aggregative manner, while the development of strategic theories unfolded in nonlinear fashion: technology set the pace and strategic theory followed.[16]

There is some truth to this, but no more. What is disturbing about this fixation on the technological engine of strategic competition is that, if taken to its logical extreme, it is certain to mislead US arms race managers in their necessary endeavours to predict future interaction chains. It is unclear whether or not Kolkowicz is prepared to endorse the notion of a technologically determined strategic convergence of the Superpowers. He declares that he will examine the hypothesis that 'the dynamics of strategic relations between the two Superpowers point to an eventual convergence of their strategic theories and policies',[17] but no very clear conclusions are reached.

American technical predilections in an arms control context may be noted with respect to problems as far apart in time as cruisers in the late 1920s and ground and tactical air forces in M(B)FR. This is not to say that American analysts have been wrong; only that it is appropriate to recognise that one is competing with a power whose leaders have an ideology that inclines them to deprecate technological factors as being of secondary importance.

Reflecting perhaps their legal backgrounds, many US arms control practitioners have tended to believe that business could always be done with the opposing advocate. Fundamentally, both sides shared enough common ground for a deal to be done. American analysts (ably supported by some of their British counterparts) do not share and have not fully appreciated the theme of political struggle which permeates Soviet international behaviour. For reasons traceable in part to their somewhat Cobdenite world view, and in part to their strategic ideology, American arms controllers have tended not to view SALT as an arena for political struggle. The appreciation that the Soviet leaders did regard SALT thus (as they did other arms control fora) need not have precluded agreement. However, an appreciation that Soviet negotiators were looking for political advantage should have had considerable impact on the scope and direction of the analytical backcloth to SALT and on the behaviour of the American delegation and of its political masters who were negotiating, in parallel (though often several steps ahead), via the Soviet Embassy in Washington.

To the extent that secrecy is still a significant strategic factor, despite the prevalence of electronic and photographic monitoring, the Soviet Union enjoys an inherent advantage over the United States: the closed nature of Soviet society and of Soviet official deliberations is non-negotiable. Ideology, history and powerful interest combine to ensure that Soviet leaders will never accede voluntarily to the opening up of Soviet society. The degree to which the Soviet political system is fragile is unknowable, but the evidence of effective Soviet action against Czechoslovakia in 1968 suggests that the present rulers are not inclined to risk experimentation. Detente is an interstate phenomenon. Any Western aspirations for the encouragement of a measure of domestic Soviet liberalisation to the point where there would be some significant popular constraint over public policy are doomed to disappointment.

Many factors have combined to produce this obsession with total control, among which are (a) official fears of unknowable consequences; (b) the arrogance of office holders and their contempt for public opinion; (c) habit and the preoccupation with security; (d) vested (institutional and personal) interests; (e) strategic advantage – an arms race 'plus' – and a guaranteed stability on the home front; (f) the clandestine origins of the party; and (g) traditional Russian attitudes. Great Russian chauvinism and near paranoia are not the products of Soviet rule. Suspicion of foreigners and fear and envy of the outside world were all inherited by Lenin (along with a very substantial secret police apparatus). The contrast with American attitudes is too obvious to warrant much comment. Russians have always felt vulnerable to attack from both East and West across a landscape largely devoid of significant defensive barriers and they have envied and feared the technologically more advanced societies to the West. The United States, by way of contrast, has enjoyed the psychological security of an insular location and the benefits of a sure knowhedge, or ideology, that she constituted a civilisation superior to that of the enfeebled and squabbling powers rejected by the majority of her population through their migration.

Those who, for the best of motives, are eager to herald the demise of the political utility of strategic weapons should reflect on the Soviet situation. Ever since 1917, Soviet leaders have lived in the shadow of superior military power abroad: military power, moreover, which was assumed to be guided by men fundamentally hostile to the Soviet Union. In the early 1970s, for the first time in over five decades, the Soviet Union has attained a position of strategic equivalence with her principal military competitor. Given the evidence of American willingness to be accommodating, as Soviet strategic power has accumulated, the temptation of Soviet leaders to play their strategic cards for political advantage must be enormous.

Geopolitics and foreign policy goals

Geography, like ideology, is an influencing factor for foreign policy that political scientists tend to regard with quite excessive suspicion. None deny the relevance of geography and ideology, but most are afraid that each, taken very seriously, might seem to over-determine their conclusions. Political geography has never recovered from its analytical abuse by the German theorists of *Geopolitik* who practiced their trade in the 1920s and 1930s. Geopolitical determinism is no more and no less unsatisfactory than are the more fashionable one factor explanatory theories which abound today and which have been discussed earlier.

Soviet–American political and strategic relations cannot be understood without due attention to their geopolitical singularities and to the foreign policy concerns that are conditioned and even determined by attitudes that stem, in part, from those singularities. Whatever the ultimate foreign policy ambitions of a state, its proximate concerns must be conditioned by the appreciation of its geographical relations *vis-à-vis* potential enemies. Technology may shrink strategic distance, but foreign policy and strategic thought continue to betray the symptoms of continental or insular location. A nation's physical and economic geography explains much of its history. From that history stem very particular features of political and strategic thought and practice.

The principal geopolitical facts of relevance to this study are the following: the United States is an insular power (albeit of continental dimensions), long accustomed to a recognised predominance in her own hemisphere; while the

Soviet Union is a continental heartland power, long accustomed (with good reason) to fear her close neighbours and enjoying no uncontested hegemony over the oceanic shoreline of her heartland.

As a geopolitical right, and also as a reflection of political prudence, Soviet leaders would seem to be convinced that theirs should be the dominant voice in European affairs. Geopolitically, as the indigenous Superpower, the Soviet Union should have significant control of all Europe. It sounds somewhat atavistic to talk of geopolitical rights, but strong strains of this line of reasoning may be discerned in connection with the much increased Soviet activity in the Middle East and particularly in the Eastern Mediterranean. The geopolitical facts of the Soviet–American arms race are that the two Superpowers, one from an insular and the other from a continental base, are contending for influence over the rimlands of Eurasia. The opportunity and some of the future danger for the Soviet Union lies only a few hundred miles away in the Western European confusion that might one day combine and grow to Superpowerhood, while for the United States protecting influence must be projected over three thousand miles and more. The military, and hence arms race, implications of the principal geographical area in contention being so close to the sources of Soviet power are both obvious and often under-recognised.

Soviet holdings in Eastern Europe require the extension of no strategic nuclear deterrent writ. The very location of those territories on the marches of the Soviet Union and the possible connections between changes in their domestic regimes and the control exercised over Soviet society endow the Soviet commitment to their socialist integrity with an inherent credibility. No such automatic response or natural concern attends US links with Western Europe. Profound and varied though these links may be, American and NATO-European officials have always felt that only a great deal of conscious effort on the part of the NATO allies could sustain a credible American security guarantee.

The destruction of the intra-European balance of power system in World War II presented the victorious Soviet Union with an opportunity not to be missed. Henceforth, Soviet power would be in Central Europe and would threaten (in a capability sense, at least) to overwhelm those countries liberated by the Western allies. The Soviet–American arms race was the inevitable product of a context wherein Central and Western Europe could not sustain its political independence *vis-à-vis* the Soviet Union without very active assistance from the United States.

Whether or not Stalin and his successors ever seriously considered the possible costs and benefits of military adventure in Europe is beside the point. Soviet ground forces, sucked into Central Europe by the events of 1944–45, have remained there as a potential threat to Western Europe. The European fixation of Soviet leaders has been reflected fairly consistently in their arms race behaviour. Large continental land powers tend to maintain large standing armies; oceanic distance is not available to provide time for wartime mobilisation. Geographical factors also mean that the most valuable of the United States' foreign holdings are easily accessible to any offensive action taken by Soviet ground forces. It may be that Stalin did not consciously design his postwar military posture to sustain a condition of 'hostage Europe', but the fact remains that geopolitical circumstance provided the immediate causes of explicit Soviet–American hostility. Given their geographical relationship and the distinctive and asymmetrical military force postures developed during World War II (again in good part as a consequence of geography), it was only to be expected that each Superpower would seek what political and latent military advantage it could from its particular geographical–technological context. In the early stages, and to a considerable degree still today, the Soviet–American arms race was a contest between an air/sea power and a land power. For reasons of ideology and political structure, Soviet strategic thinking did not pass through fires of controversy as elemental as those lit by the civilian strategists in the United States. Moreover, the military history of both countries finds its echoes in current military structure and strategic doctrine.

Soviet and American strategic thought could be said to be characteristic of, respectively, a continental and an insular tradition. In the continental tradition, so the argument goes, war is deemed a total national enterprise, liabilities are unlimited and close political control of military events is impossible. This tradition may be discerned in its literary form in Tolstoy and in a somewhat selective reading of Clausewitz. Geography yields no promise, however illusory of the successful conduct of limited military operations. As a consequence of the abutment of land frontiers, all forms of military operations directly and immediately affect national homelands and national survival is immediately at stake because of the proximity to the fighting of the core areas of national power. This continental tradition is discerned, so it is claimed, in the unfriendly reception given by Soviet writers and officials to the multifarious limited war schema devised by American and British strategists.

By contrast, the insular strategist conceives of wars as being of limited liability, of operations waged 'away' rather than 'at home', and of strategic operations fine-tuned for limited political ends. Examples of this insular preference are numerous: swift descents on the French coast and the financial sponsorship of Prussian allies in the Seven Years War, Liddell-Hart's writings of the late 1930s,[18] the American practice of limited war in South Vietnam – all may be held to epitomise the insular way in strategy.

The contrast drawn above between the two schools of strategic thought and practice is of more than marginal significance for an understanding of arms race dynamics. Past apparent Soviet rejection of limited war theories may thus reflect neither conceptual backwardness, nor even an extant force posture lagging behind that of the United States, but rather a firm adherence to an alternative set of strategic attitudes which derive not from recent strategic debate, but from deep historical and geographical factors. The prospects for conceptual convergence are dim indeed if much weight is to be placed on the geographical and historical conditioners of Soviet and American thought. Schlesinger may make more flexible the strategic targeting plans but Soviet emulation is not to be expected. Of course, the world is not quite this simple. Whatever the predilections of a defence community, technological change will induce some measure of duly domesticated doctrinal change. However, as noted above and underplayed by such writers as Roman Kolkowicz and Herbert York, doctrinal preference has been known to shape the attitudes of the men who must decide which technologies will be funded through their development cycles.

Geographical factors go far towards explaining the shape of a nation's military establishment and the military and political moves of others likely to be perceived as being of a threatening character. Because of her proximity to Western Europe, the Soviet Union was able to acquire a second class Superpower status comparatively cheaply. The maintenance of large ground and supporting air forces reflects (a) the Soviet way of military preparedness; (b) the fact that large, powerful and hostile powers (or power combinations) lie beyond her borders to the East and to the West; (c) the fact that military service is a conditioning process for Soviet youth; (d) the fact that the Soviet Union is a large, proud and demographically well-endowed state, to the leaders of which the maintenance of first class (if distinctive) armed forces is a natural and unarguable requirement; (e) extensive, if flexible, foreign policy ambitions and (f) an awareness that Soviet holdings are vast and need protecting.

In all fields of military endeavour, geographical factors influence the choice of military posture and the disposition of its elements. The Soviet–American strategic arms race by no means explains the totality of the military preparations of those two powers. The gekpolitical context of each racing state greatly complicates the problems of arms control. If one proceeds beyond the crude but convenient notion of strict parity, one enters into the political and military bogs of 'equal security'. If each Superpower were to seek to itemise its military needs for the purposes of self-defence and domestic order only, it is quite inconceivable that numbers politically acceptable to the United States could be agreed upon. The Chinese danger, the threat of

German revanchism and the discreetly 'sleeping' factor of a very large police force (not to mention the KGB's army of para-military border troops), would all serve to inflate the Soviet estimate of its domestic needs. Each racing state has very distinctive military requirements and desiderata.

It was stated earlier, that, in a general sense, political conflict drives the arms race. Of recent years Soviet foreign policy has been unusually activist, perhaps reflecting in part the new-found confidence of the leadership in the relative diplomatic and strategic 'weight' of the Soviet Union. To say that the Soviet Union is expansionist is to invite misunderstanding. It is most unlikely that Soviet leaders see any value in territorial expansion. Controlling Eastern Europe is burdensome enough; the prospect of digesting Western Europe and/or China as well should be daunting even to the most imperialistically inclined member of the Politburo. Soviet leaders have been active in European affairs; they have expressed a growing interest in South Asia; they have deployed modernised and expanded maritime elements to waters wherein Soviet vessels were once scarcely to be seen; and, supporting this thrusting activity, the full military panoply of a world power with global reach has slowly (though as yet imperfectly) been developed. The backstop and symbol of the new diplomacy is the rapidly improving arsenal of strategic nuclear weapons. If this is detente, it would be interesting to see the kind of military programme Soviet leaders would endorse for a renewal of Cold War.

In military strength as in diplomatic influence, the Soviet Union has been catching up. Hence, necessarily, her role is that of the challenger of a status quo wherein the predominant world ordering power was the United States. In long term perspective, the United States is racing/walking militarily because of profound uncertainty as to the nature of Soviet medium and long term aims; general principles of prudent Great Power behaviour; and considerations of self-respect and international status. (In other words, both American pride and American interests require that the United States lead in armaments, while it is appreciated that relative military power is closely related to perceptions of the state of the international pecking order.)

In the short and medium terms, American arms race efforts reflect the accurate perception that Soviet and American desiderata are in conflict. As the Power whose influence is in the ascendant, the Soviet Union wishes to acquire some of the international assets/liabilities of the United States. No strict zero-sum relationship is here implied. Soviet leaders wish to be more influential in the councils of Western Europe, in the decision processes of Middle Eastern countries, in the Indian subcontinent and so on. It is not inappropriate to comment that, in international politics, influence (or power applied) can be its own rationale. It is unlikely that Soviet leaders have any very definite set of medium term goals in mind. Recognising that conflict and struggle are laws of international life, it would probably not occur to Soviet leaders to deny themselves the uncertain pleasures of enhanced influence, if such opportunities for influence be available.

Somewhat as with the French fixation in the 1920s on the need for *sécurité totale,* it is uncertain that Soviet leaders recognise the legitimacy of the security concerns of others. Whatever short term foreign policy zigs and zags may seem to signify to detente enthusiasts in the West, is it only prudent that Western analysts and officials recognise the strong probability of the truth of four unfashionable claims. First, Soviet leaders do not share notions of general or particular regional order that are congruent with those most favoured in the West. Second, Soviet leaders believe in the necessity and inevitability of an unrelenting (though non-lethal) international struggle for power. Third, Soviet leaders are understandably obsessed with three particular problem areas: China, the possible (if not probable) emergence of a Superpower Europe, and the enhancement of her projected image of power relative to that of the United States. Therefore Soviet weight in each particular problem area will be increased for a more favourable conflict outcome. Finally, Soviet diplomatic and arms racing activities are not defensive in character. The Soviet Union is rather intent on rolling back the tide of American influence that flowed from World War II until the mid-1960s.

The above is not intended to imply that Soviet policy is reckless (though Soviet behaviour during the October War of 1973 might be so characterised), nor necessarily that it is aggressive. Aggression implies the intent to acquire that to which one has no just and/or legal title. Soviet leaders seem to believe that Soviet activism today reflects merely the proper and responsible behaviour of a power that is now seeking its rightful place in the sun. Anyway, the Soviet guide to international right conduct is the creed of *Realpolitik,* not the norms that inspire Western *Moralpolitik.*

Soviet conflict behaviour is disciplined by many considerations, among which are the military power of foreign adversaries, the needs of the Soviet economy for foreign technology and commodities and the appreciation that an atmosphere of detente diminishes that sense of alarm which catalyses enhanced alliance cohesion and rising defence budgets in the West. The Superpowers have not misunderstood each other in general political terms, whatever the errors in detail may have been. Each stands for and advances policies that are incompatible with the best interests of the other. This incompatibility is not total and is not acute to the point where either side prefers war to limited political conflict.

The symmetrical features of Superpower concern are not insubstantial. Both sides earnestly seek to avoid nuclear war; both sides strongly wish to limit the Superpower class of states to two members only (although for

Washington the temptation to seek to play triangular Great Power politics is considerable). Both sides are troubled by unruly dependents and each Superpower holds the other broadly responsible for the actions of its dependents. The political leadership of each Superpower also faces domestic problems of some generic similarity, although the details of the problem differ significantly — for example, each side would like to be able to spend less on defence and each side must needs constrain the competitive enthusiasm of its military establishment and of its MIC/defence–industrial sector.

Overall, it is true to observe that foreign policy does not easily lend itself to direction according to timetables or master plans, 'State of the World' packages notwithstanding. Appraising the foreign policy goals of a government tends to be a very uncertain enterprise. Declaratory and action policies may not be congruent. However, there is sufficient evidence of Soviet foreign policy ambitions — reflected in statements, diplomatic activity, continuing ideological premises and arms programmes — for it to be only prudent for US officials to be determined that Soviet leaders shall be denied whatever leverage some measure of strategic superiority might yield to them. Soviet foreign policy has been and still is opportunistic. Whether it be the acquisition as satellites of the former *cordon sanitaire* in Eastern Europe, or the bid for 'parity plus' in the 1970s, opportunities have been seized and advantage, where available, has been taken.

The above interpretation of Soviet foreign policy is really the only one which fits the evidence of Soviet programmes. Symbolic representation of the momentum of Soviet political ascendancy has been provided by the strategic forces. Arms controllers in the West, obsessed with the logic of their own theories of stability and rational arms race behaviour, have all too often failed to appreciate the essentially political character of Soviet strategic (and other) programmes. On political, if not military, grounds, it must be granted that essential strategic equivalence should be the minimum American arms race goal.[19] However, it is also necessary to appreciate that the strategic forces of the United States have extended deterrent tasks that are not shared by their Soviet equivalents. One rationale for the provision of larger and more flexibly optioned American forces is that they must be deemed, in the eyes of allies and rational Soviet officials, to be capable of first use in contexts short of a direct attack on the American homeland. No such requirement need guide Soviet force planning.

Strategic doctrine and strategic weaponry

The opinion has been expressed that SALT would be about the meaning of deterrence theory.[20] In other words, it was to be a forum for mutual conceptual education. Underlying this opinion are the convictions that there are better and worse or more and less appropriate, definitions of the requirements of deterrence – that each side could possibly increase its theoretical understanding, that each side would be open to educational endeavour, that SALT was an exercise jointly intended to solve a common set of problems and that conceptual divergence bore some of the responsibility for the course of the strategic arms race. Now, in the wake of the Vladivostok accords of November 1974, it is reasonably clear that SALT was in no important sense a seminar on strategic doctrine, that the two sides probably were not addressing a *common* set of problems, and that American educational activity bore fruit only to the extent that it may have provided an intellectual frame of reference for those Soviet civilian officials who were clearly not a part of the Soviet military strategy-making establishment. As expected, SALT seems to have politicised many strategic issues. Issues of weaponry and even of doctrine were debated at the highest political level to a degree that probably was unprecedented.[21]

However, there is much to commend the argument that SALT should have entailed a very profound discussion of the functions of strategic forces and of how the differing Soviet and American understanding of those functions may serve to promote unnecessary anxiety.

It would be most convenient if it were true that policy and doctrine can be confidently deduced from the evidence of military programmes. Unfortunately, as the protracted Western debate over the character and policy relevance of Soviet strategic doctrine proves, there is no unambiguous and necessary connection between force posture and strategic doctrine. One way to bypass the unknown is simply to presume that the adversary thinks like a rational American strategist. Or, if he quite obviously does not, one may presume that he would do so were he to be offered the fruits of American strategic enlightenment. In other words, common problems are presumed to be met with common responses. Alas, with respect to the strategic arms race, it is quite evident that the identification of problems has often been as uncommon as have the presumed responses.

Robert McNamara and the arms control establishment assumed that they had devised the only practicable general and limited war strategies and that, given time, the Soviets would catch up (both conceptually and in terms of programmes). The truth in this strain of reasoning (for example, that the United States was, generally speaking, the technological path-breaker in the arms race) is less important than are the errors. Two critically important areas of analytical misconception may be cited. It was (and is still) believed that Soviet arms race behaviour was dominated by a determination to acquire and sustain an assured destruction capability.[22] As a corollary, it was presumed that educable Soviet leaders would take care not to seem to be endangering the assured destruction capability of the United States. It was also (and is still) believed that the Soviet Union would be prepared to fight a fundamentally American-style war in Central Europe. It is difficult to resist the argument that here many American analysts succumbed to a form of conceptual hubris.

There are no good grounds for believing either that a much improved Western understanding of Soviet strategic thinking would have much influence on the velocity of the arms race or that a true convergence of strategic doctrines would, in and of itself, contribute significantly to the termination of the arms race. However, improved mutual understanding should make for a better managed arms race. Strategic conceptual convergence might contribute to a slackening of the pace of arms racing, but the cost of this could well be the freezing of both sides into a strategic context pregnant with genocidal perils. Convergence on poor strategic concepts would not be a cause for unqualified celebration.

It is a very common, and indeed even attractive, academic fallacy to believe that study promotes peace. In the extreme case of the peace researchers, this worthy fallacy reaches the heights of what might be termed theoretical determinism. The scholars will save the world from ignorant officials. Alas, officials are often not merely ignorant, they may also (to a peace researcher) be malevolent. If there were to be a scholarly exercise that resulted in the uncovering, beyond reasonable doubt, of a single arms race driving mechanism, it is more likely than not that many officials would use this scholarly widsom in order to seek to prosecute the arms race more effectively.

It is here presumed that doctrinal symmetries and asymmetries are matters of arms race importance. This view is not universally shared. Very little research or even imaginative thought, has been conducted on the question of the functions and importance of strategic doctrine. At opposite extremes, the following possibilities exist: doctrine rationalises technical and budgetary decisions; or doctrine provides the criteria for the selection of weapons to be developed and of forces to be deployed.

If the former proposition is closer to the truth than the latter, then it would be only consistent to argue that interstate conceptual education is really an irrelevance. Doctrine is a dependent variable. While granting the limited validity of both propositons, some alternative and, in part, complementary functions of doctrine should be noted. Doctrine may therefore serve: (a) to coordinate the activities of different allies (bureaucratic, interstate) by codifying the consensus that exists among otherwise apparently disparate opinions and possibly by making explicit preferences that previously had lacked formal expression; and (b) to ensure that weapons, once developed and procured, will be employed in an effective manner.

As Uwe Nerlich has argued, doctrine may also be used as a signalling instrument in interstate politics (as, in part, is the case with Schlesinger's flexible options); as a tool for the enhancement of civilian control over the military establishment – in peace and in war; and as a *lingua franca* of domestic political contention.[23] In other words, on the last point, the Air Force and its corporate allies may be interested in persuading an administration to purchase large numbers of the latest models of military hardware. However, strategic rationales must be invented (or re-formulated) so that the worth or the benefits of the hardware may be presented in terms that are acceptable in public exchanges. Some strategic doctrines are more expansive in their military requirements than others. Indeed, as with the concept of assured destruction, there are doctrines whose prime virtue is precisely that they do not sanction theoretically boundless military expenditure.

It is here contended that strategic doctrine does influence the selection of weapon systems, the way in which the arms race is conducted and the determination of arms control policies. This is not to deny that official doctrine reflects the distribution of power between the relevant national security bureaucracies, nor that new weapons are often developed long before the eventual user organisations have reached any conclusions as to the most advantageous ways in which they might be fitted into operational plans. Very much to the point is the following comment by Robert Perry upon the development of ballistic missile technologies:

> That institution [missile development agencies in the armed forces] devoted itself wholeheartedly to the advancement of the technologies of missilery for most of a decade and at the end of that period had shaped a succession of marvelously contrived weapons capable of being bent to purposes about which few had thought.[24]

Despite the centralised character of Soviet defence bureaucracy and despite the annual issuance by the United States Secretary of Defense of an authoritative posture statement, it is by no means easy to specify exactly what Soviet or American strategic doctrine is at any one point in time. In very general terms the symmetries and asymmetries of Superpower strategic preferences are identifiable with confidence. This identification is the product of an overall impression received from the monitoring of declarations and defence programmes. However, doctrine is constantly shifting as a consequence of changes in senior political and military personnel, changes in the list of available or expected technological options, budgetary pressures and political reassessments. This does not imply that doctrinal progress is made, analogical to improved weapon system performance. Defence debates so miscalled, as if the identification of strategic truth was the object of contention, betray a very limited set of strategic ideas over time. The pieces are rearranged to suit the interests and possibly the convictions of the contemporary actors.

Since official doctrine is always moving (if backwards at times), its precise description is, in good part, a matter of individual preference. Those portions of Soviet and American military posture that are relevant to the arms race are not the products of rational strategic deliberation alone. Nor, to the extent that strategic theory has inspired their government, do those portions reflect the product of rational strategic deliberation at any one point in time. The strategic forces of each Superpower reflect a mix of institutional interests and strategic preferences. One broad strategic doctrine may succeed in making an honest strategic woman of a very heterogeneous collection of programmes, but the variety of interests reflected in and declaring upon the posture, provides a rich source of ammunition for interested foreign and domestic interpreters.

Strategic doctrinal convergence need lend neither aid nor comfort to the cause of arms control. Soviet–American doctrinal convergence on the worth of the following propositions is clearly not what the convergence lobby has in mind. First, both Superpowers might share the belief that strategic numerical appearances were the stuff of which international respect and influence was made. Second, both Superpowers might share the conviction that the best way to prevent war is to be able to fight it effectively. Clearly convergence, as a naked strategic *tabula rasa* concept, is not what many arms controllers are endorsing. Rather they are endorsing a convergence on a common strategic ideology that provides built-in limits to competitive strategic effort. In other words, the atavistic conceptual luggage of the Soviet defence community has to be jettisoned in favour of the enlightenment of the stable mutual deterrence only doctrine. I am not alone in noticing the direction towards which benign convergence is presumed to be in the process of inclining. Thomas Wolfe has commented as follows:

> Finally, it must be noted that there is an inherent blind spot in any discussion of the convergence issue couched – as this one has been – essentially in terms of the likelihood of a Soviet shift toward American strategic conceptions. This rather ethnocentric view of things implies that if any fundamental convergence is to take place, it will be a matter of the Soviet side coming to accept American tutelage in strategic matters. But a shift could also occur in the other direction. Thus, it is not

to be ruled out that the interaction in SALT and elsewhere between the Soviet and American sides may eventually culminate in the movement of US views closer to those held by the Soviets, rather than the reverse.[25]

To refer again to Newhouse, could it be that the American strategic 'learning curve' ought to be open to conceptual interdiction from abroad?[26] Given the fact that many discordant voices speak on nuclear strategy and that the details of targeting strategy are as unknown as are the intentions of Soviet political leaders, it is none too difficult to substitute for reliable evidence possible 'facts' built on wishful-thinking.

It may be the case that the presumption that American-style strategic thought structures defence debates in Moscow reflects the lack of foreign area knowledge or empathy on the part of most American strategists and arms controllers. On the other hand, the Kremlinological record on, say, the Soviet build-up after 1964 is scarcely impressive, while, as perhaps is to be expected, US professional Moscow-watchers are not today in agreement among themselves on the issue of doctrinal convergence.

A dynamic strategic forces posture will sustain a variety of interpretations. Even were an authoritative Soviet analogue to the posture statement to be issued, proclaiming Soviet devotion to Western conceptions of stability and deterrence, doubters could point to the varied capabilities purchased (and still being purchased) by the Soviet Union. Also, attention would be drawn to the dissenting statements that would undoubtedly appear, however guarded their tone, in the Soviet military press. Underlying the arguments of the Western convergence theorists lie the following assumptions: that technological momentum constitutes a common problem that can only be resolved by common action or by sympathetic parallel actions; and that the technological arms race problem is becoming more and more easy to resolve as the force postures and strategic doctrines of the two sides approach each other. There is something to recommend both these assumptions. In many respects, arms race adversaries have developed congruent arsenals. Imitation and parallel (or near parallel) discovery, promoted by the exertion of comparable effort[27] and by the inventive talent of comparable defence scientific communities, have naturally produced strategic force postures that, while far short of being Siamese twins, still share many common features. Regardless of one's strategic culture, the concept of the SSBN, of the airborne warning and control system (AWACS), or of the silo-housed ICBM is likely to find many takers. Strategic use concepts will vary, but the technical point that missiles are more likely to survive underground then on the surface is culture-free to the extent that one is not attracted to preventive or pre-emptive launch tactics.

Most of the major differences between the technical characteristics of the

Soviet and American strategic forces are well known and brook comparatively little argument. But there are some exceptions. As with the legendary SAM-upgrade problem (which in 1976 constitutes possible Soviet violation of the SALT I ABM treaty), technical intelligence concerning the growth potential of a particular system may leave ample scope for bureaucratic politicking. What does generate many arguments are the estimates concerning the operational intentions of the adversary. Agreement may be general on the fact that the Soviet Union has deployed, say, the 1,618 ICBMs permitted under one variant of the SALT I interim agreement on offensive arms, but how would those weapons actually be used? Why have these, as opposed to other, weapon systems been funded through deployment?

The arms race significance of doctrinal asymmetry is considerable. To the extent that strategic doctrine impels particular arms race moves and to the extent that governments act on their strategic beliefs, a failure to appreciate the strategic values of the adversary could result in substantial and unintended arms race consequences. Each side appraises the other through the prism (or perhaps prison) of its own intellectual framework: as Jeremy Stone has suggested, Soviet strategic thought is guided more by principles and ideology than it is by the understanding gleaned from (and imposed upon) carefully defined concepts.[28]

This does not mean that the United States should endorse the strategic ideology of the Soviet Union. In arms race matters, one should do what one believes to be correct, virtually regardless of the likely reaction of the other side. However, an appreciation that many reasonable Russians do not think of their strategic forces in terms congruent with those familiar to many reasonable Americans should prepare one for distinctively non-American arms race moves. Two powers may agree to sign an arms control agreement even though the attractions of the agreement are individual to each signatory. What is desirable is that each should comprehend, at least in outline, the alien mode(s) of strategic thought with which the other is transacting arms race and arms control business. If, for broad or specific political reasons, Brezhnev and Ford were determined to halt the arms race, it is as certain as anything can be in politics that their joint desire would not be thwarted by the asymmetries of national strategic thought. An ounce of political will is worth a pound of arms control.

The most important asymmetry between Soviet and American strategic doctrines has been the insistence by Soviet spokesmen that their armed forces are charged with the task of fighting in, as well as acting as a means of deterring, a general nuclear war. The difference is one of degree, but it is still significant in scope. Despite the strategic debate in the Soviet Union that followed the death of Stalin and despite Khrushchev's pretensions as a strategic genius who was directing Soviet military posture in a radical (and economical) direction, the fact remains that Soviet strategic wisdom has not been overhauled comprehensively since World War II, although there is no deprecating implication in that statement.

Unlike the United States, the Soviet Union has not had a body of civilian defence intellectuals licensed to tell her armed forces bureaucracy that all of her traditional ways of thinking about war and preparations for war must now be revised, if not reversed, as a consequence of technological change. The 'back to the drawing board' spirit that has fuelled American strategic thought would have been alien to the Soviet context. Both ideology and the institutional and political contexts have ensured that Soviet strategic doctrine has evolved through accretion. More specifically, until recently the Soviet Union lacked the men who could have rewritten national military strategy, and the powerful, near-autonomous military bureaucracies who could sponsor and nurture islands of strategic heresy. As a very practical point, those who allege Soviet conceptual backwardness need to remember that strategic conceptual frontiersmanship is properly the role of the arms race leader. Bold new doctrines could have served to highlight Soviet postural inadequacy.

Doctrinal asymmetry on the issue of the emphasis to be placed on the development of a war-fighting capability stems from ideology and from the institutional consequences of geography and history. Soviet strategists still seem to be unhappy with the logic of mutual deterrence by the threat of punishment. The notion that one must live at the strategic pleasure of the capitalist enemy is an uncongenial one. Moreover, Soviet strategists are used to thinking in terms of defending the homeland directly. Beyond such notions that imply conceptual lag, it is appropriate to comment that many Soviet strategists seem unconvinced of the wisdom of a strategy that provides overwhelmingly for punishment strikes, yet scarcely at all for the attempt to limit damage to oneself. To refer yet again to John Newhouse, many very knowledgeable Russians have come to comprehend this 'severe and novel doctrine', and – to deny the Newhouse refrain – have found it wanting.[29]

Unlike the United States, the Soviet Union has a very strong 'combined arms' tradition.[30] The Soviet armed forces have been dominated by the ground forces, as was to be expected of a continental power with restricted access to the open ocean, and which had just fought an overwhelmingly land oriented campaign to complete victory. Unlike their American counterparts, Soviet long range aviation and the Soviet Navy were overshadowed, bureaucratically, by the ground forces. Not merely is a technology dominated strategic doctrine hostile to the Soviet ideological conviction that wars are won as a consequence of the application of all elements of national strength, but the new technologies (and the doctrines that they could have been held to imply) also lacked powerful bureaucratic patrons. One reason why the Soviet ICBM programme progressed so tardily in its translation from development to large scale procurement was that the Strategic Rocket Forces were not created until 1960.

Ignoring the biasing factors of a need to rationalise the disasters of 1941 and the long extant American arms race lead, the Soviet strategic doctrinal response to the nuclear age would seem to a great degree to be somewhat along the lines of 'we will fight as before (i.e., as in World War II), only making maximum use of new technologies.' All branches of the forces are held to be important. Victory will be secured, but only through the concerted endeavours of all services and only after the suffering of unprecedented casualties. This is perhaps a slight caricature of the strategic doctrinal mainstream, but it is the most plausible interpretation that can be made of Soviet defence programmes. As in the West, schools of thought may be discerned. One may pick out conservatives, technocrats, rationalists and so on.[31] The determined Western scholar can find most of the things for which he might wish to look in the Soviet literature. There are no convincing reasons for accepting the view that technology both proposes and disposes: Soviet dissent from the principal track of American strategic arms control theorising should not be seen as doctrinaire rationalisation for the constraints imposed by an inferior technology.

While recognising the folly of attempting to prove any case by selective quotation, I nevertheless recommend as a fair illustration of genuine Soviet military belief, the following statement by a non-traditionalist Soviet defence writer:

> Our views of the essence of war and the views accepted in the capitalist states' doctrines are diametrically opposed ... Their adopted methods of warfare are distinguished by particular savagery and by the senseless destruction of the peaceful population and the material assets created by the peoples. The Soviet Union's military doctrine has a completely different orientation.[32]

There could hardly be a more explicit rejection of MAD reasoning. Quotations could be provided from Kolkowicz's Americanologists who (a) employ American strategic terminology; (b) have derived much of their strategic education from American sources; and (c) speak and write in ways designed to encourage the efforts of those in the West who are working for arms race restraint. To some extent their arguments are, of course, intended for application to the Soviet context. What is reasonably certain is that the few American-style strategic thinkers in Moscow do not determine the course of Soviet arms race endeavour.

The evidence provided both by Soviet programmes and by many Soviet analyses leads to the conclusion that the logic of arms race stability through a mutuality of assured destruction capabilities has been rejected. Soviet leaders seem to feel no obligation (not even to their own country – despite the likely arms race consequences) to seek to restrict their ability to limit the damage that the United States (and/or China) could inflict upon them. In brief, they deter war by preparing to fight and they have therefore sought to acquire an arsenal that would provide them with the best possible war outcome (a concern which, *inter alia,* requires that attention be paid to a consideration of 'the post-exchange balance').[33] In the Soviet strategic book, there would seem to be no such thing as a provocative or a de-stabilising weapon system, at least not as assessed on technical–operational grounds. Provocative weapons would not be weapons that could reduce the Soviet ability to execute American hostages. Rather they would be weapons in the hands of West Germans or weapons deployed in geographical locations concerning which the Soviets leaders are politically very sensitive. Similarly, there is scant evidence that Soviet leaders share the dominant Western belief concerning arms race, crisis or weapons system *stability*. Stability in Soviet eyes (as in many Western European eyes) is a political and not a technical concept. From Soviet programmes and declarations we may deduce that an unstable situation would be one wherein (a) the Soviet Union was unable to defend as much of her material and human bases as she would like; and/or (b) the Soviet Union was far behind the United States in strategic capabilities, thereby suffering the frustrations of seriously constrained diplomacy.

It is not claimed above that Soviet leaders expect to have to fight a general nuclear war or expect to emerge from such an unlikely combat with anything worth calling a victory. However, Soviet political leaders and certainly the Soviet military establishment believe it to be very important for morale that the chimera of victory be not abandoned. Similarly, strategic advantage is sought not principally for any military leverage that it might yield, but rather because a relative posture of 'parity plus' (or marginal superiority) is appreciated to be the necessary handmaiden of a forward diplomacy. Soviet strategic literature is not studded with any local analogue to the Western concept of parity.

Although Soviet leaders view their strategic forces in a political perspective, one important rationale – and, so far as may be judged, a genuine one – for the war-fighting orientation is the appreciation that war could occur. The logic of a context wherein nuclear war is not impossible is that as good a job as possible must be done in order to see that the outcome is as muted in its destructiveness as possible.

It is often alleged that Soviet and American strategic doctrines are distinguished by their respective defensive and offensive orientations. With regard to the Soviet Union this allegation is surely false. On the evidence of the campaign of 1812, of the conduct of World War II and above all of the enormous resources poured into air defence in the nuclear arms race, Soviet strategists are deemed to have a particular affinity for the defensive. By way of contrast, American military preferences and arms racing style, matching the American temperament, are deemed to reflect the offensive dash that expresses impatience and a problem-solving proclivity.

There is much to recommend the view that US defence policy has had a very marked offensive orientation. This has stemmed from the preferred doctrine of the politically (and financially) favoured armed service – the Air Force – from the fact that the United States has not, since the war of 1812, been compelled to defend her territory from an external enemy, and from certain society-wide characteristics of temperament. However, the alleged Soviet defensive orientation reflects a profound misunderstanding of Soviet military history. In 1812 and in 1941 the retreats into the homeland were examples of *force majeure,* not of strategic preference.

The scale of investment in air force was close to $125 billions from 1945 until 1969, but this reflected an appreciation of the scale of the American bomber threat. If it were true that Soviet strategic thought were deeply imbued with an undue respect for the power of the defensive, how would one explain the momentum of the build-up of Soviet ICBM and SLBM forces since the mid-1960s or the fact that Soviet theatre forces in and for Europe are trained, equipped, structured and deployed for the effecting of a *Blitzkrieg* strategy?

In contrast to Soviet doctrine, the United States emphasised – particularly in the late 1960s – the folly of making an extensive investment in systems and programmes designed to limit damage in a general nuclear war. Strategic stability would attend a weapons context wherein each side could visit unacceptable damage on the society of the other. In order to preserve this destructive capability, each side must eschew the procurement of weapon systems that could limit damage (for example, nation-wide, thick ballistic missile defences, hard-target killing MIRVs and MARVs, etc.).

As a force planning tool, the concept of assured destruction had the single virtue that it pointed to a 'ball park' for sufficiency. If one must be able to destroy 25 to 33 per cent of the Soviet population and 50 to 75 per cent of Soviet industry, then one must simply match the number of warheads to the number of targets (allowing for the size of the target and the yield of the warhead), add warheads to allow for the operation of expected degradation factors and finally add a percentage in order to buttress insurance with further insurance.

In practice, assured destruction was of no great relevance for force planning. Strategic posture is not the undiluted product of rational strategic planning, nor, even if that were the case, could strategic posture possibly reflect but one dominant strategic doctrine. A strategic posture is too long in the making. The idea, as propagated by Alain Enthoven and K. Wayne Smith, that the size of the US strategic arsenal in the 1960s was determined by assured destruction criteria is ludicrous.[34] From a mainstream 'arms race stability' perspective, assured destruction could not easily undo the damage done by the more rough and ready force planning conceptions of the past, nor could it paralyse the influence of non-strategic factors on strategic force posture. But it could demonstrate, in a quite explicit way (if one accepted the logic), why force increases were not needed. If adopted by the Soviet Union, in parallel, and if not subverted by the bureaucratic interests in 'more and better', assured destruction could be the key to freezing the arms competition in a state from which neither side *should* feel moved to seek to escape.

Assured destruction doctrine has some very unpalatable features. First, with only the ambivalent evidence of the ABM treaty to argue otherwise, there is no evidence to suggest that Soviet leaders have found it at all attractive. Second, it does not address the interstate political dynamic of the arms race (given political will and appropriate weapons technology, the Superpowers could settle on a MAD plateau). Third, it is, at least in its purer versions, totally unresponsive to America's foreign policy need for some extended deterrent writ. Fourth, it promises to hold the entire northern hemisphere to an unlimited liability in the event of nuclear war. Fifth, it proffers a president too few war-waging options. A lengthier discussion of assured destruction will be found in Chapter 5.

As the Soviet Union has given no substantial measure of aid and comfort to the bearers of the MAD banner, so have the Soviets also proved to be unresponsive to the various schema of the principal Western opponents of MAD. Soviet declaratory and action policies have betrayed no sympathy for any flexibility of strategic nuclear use. Soviet programmes and declarations suggest that they would concentrate on Western military targets, but no doctrine of limited strategic war (or city-bargaining) or of explicit city-avoidance has been enunciated. However, it is as well to note that selective strategic targeting options were discussed extensively in a book published in the Soviet Union as long ago as 1967.[35] As suggested above, in the alleged continental strategic tradition, wars are presumed to be total and to be beyond fine-tuned human direction. There is no convincing evidence, as yet, that would indicate any Soviet shift to a much greater flexibility of targeting.

Doctrinal divergence, technological lags, explicit political arms racing motives, a quite distinctive bureaucratic context and a unique geography have combined to produce a weapons mix that is no mirror image of the United States arsenal and that poses problems of discouraging size and complexity for arms control enthusiasts. The principal weapons asymmetries of the Superpowers which are of relevance to this study are as follows:

1 *ICBMs:* the Soviet ICBM force is larger than that of the United States (under SALT I by 1,618 to 1,054 missiles – ignoring substitution possibilities) and it has far more throw-weight (and will eventually have more still) than does the US force. With a MIRV capability now demonstrated for three and possibily all four of the new Soviet ICBMs, it is clear that a major counterforce capability against fixed, land-based ICBMs is going to be acquired before the end of the proposed SALT II regime on 31 December 1985. Defense Secretary Schlesinger has announced his unwillingness to preside over a second class United States strategic posture, but it seems, as of 1976, that a hard-target counterforce gap to the United States' disadvantage is almost certain to develop in the mid 1980s. Qualitative improvements, such as the Advanced Inertial Reference Sphere (AIRS), which will give much improved accuracy – down to 300–400ft; higher yield-to-weight ratios in warheads; new high-beta re-entry vehicles (for an improved ballistic trajectory); the deployment of navigation satellites such as in the Global Positioning System (GPS) for the provision of midcourse trajectory correcting data; and so forth will all enable the United States to compensate for the throw-weight deficiency of her missile force. But qualitative improvement is a bilateral process. With greater throw-weight, the Soviet Union can make better use of qualitative improvements. The American MIRV programmes are four to five years more advanced in deployment than are those of the Soviet Union. But the Soviet MIRVs now being deployed on board the SS–19, for example, have far higher yields than their American counterparts (6×1–2 megatons, as opposed to 3×170 kilotons for Minuteman III), thereby relaxing somewhat the accuracy requirements for the guidance technologies. The common ceiling of 1,320 for MIRV launchers that was agreed in Vladivostok as a SALT II guideline, is quite irrelevant to the scale of the counterfkrce threat implied here. SALT II will not limit the number of MIRVs that each side can deploy, nor will it restrict in any meaningful way the throw-weight of missile forces, while it will be totally silent on the question of missile accuracy.[36] Relevant to nearly all military systems, but particularly significant in the ICBM field, is the fact that the United States holds a

commanding lead in computer technology. As with all qualitative advantages, this is a wasting asset, but it is one which the West should not be over-eager to erode as a consequence of commercial opportunities. The Soviet MIRV systems for the SS–17, 18 and 19 are controlled by a computer technology that is a decade behind that of the United States.

2 *SLBMs:* under the terms of the Vladivostok accords, both Superpowers may deploy as many SLBMs as they wish, provided the total number of strategic offensive delivery vehicles does not exceed 2,400. Although the Soviet Union developed a nuclear reactor for submarines as early as 1953, technical difficulties (not conceptual backwardness) delayed the SSBN programme for many years. The new Soviet Delta class SSBN breaks from the American and erstwhile Soviet practice (on Y–class boats) of fitting sixteen launch tubes per submarine: the basic D–class boat accommodates twelve SLBMs. The first Yankee class SSBN was completed in 1967, the final one – the thirty-fourth – in 1974. The first Polaris submarine was completed in 1960. Apart from the inferiority of their nuclear submarine technologies, Soviet submarines are hampered by the fact that until they are retro-fitted with weapons of the 4,200 nautical mile (n.m.) range of the SS–N–8 most of them must pass through oceanic bottlenecks or chokepoints that can be guarded by Western ASW forces. Apart from the difficulty of achieving unobtrusive access to the open sea with their SSBNs, Soviet leaders are doctrinally ambivalent over the role of sea-based forces and are worried by the difficulty of maintaining political discipline over naval personnel on distant patrols.

3 *Manned bombers:* the Soviet Union declined to emulate the SAC armada of the 1950s. The 432 B–52 D to H range are better weapons systems than the 135 Bears and Bisons maintained by Soviet Long Range Aviation (LRA), but the Soviet Union has sustained a major air defence capability which the United States and Canada have not. The bomber defence function of NORAD was eliminated in 1974 – thereby announcing what had long been a fact, a major Soviet–American asymmetry. While the United States is almost certain to procure 241 B–1 intercontinental bombers as the follow-on system to some of the B–52s still on the inventory, the Soviet Union has begun to deploy the Backfire B as its follow-on system. Unlike the B–1, Backfire is not a true intercontinental bomber, and hence might evade constraint by SALT II. Although Backfire has proved to be a major issue in the SALT II negotiations, it seems unlikely that the Soviet Union would opt for a very large deployment of this system – *intended as a strategic weapons platform.* Manned bombers are so slow to target, compared with ICBMs and SLBMs, that the dominant Soviet strategic doctrine of damage limitation would not be well served by heavy investment in such a capability.

4 *Long range cruise missiles:* as of 1975, neither Superpower has deployed a long range cruise missile. But a major asymmetry is pending in this technical field as the United States completes the development of an air-launched and a sea-launched cruise missile (ALCM and SLCM respectively). These technologies, due to be flight-tested from 1976 onwards, will be a revolutionary military development. With a range in the order of 1,500 miles, these missiles should, within five to ten years, be able to achieve accuracies of close to thirty feet – employing terminal guidance in the form of the Terrain Contour Matching system (TERCOM) and mid-course navigational correction from the satellites of the GPS. The new cruise missiles will be of an order of magnitude cheaper than ICBMs or SLBMs; they are also small and could therefore be purchased in large numbers and carried aboard a wide variety of launch vehicles. ALCMs and SLCMs could transform nuclear-powered attack submarines (SSNs), surface vessels and converted Boeing 747s into very capable strategic offensive delivery vehicles. The arms control ramifications of the cruise missile are horrific. Tactical missiles cannot be distinguished from strategic missiles (ALCMs and SLCMs will be dual-capable, nuclear and conventional, with no externally-distinguishable characteristics). The arms control verification problem would be insoluble. Fully aware of the strategic threat posed by the long range cruise missile (a technology which the Soviet Union is in no technological condition to emulate in short order), Soviet leaders have sought to insist that this capability must be covered by the terms of the SALT II ceilings. The ALCM would pose a novel low-level challenge to Soviet air defence that even its great resources could probably not meet successfully for many years.[37]

5 *BMD:* the Soviet Galosh ABM system is deployed around Moscow, thereby providing protection for some 350 ICBM silos (more than the United States is protecting at Grand Forks), while the United States has completed its Safeguard deployment around the Minuteman complex at Grand Forks. At the Moscow summit in 1974 the ABM treaty was amended to restrict deployment to one site only.

6 *Air defence:* the Soviet Union has the most sophisticated air defence system in the world. Effectively, the United States has none at all. It is only fair to mention, however, that the Soviet Union does confront an adversary who maintains the most sophisticated bomber capability in the world.

7 *SAM upgrade:* the United States has no extensive deployment of SAMs, nor has she the radar inventory that could service any SAM or ABM system that it might be decided to deploy in haste. The Soviet Union has both radar and SAM inventories (10,000 missiles) that could be upgraded rapidly for the provision of some BMD.

8 *Forward Based Systems (FBS) and MRBMs and IRBMs:* during the period when the Soviet Union *ought* to have been rushing her first generation ICBMs into production (rationally by-passing and countering the American long range bomber advantage), priority was instead accorded to the acquisition of an impressive and (in Western eyes) quite excessive force of MRBMs and IRBMs targeted against NATO Europe. As of July 1975, the Soviet Union had 500 SS–4 MRBMs, 100 SS–5 IRBMs and 100 SS–11 ICBMs, deployed in a theatre strike mode. A new 2,400 mile range missile, the SS–X–20 (a development of the SS–X–16), is being groomed to replace the old SS–4s and SS–5s. After the phasing out of the Thor and Jupiter missiles in the early 1960s, the United States has not sought to emulate this Soviet capability. American FBS, defined as strategic by the Soviet Union, are not matched by any Soviet deployments – for reasons of geopolitics. At present, Canada, Mexico and Cuba do not provide bases for Soviet forward-based, nuclear strike systems. The American FBS that are among the targets of Soviet diplomacy at SALT comprise, essentially, the following: 108 MGM–31 A Pershing SRBMs, 316 F–4 Phantom IIs and FB–111 As and approximately 98 A–6 and A–7 strike aircraft with the Sixth Fleet.

As might be expected, the asymmetries between Soviet and American ground and naval forces are even more noticeable than are the asymmetries noted above with respect to largely strategic systems. Stephen Canby's analyses of NATO's military problems suggest that each side is preparing to wage different wars: the Soviet Union being prepared for a short war, while the United States is prepared for a long one. The outcome of a field test of the interaction of these two doctrines is all too predictable.[38] Furthermore, substantial and militarily very significant asymmetries characterise the tactical nuclear doctrines of the Superpowers. While NATO has a late tactical nuclear doctrine appended to a strategy that calls for prolonged conventional resistance (the allies differ as to how prolonged), the Warsaw Pact countries seem to be prepared for early – or , at least, pre-emptive – and heavy nuclear use for maximum theatre-wide military effect. Opinions differ greatly over the character of Soviet tactical nuclear doctrine. I have treated tactical nuclear issues elsewhere and will therefore not repeat the analysis here.[39] The military stand-off in Central Europe offers a bountiful storehouse for the scholar in search of asymmetries.

In themselves, asymmetries in weapons serve merely to complicate the tasks of arms controllers and to increase the margins of uncertainty that surround prognoses of combat. Although specific weapon systems may accommodate a variety of strategic doctrines and possible foreign policy intentions, prudent arms race managers are bound to take account of worst plausible interpretations of the meanings of the other side's arsenal. The Soviet penchant for developing and deploying large missiles with large warheads, together with complementary programmes of civil and air defence, could be dismissed as reflecting 'the Soviet way' of supporting broadly the same objectives as those that help guide American programmes. Large missile boosters need reflect no particular malevolent first strike intent; rather they could be seen as the consequence of a missile programme that was early locked into the need to deliver large and unsophisticated atomic warheads. Arguments over the political value of large payloads, rather than the desirability of maximising a flexibility of military use, probably supported the inclination of the research and development community to continue developing large boosters. Coming up from behind in the arms race, large missiles provided some political offset effect, in a context of numerical and qualitative American superiority.

However, from the perspective of Western notions of strategic stability, the Soviet SS–9 and air defence programmes were explicable really only in terms of strategic folly. Given much improved accuracy and a MIRVed payload, could not the Soviet leaders appreciate that with the SS–9 they were deploying a weapon system that must prompt an American response? The redundancy of American assured destruction capability provided a considerable margin for flexibility of response, but, as an overall judgement, sophisticated Russians, sensitive to American modes of strategic reasoning, should not have failed to expect that many Americans would see in high throw-weight ICBMs (such as the SS–9, SS–18 and even the successors to the SS–11, the SS–17 and 19) a strategic challenge of the first magnitude. In a technical sense, these weapons systems pose an unmistakeable hard-target counterforce threat for the 1980s. In a technical arms control sense, the massive and growing asymmetry in missile throw-weight (a ratio of 4:1, probably moving to 6:1 in favour of the Soviet Union) could have precluded any agreement in SALT II – as the United States sought to bargain for a formula that guaranteed them the right to purchase a strategically equivalent posture. Recognising the intractability of the throw-weight problem, Kissinger eventually decided to ignore it (as the Vladivostok accords bear witness). The Soviet Union would not agree to constrain sharply her deployed throw-weight, nor would she agree to any compensating 'side-payments' (such as an unequal MIRVed launcher limit) for a balance of asymmetries. The SS–9 and the follow-on SS–18 are to be seen neither as evidence of strategic conceptual folly, nor as clear and unmistakeable evidence of Soviet bid for that understandable obsession of different doctrinal wings of American strategic thought – a 'splendid first strike capability'.[40] To the Soviet Union, the SS–9 and the SS–18 make excellent strategic and political sense. In both

SALT I and SALT II negotiations, the United States has given every evidence of 'running scared' before the hard-target counterforce threat posed first by the SS–9 and then by the MIRVable generation of ICBMs. In a strategic sense, SALT I was an appallingly poor package for the United States. Kissinger was really attempting the impossible – to negotiate the Soviet Union out of the early acquisition of a Minuteman-neutralising capability. But there was still no need for the United States to trade a tolerably effective hard-point ABM option (Safeguard and its Site Defense successor) in return for strategically meaningless constraints on Soviet ICBM deployment.

Very large missile booster technology is cited here as evidence that a unique military capability can have significant consequences for the course of the strategic arms race. Other examples are available, the most notable of which is the Soviet ABM programme from 1960 until 1972, with its starts, stops and protracted half-life. The inferring of possible foreign policy intention from expected strategic capability is the very stuff of which the strategic reasoning (or interstate action–reaction) dynamic of the arms race is made.

Notes

[1] I am offering here a multiple asymmetry model, in contrast to, for example, Jan F. Triska and David D. Finley, 'Soviet–American Relations: A Multiple Symmetry Model', *Journal of Conflict Resolution,* vol. 9, no. 1 (March 1965), pp. 37–53.

[2] Roman Kolkowicz et al., *The Soviet Union and Arms Control – A Superpower Dilemma* (Johns Hopkins Press, Baltimore 1970), pp. 35–7.

[3] Newhouse, *Cold Dawn,* pp. 3–4.

[4] Yehezkel Dror, *Crazy States: A Counterconventional Strategic Problem* (Heath Lexington, Lexington, Mass. 1971).

[5] Gallagher and Spielmann, *Soviet Decision-Making for Defense,* Chapter 1.

[6] See Franklyn Griffiths, 'Transnational Politics and Arms Control', *International Journal,* vol. 26, no. 4 (Autumn 1971), pp. 640–74.

[7] On the Soviet defence bureaucracy see John Erickson, *Soviet Military Power* (Royal United Services Institute for Defence Studies, London 1971), Part II; David Holloway, *Technology, Management and the Soviet Military Establishment,* Adelphi Papers, no. 76, (Institute for Strategic Studies, London April 1971), pp. 4–15; and David Holloway, 'Technology and Political Decision in Soviet Armaments Policy', *Journal of Peace Research,* no. 4 (1974), pp. 257–79.

[8] Newhouse, *Cold Dawn,* pp. 111–30. My point is that the Soviet system would seem to preclude the fairly low-level bureaucratic initiatives on SALT

taken by Halperin from his ISA (International Security Affairs of the OSD) base. This is not to imply that Soviet thinking on SALT has been monolithic.

[9] *Cold Dawn*, p. 56.

[10] Useful analyses of contemporary civil–military relations are Malcolm Mackintosh, 'The Soviet Military: Influence on Foreign Policy', *Problems of Communism*, vol. 22, no. 5 (September/October 1973), pp. 1–12; William E. Odom, 'The Party Connection', *Problems of Communism*, vol. 22, no. 5 (September/October 1973), pp. 12–26; and 'Who Controls Whom In Moscow', *Foreign Policy*, no. 19 (Summer 1975), pp. 109–23; and Raymond L. Garthoff, 'SALT and the Soviet Military', *Problems of Communism*, vol. 24, no. 1 (January/February 1975), pp. 21–37.

[11] US Congress, Senate Committee on Foreign Relations, *Strategic Arms Limitation Agreements, Hearings*, 92nd Congress, 2nd session (US Government Printing Office, Washington, D.C. 1972), pp. 69–70.

[12] Roman Kolkowicz, 'Strategic Elites and Politics of Superpower', *Journal of International Affairs*, vol. 26, no. 1 (1972), pp. 48–54.

[13] See Johan J. Holst, *The Russians and 'Safeguard'*, HI–1176/4–P (Hudson Institute, New York, 18 April 1969), Appendix 3, p. 3–1; William R. Van Cleave, 'Political and Negotiating Asymmetries: Insult in SALT I', in Pfaltzgraff (ed.), *Contrasting Approaches to Strategic Arms Control*, pp. 11–14; and US Congress, Senate Committee on Government Operations, Subcommittee on National Security and International Operations, *International Negotiations, Communist Doctrine and Soviet Diplomacy: Some Observations*, Memorandum by Adam B. Ulam, (US Government Printing Office, Washington, D.C. 1970), p. 8.

[14] See Newhouse, *Cold Dawn*, pp. 191–2.

[15] See V. V. Larionov, 'The US Strategic Debate', *Survival*, vol. 12, no. 8 (August 1970), pp. 263–72; and M.A. Milshetyn and L. S. Semeyko, 'Salt II – A Soviet View', *Survival*, vol. 16, no. 2 (March/April 1974), pp. 63–70.

[16] Kolkowicz, 'Strategic Elites and Politics of Superpower', p. 42.

[17] Ibid., p. 42.

[18] For example, *The Defence of Britain* (Faber and Faber, London 1939), and much of his writing on the theme of the 'indirect approach' in strategy.

[19] Strategic equivalence, with its implied focus on military capabilities, is to be contrasted with the Soviet preference for the more heavily political concept of equal security.

[20] See, for example, Ian Smart, 'The Strategic Arms Limitation Talks', *The World Today*, vol. 26, no. 7 (July 1970), pp. 298, 304.

[21] Rather more important is the question of the terms in which the Politburo analysed its SALT options: see Newhouse, *Cold Dawn*, p. 262; and

Garthoff, 'SALT and the Soviet Military'.

[22] See, for example, Alain C. Enthoven and K. Wayne Smith, *How Much is Enough? Shaping the Defense Program, 1961–1969* (Harper and Row, New York 1971), pp. 187–8.

[23] Uwe Nerlich, 'Alternative Strategic and Tactical Doctrines in the Central European Theater', in *European Security and the Nixon Doctrine*, International Security Series, no. 1 (Fletcher School of Law and Diplomacy, Medford, Mass. 1972), pp. 82–3.

[24] Robert Perry, *The Ballistic Missile Decisions*, P–3686 (RAND, Santa Monica, Calif., October 1967), p. 24.

[25] Thomas Wolfe, 'The Convergence Issue and Soviet Strategic Policy', in *Rand 25th Anniversary Volume* (RAND, Santa Monica, Calif. 1973), p. 149.

[26] Newhouse, *Cold Dawn*, p. 4.

[27] The true scale of the Soviet defence effort has been, and remains, something of a mystery. An excellent recent attempt to lift the veil a little is William T. Lee, *The Credibility of the USSR 'Defense' Budget*, GE75TMP–1 (Center for Advanced Studies, General Electric Company – TEMPO, Santa Barbara, Calif. January 1975).

[28] Jeremy Stone, *Strategic Persuasion: Arms Limitations Through Dialogue* (Columbia University Press, New York, 1967), pp. 35–44. Also very useful is Benjamim Lambeth, 'The Sources of Soviet Military Doctrine', in Frank B. Horton III et al. (eds.), *Comparative Defense Policy* (Johns Hopkins Press, Baltimore 1974), pp. 200–16.

[29] Newhouse, *Cold Dawn*, p. 3.

[30] See Raymond Garthoff, *How Russia Makes War: Soviet Military Doctrine* (George Allen and Unwin, London 1954), Chapter 12.

[31] This particular listing is that provided in Kolkowicz, 'Strategic Elites and Politics of Superpower', pp. 50–53. Thomas Wolfe has discerned 'traditionalists', 'centrists' and 'modernists' in *Soviet Strategy at the Crossroads*, (Harvard University Press, Cambridge, Mass. 1964), p. 6; while readers of Lawrence T. Caldwell, *Soviet Attitudes to SALT*, Adelphi Papers, no. 75 (Institute for Strategic Studies, London, February 1971), may contemplate the rather extensive poles of 'modernism' and 'orthodoxy' (pp. 2–4). William F. Scott has made a persuasive case to the effect that the schools of thought discussed by Westerners are figments of the imagination. 'Soviet Military Doctrine and Strategy: Realities and Misunderstandings', *Strategic Review*, vol. 3, no. 3 (Summer 1975), pp. 57–66.

[32] Lt. Gen. I. Zavyalov in *Red Star*, 19 April 1973, quoted in William Van Cleave, 'The SALT Papers: A Torrent of Verbiage or a Spring of Capital Truths?', *Orbis*, vol. 17, no. 4 (Winter 1974) p. 1394.

[33] See Erickson, *Soviet Military Power*, p. 46.

[34] Enthoven and Smith, *How Much is Enough?*, pp. 207–8. For a very different version of why the United States deployed 1,054 ICBMs or at least why a number so close to 1,000 was decided upon, see David Halberstam, *The Best and the Brightest* (Random House, New York 1972), p. 72.

[35] See Carl G. Jacobsen, *Soviet Strategy–Soviet Foreign Policy: Military considerations affecting Soviet policy-making* (MacLehose, The University Press, Glasgow 1972), p. 75.

[36] The text of the Vladivostok accords may be found in *Survival,* vol. 17, no. 1 (January/February 1975), pp. 32–3. The technical strategic issues of SALT II are discussed in *Strategic Survey, 1974* (International Institute for Strategic Studies, London 1975), pp. 46–50, 60–65; Michael L. Nacht, 'The Vladivostok Accord and American Technological Options', *Survival,* vol. 17, no. 3 (May/June 1975), pp. 106–13; and Colin S. Gray, 'SALT II and the Strategic Balance', *British Journal of International Studies,* vol. 1, no. 3 (October 1975) pp. 183–208.

[37] Cruise missile issues are discussed in my article cited above. See also Kosta Tsipis, 'The Long-Range Cruise Missile', *Bulletin of the Atomic Scientists,* vol. 31, no. 4 (April 1975), pp. 15–26.

[38] See Steven Canby, *The Alliance and Europe: Part IV: Military Doctrine and Technology,* Adelphi Papers, no. 109 (International Institute for Strategic Studies, London, Winter 1974/75).

[39] Colin S. Gray, 'Theater Nuclear Weapons: Doctrines and Postures', *World Politics,* vol. 28, no. 2 (January 1976).

[40] The term is borrowed from Herman Kahn, *On Thermonuclear War* (Free Press, New York 1969), pp. 36–7.

4 Patterns of interaction

The many faces of reality

By definition, an arms race is an interaction process – it is a system. Implied in the interstate action–reaction theorem is the notion that, given sufficient information, the rational strategic history of the arms race could be written. Proof of intent could rarely be supplied definitively, but a persuasive case could be made for a number of similar interstate action–reaction chains that have extended for over two decades. Every weapon system and strategy change has some strategic rationale (usually several) and the arms race has been conducted in so many lines of related military business that plausible connections are not hard to discern.

Analytically considered, there are a number of arms race histories that could be written. The arms race has a strategic history, a bureaucratic history a political incentives history, a technology history, and so on. Each would provide one window on the total reality.

Many traps await the unwary who seek to impose a rational pattern on believed arms race actions and reactions. The most dangerous of these traps is the assumption that there is a generality of strategic wisdom: that a long and detailed familiarity with American strategic thought should enable the intended functions of particular weapon systems to be identified (deduced) with high confidence, whatever the legislative and non-rational domestic processes may have been that produced particular strategic resultants. However, with what degree of confidence can strategic intention be deduced from the evidence of Soviet hardware deployed? In strategic terms, to Soviet leaders and military officials, the SS–18 Mod. 2 means what? One can argue that the question is unimportant, because the American defence community should consider what the SS–18 Mod. 2 *could* be used for and that good enough answers can be provided. Unless completely random arms race behaviour is presumed to be 'the Soviet way', the product of so many factors interacting that policy consistency is not to be expected, it is reasonable to presume that an understanding of the strategic, bureaucratic, technological and political factors that coalesced to produce the SS–18 Mod. 2 programme could tell us a great deal about future Soviet arms race behaviour.

On the other hand, it can be argued that the factors that combined to produce an SS–18 Mod. 2 are discernible to those with sensitive antennae from the evidence provided by the missile itself. From the point of view of the arms race managers of the United States, could it not be argued that a close examination of past and present Soviet arms race behaviour should provide a good enough guide to future behaviour? Detailed weapon system case studies might tell us more than we wish to know and certainly far more than is at all useful for American arms race managing purposes.

It could also be argued that the domestic dynamics producing arms race moves by the Soviet Union are 'nice to understand' rather than 'essential to know,' because of the long lead times for major weapon systems, the variety of major weapon systems and the momentum and broad front of American research and development activities. As a policy scientific exercise, arms race analysis should provide the basis for improved guesswork. The logic of the above points is that improved predictive skill may not be very important. The broad front of American research activities ensures that the scientific basis for very varied weapons development is always available. A technological surprise by the Soviet Union should not find the United States unable to develop an emulative, an offsetting, or a by-passing technology before strategic imbalance ensued. Also, however poor our predictive wisdom may be concerning future Soviet arms racing decisions, the redundancy that each side maintains in its strategic triad should guarantee that no technological surprise could result in a strategic or political ambuscade.

A slightly more mundane point is that no new weapon system is ever deployed without its having been tested extensively. The years that separate prototype testing – a process that is not easily concealed – from a full operating capability are years in which the 'surprised' and prospectively vulnerable arms racer may take quick action to offset the threat. In the present and in prospective strategic contexts, the *ultima ratio* of the arms racer in acute distress would be the announcement of a 'launch on warning' or 'launch through attack' firing policy.

Furthermore, a close study of the domestic politics of arms race moves may yield no greater wisdom than could be gleaned from technological forecasting. While granting that technological momentum is in part guided and controlled by the needs of different bureaucratic interests expressed, in part, in the language of strategic doctrine, we now have over twenty years of Soviet and American technological histories as evidence of trends and preferences. Although the precise details of performance and actual phasing will be unknowable, no great measure of understanding of Soviet arms race behaviour is required in order to isolate those technologies that could or could not be developed by, say, 1980 or even 1985. Without proceeding very far into the details of Soviet policy making (not many of which are known anyway), a good enough prognosis of future weapon system decisions should be attainable. Lest the point be forgotten, it is worth repeating that this exercise in technological forecasting and the construction (and re-construction, since many of the vital decisions that will affect the strategic context of 1980 and 1985 have already been taken) of strategic rationales must be explicitly Soviet in orientation.[1] Naturally, the possibility of major arms control events, such as a SALT II and possibly III agreement, reduces the amount of confidence that should be placed in surprise-free strategic projections. However, arms control agreements are not the acts of a capricious *deus ex machina,* they reflect the interests of the parties and the content and trend of relative advantage in the strategic balance. The difficulties that have attended the SALT II negotiations were inherent in the unbalanced asymmetries of SALT I and were identified long ago by the critics of that agreement package.[2]

The above argument is not intended to subvert the case for the full analysis of arms race processes, but to subvert the argument of those who may believe that unless one knows all about how the United States and the Soviet Union decide on defence matters, one really knows little of consequence. To peel the arms race onion may be to discover truths that are different in kind from those yielded by the outer layer only. Americans presumably wish to know what the SS–18 Mod. 2 can do; what Soviet leaders may believe should follow politically from that capability; and what the Soviet military establishment plans to do with it in the event of war. Extreme domestic process probers of Soviet arms race behaviour might discover that the SS–18 Mod. 2 was deployed because of the uncontrollable nature of weapons technology, because of a deal made between the military and a political leadership that needed to keep the military on board for a SALT II treaty and so on. In other words, different questions would be answered. From the arms race perspective, considered from the point of view of American policy interest, the important questions are: 'What is the SS–18 Mod. 2 and what can it do?', 'What is the SS–18 Mod. 2 for?' and 'What is believed by Soviet leaders to be its political exchange rate?' – not 'How did the SS–18 Mod. 2 come to be deployed?'

This line of reasoning is not totally satisfactory, even from the point of view of American policy interests. One cannot presume *a priori* that Soviet and American weapon programmes are really autonomous, with genuine perceptions of interstate adversary behaviour providing no interdicting arguments of significance. In other words, the study of arms race dynamics should help to sensitise American officials to an awareness of those weapon programmes and signals of political interest that promote particular concern in the Soviet Union. It is only through the study of the internal politics of arms racing that one can comprehend how the alleged interstate action–reaction mechanism(s) works. If it could be shown that Soviet arms race behaviour is largely the product of such factors as the momentum of technological innovation, bureaucratic interests and international political ambition, understood, in convoy, as constituting an independent arms race dynamic, then American arms programmes and strategy should cease to be constrained by an ill-informed, if laudatory, concern to mitigate arms race consequences.

This study seeks to explore the extent of arms race understanding and to consider the arms race consequences, if any, of the alternative strategic postures that could be adopted in the late 1970s. It is not concerned with telling the story of the Soviet–American arms race, nor highlighting the costs. Arms races tend to be waged for sound political reasons: to brake and eventually to halt them are secondary goals. An arms race is, however, to be preferred to the purely unilateral exercising of military competitive restraint. A state may conduct an arms race 'tango' on its own: determined to place as much strategic distance between itself and its political adversary as possible, it may elect to build very rapidly to a purely self-generated goal identified as being sufficient. The enemy of arms controllers is not a reified arms race; it is the political interests of the contending states that inspire military competition.

Although many analysts are willing to discuss interstate interaction processes at a level of considerable generality and a few have considered in near exhaustive detail the development cycle of particular weapon systems, no analyst has as yet undertaken to provide either a history of the entire course of the strategic arms race, presented in such a way that possible actions and possible reactions are identified explicitly in sequence, or even a systematic listing of possible alternative interaction processes.[3] Strongly held opinions now proliferate on the question of what drives the arms race but little useful conceptual, let alone historical, work has yet to appear. At present, because the available information on Soviet defence policy making processes is inadequate, the Soviet side of the arms race cannot be presented with any confidence. Also, much work remains to be done on the domestic processes that have produced American arms race behaviour. Granted that there is a daunting list of unknowns and unknowables, it is still useful to present a family of interstate action–reaction models, each of which seems to fit some of the evidence of Soviet–American arms race behaviour. Their deployment here should have heuristic value for the research of others, though it is not pretended that each is of equal plausibility. Every one of these six model sets (each is capable of sustaining considerable variation) does not imply a plausible alternative arms race history, inviting the reader to elect the analytical victor. Rather they suggest different meanings of the action–reaction mechanism. In summary form, the six model sets are as follows:

Model 1: *Eigendynamik*.
Model 2: random response.
Model 3: macro response.
Model 4: limited response.
Model 5: differential response.
Model 6: mechanistic response.

Model 1: Eigendynamik

Model 1 provides comment upon, rather than a variant of, action–reaction theorising. According to this model, once an arms race is catalysed by the interaction of (possibly misconstrued) threat signals, the domestic processes of each racing state may be relied upon to sustain military competitive activity.

Relying fairly heavily upon the insights and data generated by the schools of bureaucratic political analysis and MIC theorising, the *Eigendynamik* theorist need make scant reference to the fact that the country whose defence policy he is discussing might well have some quite serious external foe. Foreign threat is, in effect, dismissed as grist for the domestic arms racing mill.[4] Scholars to the left of the political spectrum tend to presume that the conventional presentation of threat assessments either is intended to fool the gullible public or reflects a conflict ideology which is honestly held. In either case, the conflict ideologists – the national security managers – are *really* (consciously or not) rationalising activities that are conducted for the benefit of domestic interests.

At the centre and to the right of the political spectrum, scholars may be found who believe that each racing state tends to 'do its own thing', but also hold that the arms race is a necessary expression of political conflict. The conservative interest in the *Eigendynamik* model is quite obvious: if each, or one particular, side does what it will, almost regardless of the programmes and beliefs of the other, then the strategic programmes of one's own side should not be constrained by fallacious 'arms race consequences' reasoning.

The evidence for the *Eigendynamik* model set (many variations may be played upon the domestic processes theme, as was illustrated in Chapter 2) is impressive yet controversial. The problem of assimilating the interstate adversary is one that few analysts have yet sought seriously to resolve. After all, if arms race activity is self-generated and domestically oriented, how did the whole process begin and how could it end? Some arms races have been resolved by explicit political agreement, while others have just faded away.[5] Also, despite the abundance of seductive domestic detail that supports Model 1, the history of Soviet–American relations since World War II suggests that it is unlikely to provide sufficient explanatory power.

No *Eigendynamik* or domestic process arms race analyst can deny the step level jumps in American strategic programmes that occurred in the early 1950s (the Korean rearmament programme) and in the early 1960s (the military arm of the New Frontier). Similarly, the evidence and apparent evidence pertaining to the bomber and missile gaps and to the momentum of Soviet missile programmes in the late 1960s, had marked and easily identifiable consequences in terms of American doctrine, strategic programmes and arms control policies. Furthermore, no student of American defence policy could fail to note the major controversies sparked off by the ambivalent evidence of Soviet ABM deployment after 1960.

What should disturb the careful scholar is not the fact that these external stimuli clearly had substantial impact on American policy making, but rather that these stimuli may so easily be shaped to the purposes of *Eigendynamik* theory. Domestic process theory often provides explanations inferior to those proffered by the variants of interstate action–reaction. Explanations that explain away everything really explain very little. Bureaucratic political reinterpretations of arms race behaviour, amongst other things, could well blind analysts to the many facets of the evidence. To grant that, say, the Air Force will seize on the counterforce potential of 313 SS–9s and SS–18s and will deploy this threat to its own maximum budgetary advantage is not to say that those 313 ICBMs will not constitute a threat. Defence bureaucracies certainly manipulate intelligence guesses for their own advantage. But comparatively few totally phantom threats are deployed for self-interested ends and when they are, the variety of bureaucratic interests guarantees that special pleading masquerading as objective threat analysis will be challenged.

The conservative wing of the *Eigendynamik* modellers has the better argument. It presumes the reality of the threat but stresses the individuality of the total arms race response. Threats will be made and taken seriously but the responsive mechanism does not consist of a *yin* and *yang* process. Rather, each racing state sustains a momentum of programmes that reflects its unique mix of doctrines, geopolitical problems and opportunities and so on. By racing comprehensively, sharp zigs and zags in response to evidence (or projections) of adversary activity may be eschewed. The examples of apparent technological emulation are difficult to assimilate in this model. Each side may race as it thinks fit in its own way, but good technical (if not doctrinal) ideas are copied. Of course, apparent emulation may be dismissed as parallel discovery. The MIRV 'bus' concept, variable geometry aircraft wings, missile silos, laser and TV optical guidance technologies, should all in the end have occurred to competent defence communities, regardless of examples provided abroad.

Model 1 accommodates the arguments both of convergence theorists and of their critics. Autarkic arms race processes, in which each country's racing agents are racing between themselves, do not preclude 'the common logic of technology' theme. However autonomous Soviet and American arms programmes may be, one could argue that these autonomous arms race (sub) systems are, increasingly, making very similar decisions on technology and doctrine.

Model 2: random response

Probably the least vulnerable of interactive beliefs is the notion of random response. This is the kind of intellectual position that provides its adherent with an all-purpose 'yes, but' response to any arms race hypothesis. This model suggests that there is an interstate action–reaction mechanism but that it runs slow, fast, and even appears to stop for periods, according to no single dominant logic. Each arms race move is deemed to be unique, in that the constellation of bureaucratic forces, the budgetary constraints, the credibility of the threat, etc., will differ from instance to instance. Arms race decisions are random only in the sense that they are not predictable. It is not contended that they are irrational. The random response model should sensitise analysts to the fact that rationality has many dimensions. Given the facts of the international strategic and political contexts of September 1967, the decision to deploy the Sentinel ABM system (at least for the leading reasons officially presented) may be deemed strategically irrational. However, as Halperin and Adams have indicated, the decision was very rational indeed in the context of American electoral politics.[6]

Random response is clearly unhelpful to the policy maker. A man who needs to be acquainted with the best possible guess concerning probable Soviet responses to, say, the deployment of an ALCM is unlikely to derive much benefit from a study that suggests that no single arms race decision is to be considered in the context of the past decisions taken upon this particular class of arms race problems. Random response (or initiative) does not suggest irresponsibility or 'crazy state', 'counterstylistic' behaviour. Rather it suggests that our need of arms race prediction must not lead to the courting of procrustean dangers. The United States-oriented Chapter 2 of this book examined eleven arms race dynamic factors. The identification of the balance of influence among these for some point in the future, particularly for a country as impermeable to Western analysis as the Soviet Union, should induce extreme caution, if not humility, on the part of any policy scientist.

The random response adherent can argue that a different balance among factors at different times produces very different kinds of arms race decisions. However, at any one point in time, the imbalance among factors leading to the taking of a particular decision may have been very great — and indeed should have been predictable some time in advance.

Looking back over the arms race record of both Superpowers, with few exceptions it is difficult to conceive of alternative arms decisions. Since major arms race decsions tend not to be taken capriciously, the constellation of forces that determined X rather than Y or Z should be discernible to the trained eye. Adherents to the random response model would need to consider how random was random. It may be almost impossible to predict at what point in time 'ripening plums', perceived foreign threats and various political interests will coalesce under the impetus of the budgetarty cycle to produce the decision, say, to undertake development of a strategic cruise missile — but the only uncertainty should be over the timing.

Policy making personnel, bureaucratic actors, technologies, doctrines, levels of budgetary support and threat assessments, all tend to persist. Foreign threats, in detail, may rise and fall in credibility and as a reasonable cause for the sounding of alarm, but many arms race responses can only be made when the technology is ready. No matter how random defence decision making may be, no matter how unique the circumstances at any one point in time, the scope for random arms race behaviour is very sharply delimited by technological and industrial constraints.

The value of the random response model depends critically on the time scale appraised. Considered over a period of ten years or more, arms race behaviour looks anything but random. One knows that weapon systems tend to be succeeded by similar weapon systems that incorporate refinements valued by the user organisation. Similarly, one is aware of technological preferences, buttressed if not generated by doctrinal preferences, that incline a country to pursue particular technological tracks through research, development and procurement. There is sufficient structure in the equation for general projections to be made. For example, it was a certainty that the Soviet Union would pursue MIRV technology and that the United States would explore terminal guidance technologies. The only unknowns of importance pertained to the details of timing and precise performance parameters. (Even this latter unknown is unknown only with regard to precise dates).

Underlying the random responder's case is the assumption that each racing state will feel itself obliged to offer some response of some character and at some time to every major military programme devised (if not actually deployed) by its rival that is plausibly of arms race relevance. As Andrew Marshall has suggested, the responses will more likely than not be 'muffled, lagged and very complex',[7] but responses they will be: random in the short term but inevitable in the medium and long terms.

Model 2 proffers no advice concerning the probable nature of responses. From time to time strategic logic will suggest an arms race move but strategic logic, alas, tends to be specific to culture and even, to some degree, to time and hence to technology. Model 2 might therefore be identified as the preference of the strategic agnostic.

Model 3: macro response

Model 3 suggests that the record of the strategic arms race shows a series of often severely time-lagged, broad-fronted, almost lurching responses. While granting, in principle at least, that individual responses may be made to individual weapon threats (extant or, more likely, anticipated), these should be understood to be the small change of arms race history. In this view, to seek to demonstrate that ABM possibilities begat the MRV concept, which evolved into MIRV, which induced Soviet leaders to augment their ICBM programme, etc., is unsatisfactory because there are too many variables to be weighed and attention is concentrated on the weapon trees instead of the arms race wood.

Typical Great Power reasoning ensures that the Soviet Union and the United States will each seek to deny the other any clear lead in military technology that could be of strategic/political advantage. The weapons laboratories, defence industries and armed services ensure, moreover, that the flow of product improvements does not falper. What sustains these parallel domestic weapon generating processes are the broad political and strategic concerns of governments. Model 3 suggests that the significant action–reaction process is the one that pertains to the perceptions of major shifts in the political intentions of the adversary and/or major shifts in his overall strategic capability. The fine print of one's arms race response may be geared, to the degree possible, to the detail available concerning the shielding on SS–11 Mod. 3 re-entry vehicles (RVs), or the noise signatures of the propellers of Yankee class submarines, but the analyst interested in what moves the arms race adversaries to act and react must focus (at least initially) on macro rather than micro activity.

Model 3 is an attempt to politicise what is all too often a technical exercise – the analysis of plausible arms race action–reaction chains. Furthermore, it emphasises the momentum and the sweep of the arms race lurches mentioned earlier. Action–reaction, in this view, is no tidy, hygienic thrust and parry exercise. The arms race activity of a state moves from one plateau of effort to another, as a consequence of a shifting of arms race controlling gears by the political leaders. The transmission is far from automatic. Broad responses to broad perceived challenges may have to await favourable electoral political circumstances, and will not be reflected in weapons developed and deployed for many years to come. Nevertheless, as a signal of political intent, shortly to become, in Robert Jervis's sense, an index,[8] declared shifts in arms race strategy should be understood as having an immediate political effect. An obvious example of a declaration of an intended shift in the scale of defence preparation was the 'Special Defense Budget Message' sent by President Kennedy to the Congress on 28 March 1961. In part, the President's political needs were immediate, to meet electoral commitments and to demonstrate political resolve to Khrushchev, but the consequences of his needs of 1961 were to be felt for the remainder of the decade.

There is good reason to claim that the arms race had its genesis, has been sustained by and has been moved into higher or lower gear as a consequence of the perceptions of broadly understood political threat. Model 3 in no way denies the analytical merit of any particular, plausible, micro action–reaction concept. Furthermore, Model 3 requires a willingness to accept a considerable blurring of the line between what may be understood to be strategic and what political. The macro response model suggests that the following should be seen as the major arms race events or event sequences (contemporary perceptions rather than hindsight is the guide):

1   A Soviet political challenge to the West in the period 1946–50. The military action by North Korea was the index of aggressiveness that occasioned America's major post-war rearmament move.
2   Khrushchev's missile diplomacy, particularly over Berlin, was the stimulus to the second major American shift of arms race gear – under the Kennedy Administration.
3   The political humiliation of the Soviet Union in October 1962, plus the great momentum that was driving the American ICBM and SLBM forces to greater heights of superiority over their Soviet rivals, induced both a much-chastened Khrushchev and (particularly) his collective successors to sustain a major arms race response (which was probably initiated in 1961).
4   By 1973–74, the momentum behind the Soviet response of the 1960s had carried the Soviet Union to the point where cautious Americans could plausibly sell the idea that strategic superiority was the Soviet aim. Fearing for the possible political, if not military, consequences of an unfavourable strategic imbalance, the Nixon Administration began issuing serious warning signals to the effect that it was prepared to engage in a 'trial by missile race' if necessary. Declared alterations in American strategic targeting plus the initiation of new strategic research programmes in the 1975 budget request,

were intended to make explicit the depths of American concern and the probability of a major American arms race response.

The period 1946–50 in Soviet–American relations is somewhat analogous to Anglo–German relations in the period 1898–1902. As I have suggested elsewhere, it is appropriate to identify a period of 'arms race in embryo'.[9] Britain was certainly not racing against Imperial Germany from 1898–1902, while it is difficult to accept that the United States was racing against the Soviet Union from 1946 to 1950. Those who, like Samuel P. Huntington, contend that the nuclear arms race began in 1946[10] have a great deal to explain. United States officials (and the general public by 1946–47) had certainly fixed on the Soviet Union as *the* enemy (in a somewhat vague, non-military sense), but this was scarcely surprising. What is perhaps surprising is that the pace of American defence effort was so relaxed from 1946 to 1950. Many reasons may be advanced in explanation: defence reorganisation traumas; post-war demobilisation confusion; public mood so soon after World War II; contemporary strategic doctrine, stressing a replay of World War II, with wartime mobilisation; technological hubris and so on. However, there is little to be discerned in this period that projects the concept of an arms *race*. Even if a relaxed approach to the military prowess of the Soviet Union was appropriate in this period, some of the facts of American casualness just do not accord with even the most minimal definition of an arms race. For example, in his excellent study on nuclear diplomacy George Quester has noted the following facts:

> For some of the post-1946 period, the US stockpile of nuclear weapons apparently was kept concentrated in a single location at Los Alamos, New Mexico, outside of Albuquerque with the bombs left unassembled as a collection of components in the custody of the Atomic Energy Commission.[11]

Radar warning coverage was virtually non-existent (military radars were used for training purposes only), while high altitude air sampling to monitor possible Soviet atomic testing was initiated only in 1949.

A Soviet political challenge was perceived during the period 1946–50 but the United States made no substantial arms race response until 1950. The Korean War was the occasion for the American postwar rearmament programme. Joint State-Defense analysis (NSC–68), initiated formally as a consequence of the presidential decision of 30 January 1950 to permit the development of an H-bomb, had already specified the political and military threats and had, in a very general way, indicated the directions that should be taken by the United States defence programme. Intensive intellectual 'limbering up' for a major arms race response had been under way for over a year prior to the North Korean invasion.

The American arms race move of the period 1950–51 was both a military and a political reaction to the perceptions that the Soviet Union (a) was prepared to use, or to sanction the use of, force (Korea); (b) would acquire by 1954 ('the year of maximum danger') the capability to strike at the United States in atomic strength; (c) could expect to negate American atomic power by the deployment of her own atomic power, hence giving her a free hand to attack Western Europe; and (d) was enjoying a favourable political tide (the 'loss' of China, disunity in the West over defence coordination). In short, the discovery – the Soviet Union did not announce the fact – that the Soviet Union had become an atomic power (though only just) was by no means the sole source of American disquiet. The perception of political will was quite as important. Korea seemed to demonstrate that former judgements concerning Stalin's propensity to take risks had been unduly optimistic.

To rephrase Parkinson's Law, military programmes will expand so as to take up the money available. The somewhat frenetic American missile programmes after 1954 owed their budgetary existence to the new plateau of annual defence expenditure attained as a result of the threat assessment of 1950–51. US arms race behaviour in the 1950s was critically a function of the level of dollars that could be spent on defence, a level determined by Congress and the President, once the initial rearmament frenzy had subsided. The lowest figure of defence expenditure under the Eisenhower Administration was $35.53 billion (FY 1955) and the highest was $43.23 billion (FY 1961). Expenditure and therefore programme stability over 'the long haul' (as Eisenhower termed it), was generally understood to be desirable. More to the point, given the inertia that accounts for so much of defence expenditure, not to mention the bureaucratic, political and emotional commitments of individuals and organisations, the degree to which arms race behaviour can be reoriented at short notice is clearly limited. However, solemn and very public declarations *may* serve as a short term substitute for long lead-time hardware.

Whether the first generation long range bombers and ballistic missiles of the Soviet Union should be seen as examples of the Soviet response to the American response of 1950 onwards is very unclear (though it would seem, given the timing, to have been extremely unlikely). There is no doubt that Soviet ground forces, in particular, were augmented considerably from their postwar trough of 1948–49 as a consequence of the US rearmament programme and the parallel activation of NATO as an integrated military organisation controlling multi-national armed forces. It seems rather more likely that the bomber (Bear and Bison) and missile programmes that were to create such 'gap' hysteria in the West from 1956 to 1961, were essentially the product of long-established Soviet development programmes. Certainly, it would be very difficult to seek to blame the American rearmament programme of the early 1950s for Soviet weapons developments that must have been under way long before 1950.

The political mileage that Khrushchev sought to derive from his under-funded and lagging missile programmes promoted the fear in the West that the Soviet Union would soon be able to indulge in quite blatant political coercion resting upon her generally acknowledged margin of strategic superiority. The arms race response of the Eisenhower Administration was strategically more than sufficient but was politically inadequate. The general public seemed to record its wish for a more vigorous waging of the race by the slim majority given to John F. Kennedy in the presidential election of 1960.

Having campaigned on the platform that the nation was in danger, Kennedy had to deliver arms race action in 1961 (regardless of the good news of the absence of any large scale Soviet missile build-up that was received via satellite reconnaissance). The scale of the Kennedy shift is indicated by the following figures: the Eisenhower budget estimate for defence expenditure during FY 1962 was $42.9 billion; the actual figure for FY 1962 was $48.2 billion. In other words, the shift was noticeable but was several orders of magnitude less than that recorded between 1950 and 1953.[12] Prior to the major intervention in Vietnam in 1965, it is accurate to say that the shift of arms race gears effected by the Kennedy Administration had taken the defence budget from a level close to $40 billions to a level close to $50 billions.

The arms race 'response' of 1961 is somewhat confused, in an analytical sense, by the domestic constraints and opportunities that disciplined Kennedy's policy freedom. 'Ripening plums' in the forms of Polaris and Minuteman were then ready for deployment (deployment of Polaris had already begun), while a good proportion of the amendments to the Eisenhower estimates for FY 1962 were directed towards an improvement in the size and readiness of the general purpose forces. An accompaniment, if not clearly either a cause or a consequence of the Kennedy arms race response, was a shift in strategic doctrine. 'Flexible response' was the umbrella concept for both general purpose and strategic forces. For both categories, the doctrinal preferences of the Kennedy Administration suggested a need for larger forces than had been the case under the former doctrines.

For reasons of bureaucratic and congressional peace, as well as for putative international political advantages, the missile programmes of the early 1960s were not sharply reduced when incontestable evidence of the dilatory pace of Soviet programmes was received. In contrast to the reasoning of many Western arms controllers, Soviet leaders seem to have determined in the mid-1960s that the balance of strategic forces was of political significance. The collapse of Khrushchev's ambitious foreign policy in 1962 and the lessons learnt by the Soviet Union from the Cuban Missile Crisis must have persuaded the collective leadership of Brezhnev–Kosygin (Khrushchev having been deposed on 15 October 1964) that Soviet foreign policy, as well as Soviet dignity, required the backing of a first class strategic posture.

It would be a mistake to exaggerate the pace of the Soviet strategic build-up since 1965. The Soviet–American missile race, in quantitative (launcher) terms, happened to occur sequentially rather than by temporally parallel effort. As the United States moved from eighteen ICBMs in 1960 to 1,054 in 1967, so the Soviet Union moved from 200 in 1964 to 1,590 in 1975. The asymmetrical quantitative freezes imposed in the Moscow Agreement of May 1972 and the common ceilings agreed on at Vladivostok have and promise to have, no notable impact on the momentum of Soviet strategic force improvements. By mid to late 1973, it was beginning to be very difficult to argue that the Soviet Union was following an arms race strategy that called for effective or rough parity.[13] American contentment with the terms of the SALT I interim agreement on offensive forces had rested in good part on the conviction that US qualitative advantages balanced Soviet quantitative advantages. Soviet testing of MIRV systems earlier than had been expected – on three of four new ICBMs – plus Soviet pre-Vladivostok endeavours to perpetuate in SALT II the *temporary* numerical asymmetries of SALT I, promoted the conviction in the United States that some broad arms race response was required.

As with the broad responses of 1950 and 1961, fears were essentially political. The Nixon Administration was worried lest Soviet leaders should come to believe that they could build a strategic forces mix that would be politically exploitable. In military terms, American strategists were and are, worried both about the asymmetrical counterforce advantage that the Soviet Union will enjoy as a result of its numerical and throw-weight edges in ICBM capability (despite the SALT II ceilings) and also about the political effect of the appearance of Soviet strategic superiority. The Schlesinger shift to *more* flexible strategic targeting options and away from assured destruction ideology, supported by research programmes that will enhance warhead yield to weight ratios, accuracy and rapid missile re-targeting, is the beginning of what could become a considerable arms race response by the United States.

Model 3 fails therefore to provide any guidance as to the direction that a particular arms race response will take. For that prognosis there is no substitute for the detailed examination of domestic processes.

Model 4: limited response

Complementary to Model 3 is the idea of Model 4: that limited sequences of strategic *yin* and *yang* may characterise arms race behaviour. Denying any general wisdom either to the *Eigendynamik* theorem or to the notion that the arms race is a protracted exercise in which a rational strategic Russian interacts with a rational strategic American, sharing a common strategic ideology, the limited responder believes that *some* patterns of rational response are discernible. Granting the individuality of domestic circumstances, foreign ambitions and strategic doctrine, so the argument goes, it is still a fact that interests overlap at times and that much arms race behaviour necessarily reflects a technical logic that is culture neutral (e.g., SAM's counter manned bombers in any strategic language).

Model 4 does not require the acceptance of the proposition that the strategic arms race is driven by the interaction of particular weapons systems. It allows for the strong probability that there is no detailed strategic interaction among many weapons systems and that overall political direction will ensure that a way will be found to prosecute the arms race, should particular tracks be blocked by effective offsetting activity by the adversary. No laws of arms race action and reaction are proposed.

Four possible patterns of limited response are identifiable: defence–offence; offence–defence; offence–offence; and defence–defence. Offence and defence refer only to technical capability, not to the political intentions of the deployer. To complicate matters further, reactions (defensive or offensive) can be either sequential or anticipatory (i.e. possibly reaction–(in)inaction). Moreover, the possibility of inaction–reaction and action–inaction sequences must also be taken into account.

If it is granted that each side monitors the arms race behaviour of the other very carefully, it is only reasonable to presume that a very weak form of action–reaction logic (at the least) must attend every contemplation of the performance of the other side. A decision not to react is a reaction, albeit a negative one (action or inaction–inaction?). Similarly, the perception that the other side has not acted as expected could serve to encourage behaviour that might otherwise have been deemed unprofitable (inaction–reaction).

Action–inaction possibilities might be labelled arms race deterring moves. In recent years this argument has surfaced in connection with MIRV. It has been argued that the best way to induce the Soviet Union to desist from deploying a nation-wide ABM system is to fund a very large MIRV programme – and to make the connection quite explicit.[14] The sequence in this case should be possible action–anticipatory (over–) reaction–inaction. This is very close to what has happened since 1966. As a consequence, MIRV is now deployed but ABM is not (beyond the one site token level of the amended ABM treaty).

The classic example of the arms race deterring strategy is the declaration of an intention to maintain a fixed ratio of military or naval power. Among the difficulties that attend attempts to maintain a fixed ratio are the facts that units of strategic strength may differ in effectiveness and that the race may be conducted on a fairly broad qualitative and quantitative front.

The history of an arms race could well be marked by action–inaction sequences. 'Two keels for one' or 60 per cent superiority (Winston Churchill's proclaimed naval race strategy in 1912) should persuade any arms race competitor of the folly of racing. The greater one's competitor's efforts, the larger one's absolute margin will be. However, domestic enthusiasm for a large measure of arms race superiority is rarely sustained. The benefits of being ahead can be difficult to identify (they are probably negative – one cannot demonstrate humiliation averted), while the marginal cost of arms racing is rising with every additional dollar taken from alternative uses. If the Johnson Administration had been prepared to brave the wrath of the arms control community and imperil its preferred South East Asian policies and 'Great Society' programmes, it could have declared to the Soviet Union that the United States had decided to maintain (for example), either a 2:1 missile superiority or a 2:1 ratio according to some composite index of strategic capability. Despite the exponential expenditure promise of this strategy, it could have firmly discouraged Soviet programmes, had it been believed. Needless to say, it would have denied the validity of much of assured destruction reasoning (and almost every other item in the arms control creed). The United States has raced sufficiently vigorously to impose enormous (and, of course, disproportionate) costs on the Soviet Union but not sufficiently vigorously as to discourage Soviet competitive endeavour. Could it be that sophisticated notions of sufficiency are not really so sophisticated? Many arms controllers seem to confuse the domestic and international contexts. The Soviet Union has no inherent right to strategic parity (whatever that may mean) or to a place in the sun co-equal to that occupied by the United States. The arguments that it is in the American interest that legitimate Soviet interests be accorded due recognition and that the Soviet Union should be encouraged to assume her rightful place as a co-equal first class Superpower, meeting the responsibilities that devolve upon such states, are no more than arguments. As stated here they should promote no unease; the problem is that they beg crucial questions pertaining to the similarity of the interests and ambitions of the Superpowers.

The principal difficulty with the limited logical responsive patterns identified earlier is that they defy attempts to demonstrate their validity.

Offence–offence and defence–defence interactive chains refer to that hardy perennial of arms race analysis, strategic emulation. However, the fact of approximate parallel discovery much weakens the emulation case. Equally competent Russians and Americans, operating with not too dissimilar budgets and enjoying a rough equivalence of past technical accomplishment, are likely to discover similar technologies. Their countries may deploy them for very different purposes, but even highly individual operational strategies may derive from a fairly common technological path. In support of this argument it is worth recalling that within the United States the MIRV concept had at least five identifiable parents or groups of parents. (The autonomous nature of each parent's process of discovery is not at all certain, of course. Research and development is a community business).[15]

Emulative patterns, if they truly are such, may stem from a variety of rationales. First, on the grounds of political and strategic appearances, no racer would like it to be believed that his competitor had mastered a technology that he had not mastered himself. Secondly, evidence that the rival is doing something inclines one to believe that it could well be worth doing, and the only way to find out is to follow suit. Third, there is an irrational emulative drive that appears from time to time: 'they have it, are about to have it or could have it; therefore we must have it'. Like strategically and politically unreflective preferences for superiority, the desire to emulate is usually clothed in respectable doctrinal garments. Beyond such points as the maintenance of a strategic triad, the (somewhat dilatory) hardening of ICBMs in silos and the placing of sixteen missile tubes on Yankee class SSBNs, what evidence is there for the operation of limited defence–defence and offence–offence mechanisms?

At the level of the detail of likely performance, one naturally finds that systems are configured so as to maximise their chances of operational success. However, defensive weapons do not fight defensive weapons, while offensive weapons are countered, if at all, by the defensive features of offensive weapons. For example, one response to an SLBM threat to manned bombers is to procure a system such as the B–1 that can be dispersed to a large number of airfields in an emergency because it has a relatively small runway requirement. Its required safe escape time would be shorter than, say, for the B–52. Much more to the point is the question whether any offence–offence deployment races are discernible?

The B–47 and the B–52 cannot have begotten the Soviet Bear and the Bison – they were developed in parallel. Moreover, long range strategic bombers were implied by the geography of Soviet–American relations and were the logical next step following the development and deployment of the B–29 and its Soviet copy, the TU–4. Did the missile programmes of either side inspire those of the other? Yes, but only with limited respect to timing. American official interest in ballistic missile technology was certainly encouraged by the very sparse information that was available concerning Soviet research in this field, but the crucial pacer of American effort was scientific and engineering knowledge (and confidence). The technical catalyst for the ballistic missile programmes of the mid–1950s (Atlas, Jupiter, Thor, Polaris, Titan) was the explosion in November 1952 of a thermonuclear device. A compact thermonuclear warhead with a yield measured in megatons rather than kilotons would render the ballistic missile an attractive weapon carrier, given its anticipated inaccuracy (in excess of five miles).

The organisation, management and funding of the missile programmes was certainly much helped by the fact that the administration, Congress and the public knew that the Soviet Union was also developing missile technology. However, *Eigendynamik* with very few qualifications seems most appropriate for the explanation of the ballistic missile programmes. Ballistic missiles offered prospective strategic and political advantages such that they would have been developed regardless of the interest shown in them by the other side. The Minuteman and Polaris programmes were particularly attractive in that they offered invulnerable weapon capabilities, but they also reflected the bureaucratic interests of their sponsors and improvements in fuel, electronics, metallurgical, etc. technologies.

Model 4's offence–offence variant could be held to suggest that the American MIRV begat the Soviet MIRV. The variety of arms race doctrinal utilities of MIRV suggests the limited credence that should be accorded to any one or any particular combination of them. On what basis could one assert the MIRV-MIRV connection? First, American MIRVs, however low their individual yields, should one day (via improved accuracy) threaten to eliminate all but a handful of the Soviet ICBM force. By MIRVing its ICBM force, the Soviet Union multiplies the number of warheads that will spread death and destruction in the United States – ignoring the long range bomber and SLBM forces, that is. Hence they contribute to deterrence. Second, the Soviet Union could not acquiesce in the American attainment of a unilateral counterforce advantage such as might be a consequence of the American MIRVing. Third, the Soviet Union could not acquiesce in the unilateral American demonstration of MIRV virtuosity. A Soviet Union that is to be seen as at least the political and strategic equal of the United States needs MIRV.

Unfortunately for the offence–offence case of Model 4, there is an impressive list of arguments suggesting that MIRV should have been very attractive to Soviet defence officials regardless of the technological path followed by American arms racers. Given the very large throw-weights of

Soviet missiles, the Soviet MIRVing potential could not fail to be far greater than that of the United States. Also, the *Eigendynamik* theories, duly shaped in a Soviet mould, must have applied with full force. Granted that the kind of bureaucratic coalition that vastly facilitated America's progress towards MIRV probably did not obtain, the fact still remains that with five or more separate parents in the United States, there must also have been a number of Soviet scientists who perceived the technological possibility.

Offence–defence and defence–offence chains are believed to be the very core of arms race reality. 'Every weapon will find its counter' and similar maxims emboss this region of analysis. In a generic sense, an air defence system is deployed because a bomber threat is materialising, although the manifest inadequacies which it demonstrates 'in action' against one's own manned bombers provide the impetus for the deployment of a bigger and better air defence system. The history of the air defence of North America, following the conceptually crucial Lincoln Summer Study Group of 1952, offers fair support for the offence–defence action–reaction model. The programme was instigated on a 'crash' basis and was duly decimated when the expected Soviet bomber armada was not procured.

The Soviet air defence programme has clearly been, overall, a rational response to the American bomber threat. In detail, however, Soviet strategic rationality has been less certain. Throughout the 1950s, Soviet air defence was heavily dependent on tube artillery pieces (useless against high flying jet aircraft) and on day and fine weather only interceptors, particularly the MIG–15. These would seem to be clear instances of strategic error. However, contrary to some implications of the 'idiosyncratic doctrine' and 'organisational momentum' components of the *Eigendynamik* model, one is able to argue that, however poorly it was configured against the likely threat, air defence was clearly *intended* to reduce the damage that SAC might cause. Motive rather than performance is of importance here.

There are many examples of the defence–offence variant of Model 4. Penetration aid technology and tactics (for example, high-low-high flying to evade radar warning screens) are monuments to the truth in the assertion that every major defensive technology will call forth an offsetting or by-passing offensive technology. However, this does not mean that every offensive technology will be procured or if procured, will necessarily be procured as early as possible.

MIRV was probably born in the Preliminary Report of the Bradley Committee (Re-entry Body Identification Group), which was dated 30 January 1958. Rationales for the system have shifted but the shifts have only been shifts of emphasis. At least until the signing of the ABM treaty in May 1972, the principal reason for civilian official enthusiasm for MIRV was its promise as a high confidence penetrator of BMD systems. Briefly, during the McNamara counterforce period of 1962–64, the principal rationale became MIRV's utility for the coverage of the maximum number of targets. However, those arms control analysts who have sought to argue that MIRV has been intended as a counterforce weapon all along, and/or has been developed and procured with scant reference to the arms race adversary distort the available evidence.[16] One of MIRV's user organisations (the Air Force, but not the Special Projects Office of the Navy) has indeed always favoured MIRV, along with any other weapon of similar promise, for its counterforce utility. Such hostility as MIRV encountered in the Air Force would seem to have stemmed from the belief that an ICBM force with single warheards would have better hard–target kill probabilities than the low yield MIRVs.

The Air Force was not opposed to the development of weapons that would minimise the utility to the Soviet Union of any BMD system that it might acquire. It simply wished that such a penetration capability be congruent with a capability to strike as many Soviet hard military targets as possible. While granting the operation of all the identified domestic factors that pushed for MIRV deployment, the fact does remain that the Johnson Administration (meaning, in this context, McNamara himself) valued MIRV primarily as a penetrator of an ABM system. In Ted Greenwood's words:

> It is the complex interplay of technological opportunity, bureaucratic politics, strategic and policy preferences and the existence of great uncertainty about Soviet activities that led to MIRV.[17]

By 1969–70, in addition to its strategic roles as hedge against Soviet ABM progress and (potential) scourge of Soviet hard targets, MIRV had assumed the politically untouchable (or difficult to contradict) mantle of being a major SALT bargaining chip. Strategic programmes are not driven by one factor alone. Although rational strategic (say, defence–offence) motives may be dominant, such motives must be located within organisations that wield bureaucratic influence and must be capable of persuasive expression in familiar strategic logic.

Model 5: differential response

Whereas Model 4 eschewed any sensitivity to the possibility that each side might have its own distinctive style of racing, Model 5 proposes that strategic individuality does mark the arms race behaviour of each party. Model 5 will bear a number of different interpretations. The most elementary of these is the proposition that one side has been more reaction prone than has the other. A more complex case to argue would be that each side has a distinctive pattern of arms race response.

On the last point, a familiar refrain among arms controllers is that a clutch of mutually supportive factors has produced a habitual and therefore predictable American arms race style. In short, the United States tends to over-react in anticipation of Soviet programmes that (a) do not materialise; (b) appear much later than expected; or (c) appear in forms and at levels quite different from those anticipated.

The reasons for this allegedly quite distinctive American arms race tendency (the Russians are also alleged to be guilty of this form of behaviour but not to the same extent) are the following: US technological leadership; the asymmetrically closed nature of Soviet defence policy making processes; the conservative bias that seems to be a required qualification for employment as a military force planner; and, finally, general uncertainty about the future. (The second two points are not, of course, specific to the United States.) Overall, the prudent maxim that 'it is better to build too many rather than too few' serves generically to excuse the practice of arms race over-reaction. Is this a caricature of the United States' arms race record?

The evidence is mixed, but it is good enough to enable the proponents of the argument to advance an impressive case. As usual, the less detail provided, the better the case may be presented to the unwary. In support, the following points, *inter alia,* may be deployed:

1   In the period 1954–59, the United States and Canada overbuilt a very sophisticated (too sophisticated in the case of SAGE)[18] air defence system – to counter a Soviet long range bomber fleet that never exceeded 210 aircraft.
2   In the period 1955–57, the United States over-reacted to an apparent emerging 'bomber gap' by accelerating and augmenting its B–52 and KC–135 (aerial tanker) programmes.
3   From 1957 until 1961, the United States over-reacted to a fictitious 'missile gap' and, as McNamara claimed in September 1967, determined to purchase far more missiles than were needed.
4   Throughout the 1960s, beginning in 1961 with the so-called Leningrad System, heavy, nation-wide Soviet ABM deployments were anticipated, lending strategic rationales to the support of (at best) premature offensive missile programmes (i.e. MIRV).
5   Worthy of a special mention is the internal American debate (really just the counter–assertion of bureaucratic interests) on the BMD worth of the Tallinn Line, first discovered in 1963 by the intelligence community. The possibility of Tallinn–upgrade has been a perennial feature of the case for

augmenting the scope and the scale of US offensive 'hedging' programmes.

6 In 1969, the SS–9 was proclaimed to pose a deadly threat to Minuteman. Again, whatever the truth in this argument, and whatever such truth might betoken concerning Soviet strategic and political intent, it was grossly premature. The SS–9 threat was manipulated in order to boost the credibility of the case being made for the Safeguard ABM system.

7 In 1967, irrational Chinese brandishing their as yet undemonstrated ICBM capability were invoked as the star rationale for the deployment of the Sentinel ABM system.

8 In recent years, the naval lobby has exaggerated the vulnerability of the West to the emerging capabilities of the Soviet Navy. The effectiveness of American foreign policy is being threatened by Soviet forward naval deployment off the coasts of friendly, allied and non-aligned countries, while vital supply routes are vulnerable as never before. In fact, so it is argued in rebuttal, the Soviet Navy is heavily committed to defensive tasks, its quantitative increase is none too spectacular, its geographical disadvantages are essentially ineradicable, and its development is, as yet, of an unbalanced character.

9 Anticipatory over-reaction was institutionalised by McNamara in 1965 with his introduction of the force planning tool known as 'The Greater than Expected Threat'.[19]

Many commentators see America's apparent proneness to arms race anticipatory over-reaction not as evidence of strategic folly, but as evidence of villainy. Arms programmes may be promoted on the argument that 'the Soviets will surely develop X – and even if they do not, it is only responsible for us to assume that they will. After all, it is only dollars that are involved?' Weapon systems are technologies in search of rationales. The principal function of the Soviet Union is to provide those rationales. Since the United States has tended to lead in arms technologies, actual evidence of the (putative) Soviet capability in question is almost bound to be lacking.

The above argument has a great deal of merit, but not as much as many are inclined to believe. In order to present the case fairly, the negative interpretations were appended to 'the facts' of the examples. Two kinds of responses may be offered of significance to this book. One can argue that the discerned proneness of American policy makers to indulge in anticipatory over-reaction is but a figment of jaundiced imagination – the evidence is mixed. Alternatively one can grant the substance of the case, yet claim either that it is endemic to all arms race decision processes, the Soviet no less than the American, or that it is the product of entirely rational strategic considerations, in which case the pejorative comment that tends to accompany its presentation should be expunged.

On the veracity issue, the following selection of points should be noted:

1   From 1946 until 1949–50, the pace of development of Soviet atomic capabilities was underestimated.
2   In response to the evidence of Soviet long range bomber procurement, the United States took no more than minimal, prudent measures. The B–52 programme was accelerated and augmented (though keeping the same planned SAC wing structure) under the aegis of a strategic doctrine that called for sufficiency, not for some mindless margin of quantitative superiority.[20]
3   High-confidence evidence of the slow pace of the Soviet ICBM programme was not available until the late summer of 1961. The scale of the American missile programme was reasonable, given the contemporary shift to an explicit counterforce strategy.
4   The scale of planned air defence preparations was always appropriate, given the strategic intelligence information available at the time.
5   Given the past Soviet record of massive air defence deployment, and given a Soviet high altitude, ABM-oriented, nuclear test programme in late 1961, it was quite reasonable to believe that large scale ABM deployment would be authorised by the Soviet government.
6   The anti-Chinese rationale of Sentinel was admittedly weak, but there were many excellent reasons for deploying Sentinel (i.e., a hedge against small-scale accident; insurance against small-scale ballistic blackmail; the beginning of the breaking of the assured destruction stranglehold on American defence policy; a small start towards the active defence of ICBM silos).
7   From 1962 until 1975 the pace and even (eventually) the quality of the Soviet missile build-up have been underestimated. A recent example of American intelligence under-reaction has been the technological surprise the Soviet Union has effected with its mobile SS–X–16, and its MIRVed SS–17. SS–18 (two models, one MIRVed) and SS–19.

Can it be that conservative defence planners reside only in Washington D.C.? George Rathjens, one of the leading apostles of action–reaction believes not:

> ... if doubt exists about adversary capabilities or intentions, prudence requires that one respond, not on the basis of what one expects, but on a considerably more pessimistic projection. The United States generally bases its plans – and makes much of the fact – on what has become known as the 'greater-than-expected-threat'. In so doing, the Americans – *and presumably the Russians* – have often over-reacted. *The extent of*

the over-reaction is directly dependent on the degree of uncertainty about adversary intentions and capabilities. (Emphasis added.)[21]

Rathjens' analysis is stronger on logical inference than it is on plausible historical evidence. All weapon systems are deemed to reflect overdesign, as technologists and military men assume the best of adversary systems and the worst of their own. The last sentence in the Rathjens quotation above is a very mechanistic oversimplification. There is ample evidence to suggest that there is no inevitable direct relationship of dependency between over-reaction and ignorance. Rathjens suggests:

> Because there has been no corresponding effort by the Russians [of unilateral disclosure of strategic information, capabilities, reasoning, etc.] the United States probably over-reacts to Soviet decisions more than they do to American decisions. (At least, it is easier to trace a causal relationship between Russian decisions and US reactions than vice versa.)[22]

Plausible evidence of Soviet over-reactive behaviour is very thin on the ground. Rathjens makes a reasonable case for the Tallinn Line being a Soviet anticipatory over-reaction to a deployment of the B–70 that did not occur. However, one swallow does not make a summer, not even in this region wherein argument by isolated example or alleged logical necessity is very popular. Readers should also be reminded that the claim that weapon systems are overdesigned is a claim not totally innocent of doctrinally induced bias. As a very general statement, the claim is really meaningless. By what criteria does one judge a weapon system to be overdesigned? Presumably the critical question is, 'How good does the performance have to be for one to be sure beyond reasonable doubt that it is good enough to perform the task for which it has been designed?' Marginal performance improvement tends to be very expensive. However, military operators will argue that survival or oblivion in war is a matter of margins. An interceptor good enough for the Office of Management and Budget is unlikely to be good enough for the Air Force. Naturally, the pursuit of the best may easily compromise the deployment prospects, and even the performance, if deployed, of the good.

By 'overdesign', arms controllers tend to mean not so much that systems incorporate very expensive 'nice to have' features, but that they have a performance promise that exceeds their strategic justification. For example, arms controllers are happy with multiple warheads for the guaranteed penetration of any ABM defence system, but they observe, quite correctly, that ABM penetration requires only that the warheads be separated sufficiently as to require a separate ABM interceptor to target each re-entry vehicle. Highly accurate MIRVs should not be the result of a development programme intended primarily (by the politically responsible actors) to negate ABM effectiveness.

At the level of Model 3, the macro response, it might be suggested that Soviet missile programmes reflect an over-reaction to the lessons of Berlin and Cuba. Having been taught by formerly arrogant Americans that 'strategic superiority pays,' the Soviet Union, so the argument goes, is now seizing her historic, and thus far unprecedented, opportunity to secure a marginally superior strategic position. To the extent that it may be viewed in the context of arms race reactive behaviour (not to any very great extent in my judgement), one would have to conclude that the Soviet strategic thrust of 1954–64 reflected an under-reaction. Too few bombers and missiles were produced.

The over-reaction thesis applied to the SS–9, SS–11 and SS–13 programmes (plus their successors) implies a particular strategic doctrine for the provision of criteria of sufficiency. *In vacuo* one cannot produce too many missiles. Presumably, the Soviet Union could be held to have overproduced in that, if she were aiming for a secure second strike capability that met the criterion of optical parity, she should have halted the ICBM programmes at around the 1,000 mark. The American qualitative lead was obviously a wasting asset, while the assured destruction mission for the Soviet armed forces requires fewer one megaton equivalents on target than it does for the American armed forces (because of strategic demography). In short, granted that some Soviet strategic actors seem very much *au fait* with many of the items of the leading Western strategic creeds, the *excessive* missile build-up must be held to betray a conceptual lag.

There is no convincing evidence that this over-reaction thesis is correct, nor that Soviet monitors of Western strategic literature suffer from selective comprehension. It is simpler and, to my mind, more persuasive to argue that the Soviet missile build-up is a reaction both to historic opportunity and to a past sequence of humiliating events, the interpretation of which suggested that such an opportunity ought to be seized.

Thus it would seem that there is something to Model 5, in that a differential proneness to over-reaction *could* be held to be one feature distinguishing Soviet and American arms race behaviour. However, the *ex post facto* identification of over-reaction is an exercise fraught with peril for the unwary. Have over-reaction theorists not heard of the self-negating prophecy? Ingenious Soviet arms racers may well be writing memos proving, at least to their own satisfaction, that early and heavy deployment of the air defence system known as the Tallinn Line deterred American procurement of the B–70. Certainly Soviet arms race managers ought to have a good track record concerning strategically rational arms race decisions. They know infinitely more about American strategic programmes and thinking than Americans do about Soviet equivalents, while, in coming up from behind in the arms race, the evidence of American arms race action has been quite explicit.

The arguments and evidence presented above suggest that arms race over-reaction is, at most, no more than a tendency. Moreover, many of the judgements that are made alleging over-reactive practices are in fact value judgements masquerading as objective analysis. Over-reactive possibilities are endemic to all arms race decision processes, and these possibilities may find sufficient explanation in such factors as uncertainty and an awareness of the possible consequences of guessing in too optimistic a fashion. However, it cannot be denied that threat projection is a tool of bureaucratic combat and that this tool may, from time to time, be wielded in an unscrupulous way. Commonsense in this much disputed area has been provided, most succinctly, by Albert Wohlstetter:

> That the military nearly always exaggerate enemy capabilities and that this leads to intervention is a cliché and a vast exaggeration. It isn't so. The truth is that they sometimes overestimate and sometimes underestimate – and sometimes even get it right . . .[23]

It ought to be profitable to enquire whether the Soviet Union and the United States are distinguished by a differential reaction proneness to offensive or defensive arms race action, and whether any such reaction proneness leads to responses of a defensive or offensive character. Statistical analysis *ought* to be able to test these possible relationships, but a prime difficulty resides in the ambivalence of the data. What is an arms race action and what is a reaction? Are all arms race moves simultaneously actions and reactions? Given the strategic doctrinal differences between the parties, given lead-time problems, and given an apparently irreducible ignorance concerning particular Soviet policy motives, it is just not feasible to list with a high degree of confidence the major candidate Soviet arms race reactions from 1950 to 1975. Unfortunately, the key word would be candidate.

Reflecting the respective dominant strategic creeds and the bureaucratic forces whose interests these doctrines promote, the Soviet Union has tended to react more to American offensive than to American defensive arms race actions, but no particular preference for a defensive or an offensive response is discernible.[24] American bomber and missile programmes have certainly prompted the Soviet decisions to fund major air defence, fairly economical civil defence, and only token ABM programmes. However, Soviet missile programmes initially seemed to offer a neat counter to SAC's manned bomber armada, while a decade and a half later the Soviet response to the American missile force was a missile build-up that seemed (and still seems) bent upon limiting damage to Soviet society by means of a pre-emptive counterforce blow.

American arms race behaviour, by contrast to that of the Soviet Union, has tended to respond to Soviet defensive deployments (or to the expectation of them) and to offensive deployments that seemed directed at US strategic forces. Since the early 1950s, United States military planners have been determined to ensure that the Soviet government would be unable substantially to limit damage to its society. The city avoidance strategy announced by McNamara in 1962 was a strategy which, if ever effected in trial by combat, would be enforced by means of intrawar deterrence (not denial). City avoidance was a preferred strategy, not one to be followed as a consequence of programmes intended to reduce the vulnerability of urban populations.

For nearly three decades there has been little doubt that SAC bombers have maintained their ability to penetrate the eventually very sophisticated Soviet air defences. The prospect of a nation-wide Soviet ABM system sustained a very costly and technically fertile research and development programme into penetration aids. The most pleasing penetration aid of them all, to the technologists, has been the MIRV — and now the MARV. Perceived threats to the ability of American strategic forces to inflict sufficient damage on Soviet society have never failed, as yet, to elicit noticeable American responses.[25] Although there have been substantial American defensive responses to perceived offensive danger from abroad, these responses have tended to lack bureaucratic, congressional, industrial and public support, compared to the support enjoyed by their functional rivals on the offensive side. In the context of the three major threats here considered (bombers in 1955–57, missiles from 1957–61, and missiles anticipated from, say, 1980 onwards), there has been no purely defensive response.

The distinctive reactive biases of each Superpower reflect quite clearly the central concern of its enduring strategic doctrinal preferences. The Soviet Union has tended to react as a consequence of, and in ways consistent with, its determination to do the best it can to defend its domestic civilian and political values. On the other hand, the United States has tended to react in ways consistent with a determination to ensure that the Soviet Union will be unable to defend those values.

The ABM treaty was defensible in terms of the separate strategic logics here specified. To the United States, it signified Soviet acceptance of the logic of mutual assured destruction. Neither nation would seek to defend itself by a strategy of defence by denial. To the Soviet Union, the ABM treaty was probably acceptable because it removed the potentially very serious complication of hard-target defences from the problem agenda of its military planners. The best way to defend Soviet society is to be able to destroy as many American weapons as possible at source. Thinking of the medium and long terms, Soviet leaders were probably persuaded that more Soviet lives could be saved as a consequence of Soviet ICBMs and SLBMs being granted unrestricted access to American ICBM silos and bomber bases than as a consequence of the defensive efforts of the Galosh ABM system and its successors.

Model 6: mechanistic response

Model 6 should be seen as expressing the commonsense strategic logic of arms race behaviour. Unlike Models 1 to 5, Model 6 steers the analyst clear of the messy details of politics (domestic and foreign), of the fine print concerning the development and procurement history of weapons, and of complicating asymmetries between the racing actors. Whether or not mechanistic response theory grants the possibility of some autarkic weapons developments is not at all clear. If one believes that the engine of the arms race is a tight pattern of interstate action and reaction, one can leave possible deviant examples (if indeed they exist) in a discreet silence.

Most people beyond the ranks of strategic analysts probably believe that US arms moves are very closely related to individual moves by the Soviet Union, and that this is the way things ought to be. Vigilant guardians should 'block the shots' of the adversary. At a yet more general level, many people probably believe that a tight action–reaction pattern is practically synonymous in meaning with the term arms race.

Mechanistic response provides for the explaining of all major arms race decisions. Adhering to the scientific watchword of parsinmony, mechanistic response enables one to cut through thickets of otherwise apparently impenetrable variables. Although the mechanistic response model was popularised in the late 1960s by Robert McNamara and George Rathjens,[26] its total reliance on the assumptions that strategic rationality moves collective actors and that strategic rationality transcends frontiers are characteristic of much of the deterrence, limited war, and arms control theory produced from 1954 until the end of the 1960s. The logical achievements of such theorising have been impressive. Less impressive has been the apparent disinclination of many theorists to recognise that the world of theory and the world of action are very different. Theory may educate and may suggest ranges of logical alternatives with the logical advantages and disadvantages of each duly noted. However, the rational theory of strategy can neither predict in detail how states will interact in an arms race, nor can it reconstruct an arms race history save in the sense that only one version of reality is presented.

Strategic rationalism is now somewhat out of favour, its principal limitations having been exposed. Nonetheless, mechanistic arms race thinking tends to intrude upon the unwary. As Graham Allison has argued, men naturally tend to explain the world in rational terms.[27] If an action is perceived, we are inclined to believe that that action is the result of a clear decision, taken for identified ends. Since we live with and by our perceptions of reality, we can scarcely avoid interpreting the behaviour of others in the light of our own perceptions. When a rational American strategist reflects upon the possible meaning of the SS–19, what he is very likely to be asking is 'What would I, as a Soviet strategist, mean by deploying the SS–19?' The more pertinent question would be, 'What would I, *thinking* like a Soviet strategist, mean by deploying the SS–19?'

Unlike the other models discussed in this chapter, Model 6 will brook no serious measure of compromise. Awkward facts are to be ignored or made to fit the procrustean scheme. The puritanical single-mindedness of the mechanistic response theorist has been well explained by Graham Allison. Demonstrating the exacting demands of the model (in commenting upon McNamara's Sentinel deployment speech of September 1967), Allison writes thus:

> McNamara's answer to the question about the nature of the US–Soviet strategic interaction could hardly be clearer: *actions by one nation trigger specific reactions by the other that offset whatever advantage the first nation gained by its initial action.* (Emphasis as in the original.) [28]

The clear implication of the Allison summary is that the mechanistic responding theorist believes that strategic actions must meet with their appointed rational strategic responses. The logical excesses of mechanistic response exercises have duly brought forth their antitheses: analysts who claim that threat rationales are no more than rationalisations; or that the threat is *really* perceived, but that the strategic forces of each side do not interact at all, one with the other. The rational strategists of the world of interstate action–reaction are not totally in error. Some major strategic decisions do find their way to the desks of a President or of Politburo members. These men are charged with, and from time to time take very seriously, personal responsibilities for the protection of the interests of their state. Interstate arms control negotiations do ferment bureaucratic combat, but they also serve to elevate programmes to the level of presidential decision making, when otherwise bureaucracies would probably produce negotiated semi-decisions that the President would only ratify.

While granting that every weapon system has a strategic rationale, good, bad and indifferent; that every weapon may logically be related to another (all weapons cohabit within the bounds of strategic posture); and that states locked into an arms race system will pay the closest attention to each other's activities, there are still many reasons why an invitation to endorse the mechanistic response model of the arms race should be stoutly resisted.

Firstly, *Eigendynamik* factors are ignored or are mentioned only in passing. Within its own bounds, the model makes no provision for the demonstration of its superior explanatory power. Secondly, the model embraces circular reasoning. A state will respond to a perceived threat in an appropriate manner. How do we know that the response is appropriate? Because all arms race responses are appropriate. Given that troubling logic, could it not be that the analyst has constructed his model upon the false presumption that he can identify all actions and their related responses? In theory yes, but in practice no, because the model builder locates his action–reaction events as a result of (his) strategic logic. With this logical licence, and the ambivalence and variety of arms race dynamic factors, the proposition that each action must meet with an appropriate reaction is quite literally unfalsifiable, and hence unverifiable. Thirdly, too many contrary facts and contrary possible facts are left unaccounted for.

Fourthly, the model is not plausible to those reasonably knowledgeable in the ways of government. The advancing of good as opposed to bad strategic argument should yield a debating advantage, but since when has defence policy been determined solely on the basis of which strategic argument won a debate? Fifthly, the model is dangerous. It induces a misunderstanding of the meaning of policy (one's own and that of the adversary), and it carries implications regarding fruitful approaches to arms control problems that are oversimplified and are almost certain to prove inoperable. If one misunderstands the nature of interstate interaction, one is unlikely to be able to prescribe usefully regarding the braking or deceleration of that interaction.

Model 6 suffers in esteem because of its pretensions. Analysts are not misguided in their pursuit of strategic interactive chains; the error occurs if they come to believe that interstate strategic interaction is the only engine driving the arms race, or that the related arms race events may reliably be identified in all cases.

Notes

[1] The Western strategic predictive record since World War II is far from

impressive, but the sources of error are not difficult to isolate. See Colin S. Gray, 'Predicting Arms Race Behaviour', *Futures,* vol. 6, no. 5 (October 1974), pp. 380–8; and Wohlstetter, *Legends of the Strategic Arms Race.*

[2] For example, Donald G. Brennan, 'When the SALT Hit the Fan', *National Review,* 23 June 1972.

[3] The US Department of Defense has commisioned a mammoth, highly-classified, team-written and researched history of the arms race. The writing of this 'Pentagon Papers' of the arms race is being co-ordinated and directed by Dr Andrew Marshall, Director of the Office of Net Assessment.

[4] *Eigendynamik* (or, loosely translated, inner-directed or driven) models tend to filter out unwelcome data. Foreign threat, save as a currency for domestic exploitation, just does not fit these models. For a trenchant statement of *Eigendynamik* reasoning see Dieter Senghaas, 'Armament Dynamics as Restrictive Conditions for Changes in the East–West Conflict' (Hessische Stiftung für Friedens-und Konfliktforschung, Frankfurt a.M., Summer 1972).

[5] See John C. Lambelet, 'Do Arms Races Lead to War?', *Journal of Peace Research,* vol. 12, no. 2 (1975), pp. 123–8.

[6] Halperin, 'The Decision to Deploy the ABM'; Benson Adams, *Ballistic Missile Defense* (American Elsevier, New York 1971), Chapters 11–12.

[7] Quoted in Allison, *Essence of Decision,* p. 98.

[8] Robert Jervis, *The Logic of Images in International Relations,* (Princeton University Press, Princeton 1970), p. 18.

[9] In 'The Arms Race Phenomenon', pp. 55–6.

[10] Samuel P. Huntington, 'Arms Races: Prerequisites and Results', p. 43, note 4.

[11] George Quester, *Nuclear Diplomacy: The First Twenty-five Years,* (Dunellen, New York 1970), p. 33.

[12] Defence spending in FY 1950 was approximately $11.9 billion. The figures for FYs 1951, 1952, and 1953 were, respectively, $19.8 billion, $38.8 billion, and $43.6 billion.

[13] Contemporary usage of parity tends to be imprecise. Parity, essential equivalence, equal security, balanced asymmetries and even stability are very often used interchangeably. On the presumed salience of parity to SALT I see Newhouse, *Cold Dawn,* pp. 4, 21.

[14] A useful discussion of the arms control value of *some* MIRV technologies is Malcolm W. Hoag, 'Superpower Strategic Postures for a Multipolar World', in Richard Rosecrance (ed.), *The Future of the International Strategic System* (Chandler, San Francisco 1972), pp. 36–47.

[15] Greenwood, *Qualitative Improvements* .... pp. 51–63.

[16] For example, see Young, *A Farewell to Arms Control?,* pp. 194–5,

213–214; and Ronald L. Tammen, *MIRV and the Arms Race: An Interpretation of Defense Strategy* (Praeger, New York 1973).

[17] *Qualitative Improvements...*, p. 13.

[18] Semi-Automatic Ground Environment system. This is a command and control system for the air defence of North America that, in its design performance parameters, made excessive demands of the state of the art in computer programming.

[19] See Enthoven and Smith, *How Much is Enough?*, pp. 178–9.

[20] See Gray, The Defence Policy of the Eisenhower Administrations, 1953–1961, Chapter 7.

[21] George Rathjens, *The Future of the Strategic Arms Race: Options for the 1970's* (Carnegie Endowment for International Peace, New York 1969), p. 25.

[22] Ibid. p. 28.

[23] Quoted in Richard M. Pfeffer (ed.), *No More Vietnams? The War and the Future of American Foreign Policy* (Harper and Row, New York 1968), p. 79. See also Wohlstetter, *Legends of the Arms Race*.

[24] According to one version of MAD reasoning, Soviet anxieties prompted by American ABM development encouraged the development of MIRV.

[25] The SS–9 Mod. 4 triplet did not bring forth a good-looking Site Defense of Minuteman, but it did promote a SALT agreement.

[26] McNamara, 18 September 1967; Rathjens, 'The Dynamics of the Arms Race'; *The Future of the Strategic Arms Race;* and 'Introduction: Technology and the Arms Race – Where We Stand', in B. T. Feld et al. (eds), *Impact of New Technology on the Arms Race* (MIT Press, Cambridge, Mass. 1971), particularly p. 4.

[27] Allison, *Essence of Decision,* particularly pp. 1–5.

[28] Allison, 'Questions About the Arms Race...,' p. 34.

5 Strategic postures and new technologies

Arms control and strategic posture

The focus thus far has been on system phenomena, on the ways in which the nuclear arms race may 'work'. In this chapter, attention is partially shifted to the arena of American defence policy. Whereas possible arms race consequences are a factor relevant to every decision bearing on strategic forces, it should not be assumed that it is a factor that ought to dominate policy making considerations. Given the great limitations in our arms race predictive skills, there are strategic decisions that should be taken, regardless of arms race reasoning. Similarly, arms controllability should not be the master criterion for the assessment of strategic programmes. It is one criterion, but no more than that. The United States has not sustained a strategic triad solely in order that it might be controlled by international agreement. Some of the arms control literature betrays the existence of the tacit theory that defence policy should be subordinate to arms control policy. In this view, the real problem is the arms race, not potential threats from abroad.

The above remarks do not reflect any hostility to arms control. In the abstract, arms control must be good, being the logical opposite of arms uncontrol, presumably. However, arms control is never, save in many literary gushings, an abstract matter. It is about the balance of power between very real political entities at particular points in time. Other views of arms control are of course possible (and prevalent).[1] The power struggle view of arms control adopted here reflects both my appreciation of Soviet belief and behaviour and my judgement that arms control cannot be isolated from the conflict processes that abound in international politics. It is not denied that desire for limited co-operation in the defence and advancement of common interests also motivates state-actors, nor that technical and apolitical arms control analysis does have a certain validity of its own. Provided arms control analysts remember that they are devising strategically rational schema for the use of collective political actors, no great harm is done. All too often one finds that the arms control logician is really unaware that his rational and apolitical world is not the world in which arms control is negotiated, either within or between governments.

The arms control missionary is one of the contemporary versions of the international relations idealist, the man who simply declines to recognise that this world is not capable of substantial self-improvement.[2] A scholarly fallacy here obtrudes: the conviction (in this context) that good ideas will make for good policy and that foreign officials should be capable of persuasion. Since the arms race is expensive, dangerous, and held to be futile, surely men of good will who bear the correct arms control formulae can save the world? As suggested earlier, there are many reasons why this missionary activity is unlikely to bear much fruit. To cite but one: the arms race is seen by many officials, in Moscow and in Washington, not as a technological problem-mix to be solved, but rather as an instrument of foreign (and domestic?) policy.

By way of illustration of some of the above arguments, it is worth quoting from the most influential of all arms control studies:

> One way in which arms control could lead to a safer world is rather indirect but deserves mention. This would be to educate the Soviets in mutually desirable strategies and armament policies. For this purpose, we would first have to educate ourselves in some detail as to what these were, which hardly prevails at the present time (1960). But if we did understand these matters in depth, and if we did have specific arms-control objectives fixed clearly in our own minds, it is highly likely that we could persuade the Soviets (and others) of the desirability of such objectives. Also, if we were better prepared ourselves, we should then be in a better position to understand and evaluate Soviet proposals.[3]

Brennan went on to suggest that the habit of international co-operation in arms control could be 'catching' and might encourage co-operation in non-military areas. Arguably, Brennan's hopes were reasonable in 1960. What is not reasonable is that fifteen years later so little would seem to have been learnt by so many.

Given the substantial autonomy of Soviet strategic thought and Soviet strategic posture, it is sensible to ask not 'What kind of strategic posture is most likely to lend itself to negotiability?', but rather 'What strategic posture should be developed, and now (if at all), provided the miminum American strategic *desiderata* are met, could it be rendered compatible with arms control criteria?'. Good arms control agreements are next to impossible unless one has first decided on the desirable features of a strategic posture. If one has not decided on the value of each alternative strategic capability, how could one determine its negotiability? There need be no absolute requirements, not even notions of assured destruction; everything *might* be negotiable, provided the trade-off possibilities had been assessed in the light of strategic *desiderata*. One of the great dangers in protracted arms control negotiations is that the exercise begins to acquire its own momentum. The delegates are committed to the enterprise, and agreement comes to be valued for its own sake (just as one values the negotiating process as an end in itself).

Technology and the range of postural choice

Some technological developments are, in practice though not in theory, beyond political control. To quote Brennan again:

> To affirm that armament should be only a servant of national purposes is not to say that there is a simple cause-and-effect relation between them; the interaction is much more complex. Radical technological developments sometimes influence armament policy more profoundly than do explicit decisions of national policy.[4]

Technological forecasting is one means by which conceptual and policy lags may be prevented. However, the 'rightness' of an idea, given the trends duly extrapolated, is rarely sufficient to move bureaucratic and political machinery. The bureaucratic (perhaps merely human) tendency to continue doing what has been and is being done usually requires interdiction by disturbing external events before a serious change of direction is contemplated. Minimal policy making is the rule, not the exception. Hegel's proposition that the Owl of Minerva, signifying wisdom, flies only at dusk should not apply (at least, in all of its implications) to strategic studies. First, the specific deterrent provisions by each side are so varied and numerous and so prodigious in destructive power that the 'technological peace' should be immune even to the depredations of considerable postural error. Second, there is really no dynamic frontier to strategic and international political understanding. New weaponry does not often require novel concepts, though it may require a novel mix of old concepts.[5]

Despite the efforts of mythmakers, historical societies, and an army of professional historians, in one sense the United States is a country that has no history. Indeed(in some important ways this is a virtue. A country of apparently infinite adaptability, which holds as an item of faith that all problems can be solved, tends to produce a crop of strategic thinkers profoundly unimpressed with the past and its ideas. The conceptual lag that would seem currently to beset many strategists signifies not merely that they have failed to appreciate that new technologies require different strategic ideas for their postural assimilation, but also that they have forgotten the strategic ideas of the past.

In the SALT context, should one not have expected that American officials would have pored over the studies written by Americans who had negotiated extensively with the Soviet Union in the past? The fact that they apparently did not do this has been recorded by a former member of the American SALT I delegation.[6] Considering the analytical effort that was expended in the devising of numerous SALT agreement models, the neglect of the negotiation literature was clearly a matter of temperament and judgement rather than of limited time. However, the American arms control establishment (and even the intellectual wing of the defence community as a whole) has always tended to neglect the political mechanics of arms control in favour of the armament substance. The SALT experience has catalysed, as yet in a small way, a long overdue renewed appreciation of the political bargaining aspects of arms control negotiations. These are harsh words which will, no doubt, provoke much angry dissent. Nonetheless, the SALT I record, even when portrayed by so friendly a Boswell as John Newhouse, does speak for itself.[7]

As mentioned in the discussion of the macro response model of arms race interaction, the present time is one of a shifting of strategic postural gears in the United States. Despite the vociferous protestations of arms controllers,[8] convinced that horrendous arms race consequences are likely to ensue, in January 1974 Secretary of Defense Schlesinger announced a shift in the targeting philosophy reflected in and, in particular, below the level of the SIOP and set in a train a menu of new strategic programmes.[9] The word menu is used advisedly, since the Secretary views many of the strategic improvement programmes as 'hedges' against possible and unwelcome arms race events. Briefly, the following would seem to be the major items of(and supporting, 'the Schlesinger shift':

1 More flexible targeting plans involving not the dis-targeting of urban–industrial targets, but rather the provision for far more limited strikes both against soft and hard military targets and against economic targets.
2 A declaratory signal that essential strategic equivalence is a non-negotiable United States requirement. Essential equivalence is interpreted officially as referrring both to overall force size – or optical parity – and to specific strategic capabilities (with hard-target counterforce coming high on the list). While the United States will not require strict equality on every index of relative strategic strength, she should not/will not acquiesce indefinitely in, say, a 4:1 ICBM throw-weight imbalance to her disadvantage.
3 A determination to increase the accuracy with which US re-entry vehicles may be delivered. This determination is reflected in the development of the Advanced Inertial Reference Sphere (AIRS), in the terminally-guided MARV

(though not in the Mark 500 MARV warhead for Trident I), and in the GPS.
4 Greater operational flexibility for fighting limited strategic war should be provided by the completion of the Command Data Buffer System (permitting ICBM re-targeting in thirty-six minutes), and by the eventual institution of an Attack Assessment System (for the provision of real-time intelligence data).
5 An improvement in the hard-target kill capability of Minuteman III by means of the introduction of a new warhead (the Mark 12A for the Mark 12) with an improvement in the yield to weight ratio of a factor of two (170 kilotons to 340 kilotons).
6 The continued, and expanded, funding of new weapon systems, These are the B–1, the Trident SSBN and the Trident I SLBM, and – with no commitment yet to purchase – the MX advanced ICBM concept, the ALCM and the SLCM.

The precise details of strategic programmes are less important for the course of the arms race than is the clear and unmistakable general direction taken by policy. Despite the incredulity of many commentators, Schlesinger's explicit and repeated denials of interest in the acquisition of a major damage limiting capability are not contradicted by the unmistakable drift of his doctrinal and postural package in a counterforce direction. Over the long term, unless a truly radical SALT III is signed – which is very unlikely – the United States will acquire the capability to offset the emerging Soviet capability to neutralise fixed-site land-based forces. Offset, that is, in a political, perceptual pre-attack sense. In operational terms, unless a launch on warning firing tactic is adopted, the first hard-target counterforce capability to be exercised wins, that is to say, it wins the counterforce missile duel, though not necessarily the war. Without ABM defences, American ICBM silos have, at most, scarcely more than another decade of useful second strike deterrent life. American strategic forces with counter-force equivalence to the hard-target kill potentials of MIRVed SS–17s, SS–18s and SS–19s are easily predictable, given the very low CEPs promised via AIRS;[10] the potenpial of terminal guidance; the supposed American lead in nucleonics (nuclear warhead design); and the fact that the United States will be able, under the terms of a SALT II regime that followed the principles outlined at Vladivostok, to chase the Soviet ICBM throw-weight lead. But, despite these comborting thoughts, the United States cannot(in the medium term, attain hard-target counterforce equivalence with the Soviet Union, because of the Soviet throw-weight advantage. Looking beyond Minuteman III, to the period after the expiry of SALT II (i.e., to 1986 and after) a key question for both sides is whether it might not be sensible to remove counterforce equivalence anxieties, with their explicit reference to the coercive potential of missile strikes, by the expedient of ceasing to provide fixed hard military targets.

The reasons for the Schlesinger shift illustrate many of the factors discussed earlier in the chapter on arms race dynamics. It should be appreciated that the 'shift' is only a relative one and that it has been constructed on ideas and technologies that were not totally absent from American strategic posture in years past. As prefatory comment, it is clear from Schlesinger's news conferences, posture statements and Congressional testimonies, as it is from the evidence of programmes, that the shift is seen by its authors to be away from the doctrine of assured destruction. The doctrinal drift of the McNamara years was towards assured destruction: examination of his posture statements from 1964 (FY 1965) until 1968 (FY 1969) reveals the gradual decline in enthusiasm for the promise of damage limitation. The demise of damaga limitation was, in important respects, a coerced one. Unfortunately, though for the best of reasons, McNamara chose to make a virtue of necessity.

Inadequate technology (reflecting, in part, American choices) and the momentum of the Soviet missile build-up effectively killed a major damage limitation strategy for the United States. As long as Soviet ICBMs were few in number and were conveniently deployed above ground along the Trans-Siberian railway, then US strategists could still dream of effecting a nuclear Copenhagen. Missile silos and, eventually, Yankee class SSBNs removed the option of the preclusive first strike, or even the decimating first strike. By 1973, when Schlesinger assumed control at the Pentagon in a political context wherein the President was not in the best of positions to discipline strong-minded cabinep officers, conditions had changed markedly. At least four factors were responsible for the Schlesinger shift.

First, Americans have begun to grow anxious about the state of the strategic balance. In a condition of, at best, strategic parity, the United States needed greater strategic flexibility than was provided in the extant SIOP. Somewhat incredible massive retaliatory threats *may* be appropriate to a status of strategic superiority, but they will not do for a context wherein the Soviet Union feels itself to be the stratagic equal of the United States. An assured destruction orientation is either the forced choice of a minor nuclear power, or a luxury afforded by strategic superiority. In a context of rough parity, or worse, one has to consider seriously the range of issues raised in so monumental a fashion by Herman Kahn in *On Thermonuclear War* a decade and a half ago. In brief, 'The Problem (of nuclear war) Must Be Taken Seriously' (the title of Kahn's Chapter 7). A MAD-orientation was an aberration: the product of technological accident, strategic imbalance and naive strategic theorising. The Schlesinger shift is a return to normal; it is not a dramatic departure from long established wisdom.

Second, Americans have come to be disturbe by specific Soviet strategic programmes and the Soviet posture at SALT. It was understood by many Americans, who should have known better, that the spirit of SALT I precluded any bids for unilateral advantage. The evidence of Soviet missile prototype testing in 1973–74, and the rapid progress registered in deployment of the SS–17, 18 and 19 since early 1975, has suggested to many American strategists that the Soviet Union is racing as hard as she can within the letter of the interim agreement on offensive forces and that she will race to the limits set by the agreed aggregate ceilings for SALT II. Suspicions that the Soviet Union was playing arms race games with a view to winning, rather than effecting a draw, hardened in late 1973 with the Soviet presentation of a draft treaty at SALT II that would have perpetuated the asymmetries of SALT I.[11] Whereas the asymmetries of SALT I recorded a rough extant balance between American qualitative and Soviet quantitative advantages, over the long term the American qualitative advantages must inevitably be overturned and reversed. Kissinger remarked in spring 1974 that there appeared to be no agreed conceptual base for SALT II, an admission which prompted some commentators to wonder whether there had really been any agreed conceptual base for SALT I, beyond the wishful thoughts of the Western convergence fraternity. The conceptual breakthrough that brought forth the Vladivostok accords of 24 November 1974 amounted, in effect, to a bypassing of the strategic problems that had been addressed, up to that point, in the US SALT II negotiating positions. The Soviet Union certainly retreated from some of its more expansive SALT positions (i.e., on FBS – apparently – on non-deployment of the B–1 and the Trident SSBN, and on acceptance of *equal* aggregates for offensive forces – following the numerical asymmetries of SALT I), but the price exacted included the abandonment by the United States of any serious effort to negotiate a meaningful constraint on the growth of Soviet hard-target counterforce capability. By the early spring of 1975 it was apparent that Henry Kissinger's quick conceptual fix in Moscow and at Vladivostok late in 1974 had not really provided a conceptual basis adequate even for the minimal SALT II that was envisaged. The salience of Schlesinger's readiness to wage the arms race more vigorously was in no way diminished by the SALT-related events of 1974 and 1975.

Third, the arrival and predicted arrival of new technologies meant that hard-target counterforce options began to look attractive. AIRS, the Stellar Inertial Navigation System (SINS) – for mid-course correction of SLBM trajectories – and MARV technologies (plus improved ballistic coefficients for high beta re-entry vehicles) bear the promise of much greater missile accuracy. A great reduction in unwanted collateral damage should permit the targeting of military installations close to urban centres, while advances in nucleonics would improve significantly the capability for taking-out hard-targets. Prospectively, there are no militarily significant limits to missile accuracy. For the first time since the mid–1960s, it has begun to be sensible to consider the political and strategic advantages (and disadvantages) of a major hard-target counterforce option. Very much to the point, the Soviet Union is offering every evidence of determination to acquire such an option, and the United States is unwilling to concede such a major asymmetry. Many arms controllers denounce this strain of thought as being an example of blind (strategically and politically irrelevant) imitative arms race behaviour.

Fourth, the strategic convictions of Schlesinger, his close advisers and the President, had long been unsympathetic to MAD reasoning. Anyone seeking to establish that the Schlesinger shift reflects, yet again, the fact that policy follows whither technology beckons, would have to contend with the further fact that technology permits what Schlesinger seems, quite unequivocally, to favour. For more than four years Nixon proclaimed that no President must ever be presented only with the options of being able either to annihilate Soviet civilians *en masse,* or to do nothing.[12] In Schlesinger he found a man in need of no persuasion that more options are preferable to fewer options. Schlesinger's immediate predecessors were men of a very different strategic stripe. Laird was no strategic thinker. He approved of such a shift in strategic policy, indeed it was he who established the task force which examined the targeting options, but he was not the man to preside over, lead, package and present a major strategic reorientation. Elliot Richardson had the intellectual capabilities to reorient American strategic doctrine, but his strategic beliefs would have inclined him to endeavour to prevent such a shift (at least, in its counter-silo dimension). Richardson's strategic credo seemed very close to the principal tenets of the mainstream of American arms control thought. Different Secretaries of Defense listen to different advisers. Schlesinger's strategic analytical reference group comprises men who have long believed in maintaining flexibility in strategic nuclear use (for example, William Kaufmann, Albert Wohlstetter, Andrew Marshall and Malcolm Hoag). The scholarly corollary of the Schlesinger shift may be seen in an article by Albert Wohlstetter,[13] while William Van Cleave and Roger Barnett have offered an exposition which appears to be very close to the links of official reasoning.[14]

Macro responses in the arms race may all too easily be invested with an aura of inevitability: the idea that great events must have great causes. In this case the causes are very substantial indeed, as listed above, but there is no lack of dissenting voices. It is no exaggeration to say, as I have done elsewhere, that strategic studies is now seeing its 'second wave', the 'first wave' having emerged in the 'golden decade' of 1955–65,[15] when the book of strategic theory in the West was (re-) written by the new breed of civilian strategists. 'First wave' theorists were arguing in a context of substantial nuclear policy inexperience and had to contend with pre-nuclear military impulses, or their converse, official overenthusiasm for some of the more obvious implications of nuclear technology. But 'second wave' theorists of a dissenting character must contend with officials and a host of civilian strategists who believe fervently that they know what nuclear strategy and arms control is all about. In addition, the social and political contexts of theorising are hardly propitious. Detente, thirty years without major war, and a profound disinterest in foreign threats coalesce to promote the sentiment of nuclear incredulity.

Even among some professional strategists one encounters the belief that the strategic doctrine that emerged from the late McNamara years is 'good enough'. To tamper with existing arrangements, even to question the dominant strategic and arms control credo, is to risk undermining what measure of stability has been attained.[16] Anti-intellectual, and certainly unacademic, as this reaction is, it does have some limited validity. For example, strategists (myself included) who indict the American authors and supporters of SALT I and the Vladivostok accords for SALT II have often been compelled to focus upon the potential capabilities of the Soviet Union. In so doing, one is, in a sense, acting as a promoter of Soviet interests. If it is true that Soviet leaders perceive their strategic forces in a strong political competitive light, it can only be in their interests for Western commentators to draw attention to the coercive potential of those forces. One must also consider the possibility of the self-fulfilling prophecy. Western analysts who point to the political utility inherent in the emerging Soviet strategic posture could he held, *de facto,* to be (a) encouraging the Soviet Union to practice political coercion; (b) legitimising such Soviet activity; and (c) making such activity more likely to succeed by preparing the minds of Western officialdom.

The above reasoning is not conclusive in any way, but it ought to be appreciated by strategists to a greater degree than would seem to be the case at present. On balance, the risks of the above seem worth running, because: the alternative is the lobotomisation of strategic debate; it is far from certain that Soviet leaders need Western instruction or encouragement as to the utility of their forces; the political value of a favourable strategic imbalance is denied only by American arms controllers; and one is providing limited illustration of the very nature of international politics.

When the political and technological environments alter, strategists should discern a need to amend their strategic ideas. For a variety of reasons,[17] many strategists have reacted to the multi-dimensional strategic events of the late 1960s and early 1970s in ways suggesting that they prefer to reinforce failure. The principal strategic events have been the following:

1 The step level jump in Soviet strategic power (Soviet self-promotion to the status of strategic equal of the United States).
2 The emergence of new offensive technologies that place ICBM silos under sentence of obsolescence.
3 The emergence of BMD technologies believed by some to be cost-competitive with offensive technologies.[18]
4 The experience of SALT, which, in combination with the entire arms control record since 1958, calls into question Western arms control doctrine.
5 The experience of Vietnam, which, with many qualifications, calls into question just about every facet of the strategic thought that emerged from the 'first wave' in the period 1955–65.

Many strategists have remained locked into the arms race reasoning which captured Secretary McNamara in his losing battle against ABM deployment (1965–67). Based on specious, or at best intuitive, notions of how the nuclear arms race works, the arms control mainstream came to believe fanatically in four linked propositions. First, each side must be allowed to maintain its required assured destruction capability: a condition of MAD is the meaning and *sine qua non* of strategic stability. Second, the ABM will not work, but even if it does, and at competitive prices, it must not be deployed because it could limit damage. Soviet leaders will not permit the limitation of damage; hence they will react to ABM deployments by augmenting their offensive forces. Third, offensive forces with serious counterforce potential (i.e., accurate MIRVs and MARVs) must not be deployed because they threaten to limit the damage that the Soviet Union needs to be able to impose upon American society. Hence, Soviet leaders will react to MIRV deployment by augmenting their offensive forces, deploying mobile ICBM and/or accelerating their SSBN programme. Fourth, strategic forces above and beyond a generous capability for a well-reinsured assured destruction strike have no utility – political or military.

The tacit theories that underpin the above propositions are formidable in number and in their demands for analytical tunnel vision. In effect, the adherents to MAD philosophy have sought to freeze a moment in strategic history, the technological plateau (that never was) of the mid to late 1960s. SALT has been seen as an opportunity to secure formal interstate codification of such a freeze. Alas, technology, strategic programmes, and 'international politics as usual' have left many of the arms control faithful stranded on the shore when the tide has ebbed (if one is willing to grant that it ever flowed). Later in this chapter, the three principal generic variants of strategic posture for the 1970s and 1980s are discussed. This discussion identifies the technologies appropriate to each and considers the more probable arms race consequences, if any, that they might have. The arms controllability of each posture is discussed, since an arms control agreement (if it sharply constrains behaviour) is probable the most effective way of canalising arms race reactions, thus, in effect, contributing to their predictability.

At the time of writing, the United States is swimming determinedly, if slowly, in the counterforce direction and away from the iceberg of assured destruction. The ice has been melting. However, SALT considerations seem to be having a distorting, and certainly a distracting, effect on strategic programmes and discussion. The most generous comment that should be offered on the framework SALT II terms which Henry Kissinger and Gerald Ford negotiated in Vladivostok is that they are a strategic irrelevance. Looking to the 1980s, the US defense community should be worrying specifically about the vulnerability of ICBM silos, the roles of ALCMs and SLCMs, and the value of dedicated hard-point BMD. Given the liberality of the SALT II ceilings (2,400 for offensive delivery vehicles, and 1,320 for MIRV launchers), the issues currently under negotiation are important almost solely because they have that status. SALT II does not promise to place any notable constraints on American (or Soviet) strategic posture, but it is a profoundly time and energy consuming exercise.

Assured destruction, counterforce, and defensive emphasis comprise three postural cores. Every strategist will subscribe to some unique variant of one of the core positions or to some unique combination of positions. Granting that infinite variation is a fact of life, this chapter is concerned to explore the nature, technological requirements, and arms race/arms control implications only of those positions that have either attained such a following that they may be said to be of policy significance, or, in my judgement, are so important that they *ought* to be of policy significance.

Strategic posture is a summary concept, attempts to justify a precise definition of which would lead analysis into the field of undue trivial pedagogery. Strategic posture is understood to refer to men, machines, and organisations designed to advance strategic purpose in a particular way. This particular way is deemed to be (without too much qualification) inherent in the men, machines and organisations. Strategic doctrine (and policy) is logically distinct from strategic posture, but a strategic posture is held to reflect a particular strategic doctrine. (Hence I have sometimes referred to posture and doctrine and sometimes just to posture.)

Convenience and truth are not congruent. Strategic posture need not reflect a clear strategic purpose communicated via unambiguous doctrine. Strategic posture can be mere officialese for 'our strategic forces', reflecting whatever they reflect (service credos, interagency compromises, the bequests of history, etc.). Granting that adversary capabilities, technological limitations, budgetary constraints, and politically accorded freedom of action all restrict officials in their pursuit of 'the best', what are the principal characteristics of a *good* strategic posture? From such an identification exercise, the grounds should emerge for better appraisal of the three postural cores. A good strategic posture should satisfy the following criteria:

1 Be unmistakably deterring.
2 Offer some prospect for the limitation of damage, either by making provision for intrawar deterrence and for war termination short of inventory exhaustion, or by the removal of many civilians from a hostage condition.
3 Offer a wide range of limited use options (and match the principal options of the adversary).
4 Be of such scale and character as to preclude any temptations abroad to explore political coercive possibilities.
5 Look the equal (at least) of the strategic posture of any rival state, in the light of the prominent, more obvious indices of relative strategic strength that are popular.
6 Not, by its scale and character, exacerbate political rivalries. A good posture should serve its functions without contributing to what are known as arms race and crisis instabilities. A good posture should be capable of being held in a state of high alert. Just as prior to 1914, mobilisation meant war, so in the 1980s, for example, it would be highly undesirable if an analogical *casus belli* were to be the taking out of early warning, reconnaissance, and communication satellites or the taking up of position by a fleet of SSBN-trailing submarines (offering comprehensive coverage).
7 Be arms controllable. It should lend itself to inspection by national technical means of verification. Multiple warheads and land-mobile ICBMs are examples of technologies that are not easily inspected.

The above list sidesteps much strategic controversy. The first criterion really amounts to saying that only a good deterrent is a good deterrent. The extent and nature of the promise of damage necessary for one's posture to be unmistakably deterring must clearly depend on the range of hostile acts that are to be deterred, the relative interest of the deterrer and the deterree in the stakes of the conflict, the political and human character of the hostile power, and the state of the strategic balance.

Much strategic reasoning and much strategic education in the West has been concerned with the problem of ensuring that an adversary will always find the decision not to strike more attractive than the decision to strike. This Copenhagen–Pearl Harbour focus understandably concentrates on the worst possible (though not necessarily plausible) case. However, the deterrence of total counterforce strikes by rational enemies is probably the easiest of strategic tasks (which is not to say that it is necessarily easy, as some of the minimum deterrence literature implies). After all, killing a lot of Russians and guaranteeing the deaths of most Americans is strategic simplicity today. Rather more to the point, as suggested by the Schlesinger shift, is how one promises a very limited central nuclear response to a local act of aggression that is (a) credible and (b) sufficiently damaging and/or apparently dangerous to deter.

Conceptually, at least, a limited strike may be very credible, but it may also be irrelevant in that Soviet leaders deem the expected damage to be tolerable, given their expected gains. Deterrence is not all about credibility. Not all credible threats need deter.[19]

Since a defence policy must oversee the development of strategic posture, that posture must meet the most exacting criteria of sufficiency. Whatever the possibilities of limited challenges implying a need for limited responses, in theory at least, strategic posture must be capable of deterring total challenges. As may be deduced from Schlesinger's announcements, the attention paid by previous administrations to getting the big policy decisions right (for worst cases) has resulted in many of the more probable needs for (limited) strategic use being unduly neglected.

Several approaches to the problem of how much deterrence to buy are possible. First, one can search for an absolute benchmark of sufficiency. Plotting promptly killed Russians against warheads (or dollars expended upon strategic forces) yields a marginal cost curve with a very easily identified 'elbow'. This approach, much favoured by the McNamara Pentagon, could provide a useful planning tool. It betrays no sensitivity to the question of what level of damage would actually deter Soviet leaders (in calm and in desperate moments), nor does it proffer any useful insights into the question of how a nuclear war should actually be conducted. In practice, the assured destruction criterion would seem to have been an instrument for the conduct of domestic defence politics, not the key to American strategic planning. As with the political utility of the much-lauded Programme Evaluation and Review Technique (PERT) for the Navy's Special Projects Office, management tools may have a political defensive value that far exceeds their administrative worth.

Second, one may approach the 'unmistakably deterring' problem by means of the criterion of relative damage. At least formally, this reasoning was persuasive to the Nixon Administration. Eschewing any interest in the purchasing of Soviet prompt fatalities (save as a last strategic resort), however cost effectively, it was asserted that the most sensible way to relate prompt fatalities to political considerations is to promise to inflict more damage on the other side than is visited upon oneself. This approach is not without its ambiguities. Assessing relative damage in the course of a nuclear war could be a very rough and ready exercise, for the guidance of which an Attack Assessment System may or may not provide adequate information. Also, can one presume that the two parties share a common ability to bear pain and place similar (or even identifiably dissimilar) values on comparable losses of human life, and so on? Finally, relative damage is of no use whatsoever as a force planning guide because, in principle, the Soviet Union could kill every American (though not promptly). These *caveats* all miss the important point that relative damage is of particular value when seen as a spirit that should inform strategic planning. Its intellectual adoption should incline planners to look with favour upon the provision of more as opposed to fewer strategic use options.

The above listing of the principal *desiderata* for a good strategic posture is a very Western-oriented exercise. Good strategic postures are made neither in heaven nor in the seminar rooms of an as yet non-existent Soviet–American Institute for Strategic Studies. Some arms controllers have long harboured the aspiration (noble, despite its foolishness in real world terms) that SALT should come to serve as a functional equivalent of such an Institute. The test of a strategic posture is 'Does it serve the political interests of its political masters?' Since political interests show some marked degree of variation, as argued in chapter 3, it can be presumed with fairness that the criteria for postural adequacy should be time and place specific.

The listing of criteria reflected a judgement of what is deemed politically legitimate and militarily useful in the West. Other criteria are possible. Indeed, it is the very possibility that other criteria may lurk beneath Schlesinger's prose and down the track of some of his strategic 'hedging' programmes that has galvanised 'stable deterrence and arms control first' circles into virulent critical activity.

Even if one chooses to endorse the language utilised in the listing of the criteria identified above, the specific detail of how those criteria should be translated into programmes and doctrines could show considerable variation. There is no simple answer to the question of 'What is unmistakably deterring?' Also, the determination to maintain strategic appearances, given the many weapon system asymmetries between the two Superpowers, allied to an acute sensitivity to the political coercive potential of strategic imbalance, could suggest the desirability of a posture of awesome proportions. The criterion of not exacerbating political rivalries is sensible as a general *caveat,* but what does it mean in practice? Putative arms race and crisis instabilities are very much the product of Western strategic imagination. In a generic sense, perhaps, these instabilities are, in good part, the result of insufficient

Western strategic vigour. Strategic self-restraint encourages Soviet leaders to race harder and to incite and exploit crises which, thanks to their improving relative strategic position, they believe that they have a reasonable chance of winning. In terms of theory, one can identify a range of postural, and hence arms racing, choices that extend from the most minimum of secure second strike deterrents through to a posture intended to provide a reasonable prospect for winning World War III. For political, economic, and technological reasons, neither extreme is strategically legitimate. One American postural reaction to the evidence of Soviet strategic momentum and foreign policy ambition could embrace a set of ideas and programmes that would, in Yehezkel Dror's phrase, be 'counteraccepted' (counter, that is, to American behaviour in the period 1965–1974.[20] Flouting the arms control credo of recent years, the Unite States government could decide to embark upon a strategic course that invited, and perhaps even welcomed, arms race and crisis instabilities. The arms race and crises may be seen not as unfortunate accidents, nor as diseases in need of cure, but rather as vehicles for national policy. If American policy makers were to become convinced that Soviet intentions in a SALT II regime were diametrically opposed to those of the United States (save only in the very general area of sharing a profound distaste for the prospect of nuclear war), then the American response need not be to make the best of it, or to salvage what could be salvaged in the interest of sustaining (a nearly worthless) detente. Instead, the United States could challenge the Soviet Union to an intensive trial by missile race.

Contrary to the postural implications of most, if not all, arms control considerations, one could elect to seek to promote insecurity feelings in Moscow. The probable fact that a preclusive disarming first strike is unattainable need not discourage American arms racing efforts. The race would be about politics, not about who would win, or lose the least, in the next (and probably last) world war. Given equal sustained strategic alarm on each side, over the medium to long terms there is no way in which the Soviet Union could win (politically and militarily) the arms race.

In effect, the United States would have to converge on Soviet strategic thought and build weapons which would be of some considerable, though undoubtedly insufficient, war-waging utility. The extreme case of arms race *à outrance* is cited here. A less apocalyptic version of this scenario would have the United States racing for political coercive effect. The intention would be to induce Soviet leaders to recognise that they must reduce the more expansive definition of their foreign policy interests. Far from playing down the damage limiting possibilities granted by new classes of SSNs and by an MX follow-on to Minuteman III, their counterforce potentials would be openly proclaimed and possibly exaggerated.

Few readers will find the above paragraphs attractive. However, variations on the content of these paragraphs should be considered as one legitimate track of arms race endeavour, should the international political and strategic climates deteriorate markedly. There is little in them which would appear 'counter-acceptable' to the Soviet world view.

Ignored thus far has been the fact that strategic posture may have more or fewer burdens placed upon it, depending on the adequacy of theatre military postures. However, the Schlesinger shift is desirable regardless of the range of American foreign policy interests. A fundamental rationale for the strategic doctrinal inspiration that underpins the shift to more flexible options may be found in the words of Bernard Brodie:

> Though the older expressions of the ideas contained in this book (Klaus Knorr and Thornton Read (eds), *Limited Strategic War*) may now seem somewhat primitive, it is essential to keep alive the principle that the launching of one or a few nuclear weapons even strategically need not and should not mean the launching of all.[21]

Flexible targeting plans are at a premium for a state with extensive foreign interests that could well require the first use (or the credibility of the threat of first use) of strategic nuclear weapons. Although the backstop of American strategic power is a *sine qua non* for the provision of that measure of political confidence necessary for Western European countries to engage in political and, eventually, military experiments in integration, European fears that the American strategic backstop might prematurely be weakened as a response to distinctively European initiatives serve as a brake upon regional experimentation. Nonetheless, there are good reasons for believing that the burdens of European security that have devolved upon the American forces are greater than they need be.

The need for less than massive missile strikes to figure prominently in American strategy would be considerably reduced were there to be available in NATO–Europe the capability to stop a Soviet armoured *Blitzkrieg* in its tracks. From the very beginning of the nuclear arms race, European security needs have served as a magnet attracting American policy makers towards the endorsement of those more expansive strategic conceptions, that are believed by many (including myself) to be of greater foreign policy utility than are the various minimalist notions that hover about the core idea of a small minimum deterrent. Up to a very uncertain point, local capability may act as a substitute for the threat posed by flexibly optioned strategic forces. Fearful of losing the security that stems from the transatlantic linkage to the American strategic forces, NATO–Europe has been concerned to provide just enough defence to yield sufficient evidence for administrations to fend off congressional critics: a defence that would be grossly inadequate were there to be substantial American troop withdrawals.[22]

The relevance, in a very general sense, of the US strategic forces to the security of Western Europe is a fact both political and strategic in dimensions. But the relevance of those forces in a fairly precise operational sense is less of a fact — in the sense of a necessity — and more the product of collective European choice. Although the Schlesinger shift *should* increase the credibility of fairly early American strategic nuclear use in response to a serious military reverse in Europe, it is also, paradoxically, likely to render the need for such use less pressing. Strategic flexibility could reduce the inhibitions that are almost certain to impair the military effectiveness of NATO's tactical nuclear stockpile. Knowing that non-apocalyptic strategic use options were available, NATO's political leaders should — in theory — be more willing to release battlefield nuclear weapons for early and effective defensive purposes than has been the case in recent years.

Strategic posture may be charged with more or fewer duties and its character has an impact upon the feasibility of different strategies for the deterrence and waging of theatre combat. One of the more signal weaknesses in many variants of assured destruction and defensive emphasis doctrines has been that they would neglect to provide an American President with strategic options that could credibly be invoked in defence of forward commitments.

No incoming administration can have more than a very limited impact upon the short term character of American strategic posture. The range of choice is delimited by deployed or ready to be deployed technologies, by political attitudes at home and abroad, and by the amount of bureaucratic grit that will impede any moves towards strategic revolution.

Such is the desirable redundancy in the strategic triad that even cumulatively dramatic technological developments tend not to alter the terms of strategic debate very much. Fears of technological ambush quite rightly fuel official enthusiasm for the funding of a very broad reseach and development programme, but it is difficult to identify any line (or even lines) of technological development that threatens to upset the familiar strategic relationship of offence to defence. Lest this appear a complacent opinion, some examples must be provided. Looking into the 1980s, and without placing each technology in an appropriate (multi-) postural setting, the following developments are likely either to be funded through production, or to be available 'on the shelf' for production, should political and strategic needs be established (and should bureaucratic politics be right):

1 A new family of (very) low yield TNWs designed to maximise some desired weapon effects and to minimise others: fission, fission–fusion and

eventually pure fusion.

2 When and if, the above is deployed in conjunction with precision guided munition (PGM) technologies, there will have been a true revolution in land warfare. Considered as one defensive package, TNWs (mini nukes) with PG, conventional PGMs and barrier conventional weapons (e.g., Dragon Seed, Medusa, Pandora, Grasshopper) could effectively end the reign of the tank as queen of the battlefield. Precision guidance should change the exchange ratios between offence and defence at all levels of warfare: conventional, tactical nuclear, and strategic.

3 CEPs for ballistic missiles of 100 feet or less and much improved yield to weight ratios. If preferential ABM defence of fixed site ICBM fields continues to be precluded by international treaty (beyond the one site provision currently in force), then a point must come in the mid 1980s when all that the ICBM silos are doing is adding to the length of the Soviet target list. For the sake of strategic appearance, for some first use possibilities, for their comparative cheapness to maintain, for the security of their command and control, and for the complication of Soviet attack timetables and the provision of tactical warning, the retention of vulnerable silos might be a defensible decision, but the case would not be a very good one. However, the vulnerability of Soviet and American ICBM silos would not signal the attainment of mutual preclusive first strike capabilities.[23]

4 Considerable improvements in the flexibility with which land-based missile forces could be employed. This refers particularly to the Command Data Buffer System (which allows for rapid re-targeting), to the Attack Assessment System, and to programmes designed to enhance the security of post-attack command and control. These developments will enable the United States to respond in a measured and deliberate way through many 'rounds' of a missile war, were such a conception to prove politically viable.

5 New ICBM concepts will be developed and deployed. These include land and possibly air mobile ICBMs. Arms controllers are unhappy with mobile ICBMs because they would be very difficult to count, particularly if, as is to be anticipated, the counting exercise is restricted to distant national technical means of verification. Henry Kissinger claimed that the United States could detect around 75 per cent of mobile ICBMs deployed, as of 1974–75.[24] Deployed for their relative invulnerability, land mobile ICBMs will constitute a functional continuation of today's ICBM systems. They would certainly induce an adversary to resort to different offensive tactics. A mobile ICBM could require the operational response of a 'barrage' attack. The follow-on ICBM to the Minuteman series, the MX, may well be initially deployed in silos as well as in land and air mobile modes. At the moment, the MX is a set of on-going study projects, no more than that. With a new high energy

propellant, a new large ballistic re-entry vehicle (LABRV), cold-launch from a canister, and a variety of novel navigation aids, it is certain that MX, if deployed, would be an excellent hard-target killer. But such a system could account reliably only for the fixed land-based leg of the Soviet strategic forces – and even then, only if the Soviet Union does not launch on radar warning, and if 'fratricidal' effects do not occur on a large scale.[25]

6   A family of long range cruise missiles. When silo-housed ICBMs become vulnerable (at least in theory) in the early to mid 1980s, the United States will have the option, unless it has been bargained away in SALT II or III, of deploying ALCMs and SLCMs in large numbers. With a near zero CEP, the long range cruise missile will be able to effect precision strikes. Uncertainty surrounds this technology. Strategic analysts are not sure what roles it could best perform, while arms controllers are slowly awakening to the realisation that it promises to be a technological 'wild card' that could make nonsense of the central strategic rationale for the SALT II ceilings (namely, that they will promote a stability enhancing confidence born of certainty as to deployment intentions).

7   ASW technologies and tactics will continue to improve, but not to the point where the entire SSBN fleet will simultaneously be vulnerable to destruction (unless, that is, the finder is accorded a great deal of time). The greatest potential danger to SSBNs will be the deployment of specially designed trailing submarines. However, the missile range of the D–5 Trident II SLBM (6,000 n.m.), if and when deployed – and indeed that of the SS–N–8 (4,200 n.m.) – would vastly complicate the find problem for the aspiring trailer. Apart from the fact that Trident II could be fired from within American territorial waters, there are many ways in which the trail could be broken. Since one could not trail an SSBN by active sonar (the only practicable method) without betraying one's presence, it is a near certainty that comprehensive peacetime trailing will not occur. In a context characterised by the acute vulnerability of ICBM silos, few acts would be more provocative than the institution of active trailing.

8   In the air defence area the most significant developments will be the deployment by both the United States and the Soviet Union of AWACS and Over-the-Horizon Backscatter radars (OTH–B). In synergistic combination, with a follow-on interceptor having a look-down, shoot-down capability, extant low level bomber penetration tactics will need some revision.[26] Ground clutter will no longer blind the defender's radars. However, SAC is confident that it can cope with the Soviet AWACS–Mig 25 Foxbat combination, while a new mix of air breathing (cruise missile) threats should render the task of air defence as onerous as ever. More to the point, given that manned bombers are the back-up leg of the strategic triad, there is little

reason to believe that any development in this area could markedly affect any propensity to take the utmost risks in an acute crisis. OTH–B will extend the perimeter of aircraft detection at all altitudes (unlike the line of sight limitation of the Distant Early Warning (DEW) and Pinetree Lines) to a distance in the region of 1,500 miles.

9   Real time strategic and tactical intelligence gathering and transmittal will be vastly improved. In the tactical area, as illustrated by recent tests in Europe, AWACS will enable NATO to monitor Warsaw Pact military activity as never before. In the strategic area, early warning satellites, parked in synchronous equatorial orbits, enable missile firings to be identified instantly. Such identification is backed up by a system of Over-the-Horizon Forwardscatter radar installations. SLBM firings will eventually be monitored with high confidence by means of an SLBM phased array radar warning system (the Pave Paws programme). These and related developments contribute to the stability of mutual deterrence.

Insofar as technology may be said to determine the range of postural choice, certain absolute constraints do emerge from the technological agenda provided above. There is no way, in the short or medium term, in which the mutual hostage relationship between the Soviet Union and the United States can be upset. Neither the defensive nor the offensive technologies that may currently be projected over the next decade and beyond, alone or in combination, carry any significant promise of being able to reduce expected casualties to a negligible level. However, it is important that technological determinism at this very general level should not be held to imply that strategy and politics are variables dependent on the pace and direction of the *independent* variable of technological change. Such an error has been committed in an article by Wolfgang Panofsky, who writes as follows:

> The critics seem to imply that the mutual–hostage relationship between the populations of the United States and the Soviet Union is a consequence of policy, and would therefore be subject to change if such a policy were modified. Yet this relationship is a matter of physical fact and is thus grossly insensitive to any change in strategic policy.[27]

Panofsky is, of course, correct in his assertion that neither Superpower is likely to be able to protect its population against a determined effort at massacre. But Panofsky is not correct in his critique of the schema of those strategists who expect technological developments and who wish to capitalise on such developments for the limitation of damage. The degree to which missile accuracy, with its *possible* concomitant effect of low collateral damage, is pursued and the extent to which limited nuclear use options are prepared, could have a profound impact on the chances for survival of tens of millions of Russians and Americans. Panofsky subverts his own case considerably when he grants that 'stability as it has now been achieved does not imply that there is only one preordained option with which the strategic forces would retaliate if they were subject to attack'.[28] Along with other MAD devotees, Panofsky is undertaking strategic withdrawal from the farther shores of pure assured destruction doctrine. He is now advocating a strategy of controlled central response.

Mildly to subvert the Panofsky thesis, it should be appreciated that the relationship between technology and public policy is not unidirectional. Advocates of a defensive emphasis argue that, given time, money, and an arms control agreement that sharply reduced the scale (and constrained the future qualitative development) of the offensive threat, defensive technologies could reduce greatly the number of Soviet and American citizens who must live at nuclear risk.

It seems extremely unlikely that a team of defence planners could assemble a surprise attack scheme at any time over the next ten years that would appeal to a reasonable and sceptical political leadership. However, it would be quite wrong to conclude that a very miminum deterrent could therefore satisfy a sufficient number of our criteria for a good strategic posture to be worthy of serious policy consideration. Leaving aside the political inadequacies of a minimum deterrent posture, it should be obvious that the security of the present triad is in part a function of the very sizes and diversity of its components – considered together. The fundamental unwillingness of a leader to initiate nuclear war may not be altered, but a minimum deterrent could well pose counterforce problems that were easier by several orders of magnitude to resolve than is the case with the existing triad. In a moment of desperation in an acute crisis, strategic logicians would be able to make out a better case for the launching of an attempt at a disarming attack.

Minimum deterrent proponents can bypass most of the strategic objections to their positions. They can argue that a minimum deterrent is the strategic corollary of an international condition of secure detente. Acute international crises will not happen. Or, if they grant that a small force of SSBNs could be trailed, and that a force of only (say) 100–200 ICBMs could be destroyed *in toto,* they can propose to adopt the firing tactic of launch on warning (given good management and good luck, the destruction of trailed SSBNs need not provide tactical warning). As with the mined cities *reductio ad absurdum* of minimum deterrence–assured destruction reasoning,[29] launch on warning has few openly declared advocates.

The bulk of the remainder of this chapter explores, in descending order of popularity, the relevant world of postural choice: the differences of emphasis between the arguments of those who advocate variants of assured destruction, counterforce and defensive emphasis postures. Of particular interest are the technological requirements of each posture over the next decade and the likely arms race consequences of each, insofar as they are identifiable.

The present period of policy transition from an assured destruction orientation (much exaggerated by some critics) to a heavily qualified war-fighting orientation, or flexible response, is characterised by claims pertaining to Soviet reaction proneness almost as gross and unsubstantiated as were those brought forth for the ABM debate of 1969. The question 'How must it look to the Russians?' has been posed and answered by arms controllers swift to denounce the Schlesinger shift as containing and implying provocative provisions that can only hinder progress at SALT. As was said of Louis XVIII, they have learnt nothing and forgotten nothing.

Assured destruction

Rigorous strategic logic is rarely to be seen reflected in the varied and incremental activities that comprise a defence policy in action. The nominalist fallacy in the strategic forces area has induced much scholarly and popular misunderstanding. For reasons relating to the believed requirements of political salesmanship, to the style thought necessary for the presentation of defence programmes, and perhaps to a felt need to impose an individual appearance upon a mixture which is much as before, American officials have been wont to give somewhat overblown names to their strategic packaging endeavours.

There is a distinctive kernel of strategic logic that lies at the heart of such doctrinal constructions as massive retaliation/selective retaliation, flexible response and controlled response, damage limitation, assured destruction, and flexible (or limited nuclear) options. Sufficiency and realistic deterrence are in a class of labelling vagueness all their own. They imply no specific lines of strategic reasoning whatsoever, unless, that is, one believes that something of strategic import is being conveyed by the implication that one will not be endorsing strategic forces that are insufficient or that provide unrealistic deterrence. One cause of such political discomfiture that Schlesinger may have felt over the past two years is that his policy shift has not been marketed in an optimal fashion. Commentators seem to have settled on flexible options as an appropriate appelation, but a certain elegance, or even useful pretentiousness, is missing.

One of the dangers in promoting a particular label for the policy mix in question is that many people come to believe that a single kernel of strategic logic informs all strategic policy. Furthermore, fairly acrimonious strategic debate among fellow strategists tends to promote the identification and accentuation of points of strategic divergence (errors), rather than a search for common ground.[30] It so happens that the vast majority of those strategists who are active in public debate are identifiable as favouring one in particular among the theroetical postural tendencies discussed here. However, it is also true that at the margins the differences between positions may be very small indeed.

Assured destruction reasoning has informed the strategic force posture of every American administration since 1953, and it may confidently be expected that it will continue to do so. Assured destruction means simply that under all circumstances one must be capable of imposing a level of damage deemed unacceptable by any adversay. Stated thus, there is no material for strategic debate. However, assured destruction as interpreted and employed by Secretary McNamara and by many strategic commentators thereafter has come to acquire certain rather more specific connotations. Not every adherent to a broad assured destruction position would endorse every item in this list, but there is no caricature here. A strategic posture for the United States that was dominated by assured destruction reasoning should be founded upon the following beliefs (or most of them):

1 Under all circumstances each racing state should be secure in the knowledge that it could 'destroy (for example) the Soviet Union as a viable 20th Century nation'.[31]
2 The level of promised destruction should be 'say, one-fifth to one-fourth of its population and one-half to two-thirds of its industrial capacity . . . '[32]
3 'We believe the Soviets also have a policy of keeping an assured destruction capability.'[33] Hence it should be possible to stabilise the arms race via a common devotion to the tenets of mutual assured destruction.
4 The arms race is driven by mischievous and/or foolish attempts to purchase capabilities that it is hoped will serve to limit damage likely to be suffered by one side.
5 Furthermore, the arms race may be driven by unduly conservative planning for the overinsurance of assured destruction capabilities.
6 A substantial damage limitation capability would be nice to have, but is an impossibility.
7 Therefore neither side must deploy weapon systems that might be interpreted as posing a threat to the ability of the other to sustain an assured destruction capability.
8 The sizing of one's strategic forces should be a function of the target

system and expected degradation factors. Seeking to match or to surpass the other side in numbers, in gross megatonnage, or in any particular index of relative capability is strategically and politically meaningless.

Before a Senate Sub-committee in 1968, Alain Enthoven was very explicit in his identification of the arms race reasoning that, he believed, lent vital support to the case for a finite assured destruction position.

> ... any attempt we might make to achieve more than a fully adequate assured destruction capability must be considered in the light of probable Soviet reactions. I believe that part of the Soviets' strategic policy is the maintenance of an assured destruction capability. The Soviets clearly have the means to maintain this capability. Thus, the Soviets can and would react to any steps we might take to achieve a full first-strike capability or to limit damage to ourselves significantly.[34]

To do full justice to the strategic posture of the later McNamara years, as well as to present a fair case for the second half of the 1970s and for the 1980s, it is necessary to recognise that the core of assured destruction reasoning did not and need not preclude programmes and targeting philosophies that transcend the fundamental benchmark of being able to destroy Soviet society. Damage limitation capabilities were not eschewed totally in the period 1967–69, even in a declaratory sense, regardless of estimates of their likely effectiveness. In addition, these supposedly vintage years of official devotion to the hostage cities orientation did not see convincing official American denunciation of controlled retaliatory strike possibilities, nor even of the concept of strategic superiority. But, despite the evidence of strategic doctrinal ecumenicalism, the shift towards the core tenets of assured destruction reasoning was very real.

Granting the ambivalence, or, less pejoratively, the diversity, to be found in past American policy declarations and programmes, there is little ambivalence about the view of assured destruction taken by the mainstream of the arms control community: men who, by and large, served the Democratic Administrations of 1961–69 in some capacity. It would seem that assured destruction underwent a number of metamorphoses in its function. Taken in order, the life history of assured destruction looks very much as follows: a pretentious phase of conceptual identification as the essence of a deterrent capability; an economical tool useful both for bureaucratic combat and for political presentation purposes; a deterrent concept, formally co-equal with damage limitation; and, finally, *the* deterrent philosophy, providing the criteria for assessing the worth of programmes and the acceptability of arms control proposals.[35]

In the context of this book, the fundamental weakness of assured destruction reasoning is its denial of the political character of inter-state strategic competition. The doctrine rests upon an essentially demographic–economic logic that mates none too well with political considerations. The American assured destruction requirement has been estimated to be in the region of 400 one megaton equivalents (EMT). Beyond this level, the marginal cost of killing Russians rises very sharply indeed. Even though assured destruction reasoning suggests a ceiling for the size of the strategic forces, by no stretch of the imagination could one consider it as implying a minimum deterrent. McNamara's programmes were intended (so the story goes) to ensure the *prompt* deaths of over 60 million Russians, ignoring the certainty that the number of non-prompt fatalities could easily total another 60 million (depending upon many unknowns). For a number of reasons, not all of which would stand up to rigorous strategic theoretical scrutiny, an era of assured destruction emphasis yielded an American strategic nuclear posture that (a) contained an estimated EMT figure of 4,200 (as at late 1972), and (b) should contain approximately 9,690 independent warheads by 1977.

The precise numbers are not important here; what is important is to indicate that even a vigorous counterforce adherent should not be displeased with the scale (though not with the precise character) of the US strategic posture developed under the mantle of a doctrine that was increasingly invoked to choke off damage limiting demands. This is not to argue that the scale of the United States strategic forces, considered as a whole, is politically sufficient, though.

Contrary, perhaps, to the apparent implications of the above, I personally would yield no aid or comfort to the notion of overkill. This revolting expression implies a corollary – underkill. In other words, one is endorsing the idea that it is necessary (and therefore right) to threaten to execute tens of millions of civilian hostages. Strategic forces that far exceed in their explosive promise the 400 EMT figure cited earlier should be seen as instruments of foreign policy to be wielded as a threat and, if necessary, to be used with the utmost measure of control and discretion. They should not be seen as a bludgeon for the 'busting' of Soviet society. Apart from the moral enormity of such a course of strategic action, it would serve no purpose, political or military. Similarly, there is no reason to suspect that Soviet leaders have any enthusiasm for strategies that are pregnant with genocidal probabilities.

As Wolfgang Panofsky has written, our societies are at risk – this is a technological fact.[36] What should not follow is that the technological fact is matched with a strategic fact. Even ignoring such an extra-strategic consideration as appearances (or optical parity), conservatively planned and ed strategic forces for the assured destruction mission can easily very prodigious size. What appears to some to be evidence of overkill is, in fact, evidence that defence planners have made due and proper allowance for the various factors that would degrade the effectiveness of a strategic force. Some people seem reluctant to admit that not all weapons would be ready to fire when they were needed (probably only 80 per cent – to take the nominal figure) and that not all of those that were fired would complete their mission satisfactorily. It tends to be assumed that all of one's inventory will be available for implementation of the SIOP. If the enemy attacks first and does well (and one can hardly afford to presume that he would do badly), then the overkill percentage shrinks to a point reasonably characterisable as reflecting a sensible insurance.

The size of individual strategic programmes is not, in any very precise way, the outcome of rational strategic debate. Missile and aircraft quantities lend themselves particularly to bureaucratic political contention. The political leadership may be unable to stop a programme (given the momentum that has gathered behind it), but it can seek to reduce the numbers to be deployed. It has been argued, that the assured destruction concept was a tool that enabled McNamara to ward off service demands for more missiles and for additional programmes. To some degree this is true. However, it is impossible not to recognise that the strategic forces approved by McNamara reflected strategic planning of a very conservative kind. To risk a cynical interpretation, the need to hedge against even very unlikely threats to the United States assured destruction capability could serve as a rationale that would legitimise (in strategic terms) almost any strategic programme, whatever the more salient factors bearing upon its deployment prospects may be.

Perhaps it is now clear how McNamara came to chain himself to the relentless strategic logic of mechanistic action–reaction. If one races in armaments not for putative political advantage, nor to do one's best in the event of war occurring, but rather to attain (in the Soviet case) and maintain (in the American case) a secure second strike retaliatory capability *of a certain, identified dimension,* then *ipso facto* one must respond to challenges to that capability. McNamara's mechanistic response model was the product of his own preferred strategic doctrine, not of a close observation of past arms race dynamics, nor of any general strategic necessity that must move arms race actors.

The assured destruction doctrine was employed, in its arms race dynamics guise, to impede the prospects for ABM deployment. From the point of view of an understanding of international politics, assured destruction reflects a shallow technocratic perspective. The doctrine provided (and still provides) answers for busy officials who often need to operate on the basis of dead reckoning. Unfortunately, as the evidence of Soviet strategic behaviour over the past decade illustrates beyond reasonable doubt, the rules of thumb offered by assured destruction are nowhere near good enough.

Devotion to a rigorous interpretation of assured destruction doctrine induces a poorly oriented paranoia. The central criterion of promptly dead Russians, the currency of assured destruction analyses, directs the attention of defence policy makers away from practically the whole gamut of possible strategic forces' actions in support of (and of more general relevance to) foreign policy. It is difficult to identify much strategic sense (as opposed to logic) in assured destruction doctrine. Adherents to the doctrine are of course sensible to stress the need to ensure that the Soviet Union does not even begin to approach a relative strategic position wherein some of her military planners discern disarming first strike possibilities. But the massive strike and prodigious hostage execution foci (now denied by MAD bombers in retreat) inalienably associated with assured destruction doctrine seem certain to (a) grant arms racing advantages to the adversary; (b) impede the development of weapon technologies that could be used in support of foreign policy; and (c) ensure that, if bilateral strategic operations do begin, the casualty list will be greater rather than smaller. The doctrine reflects, and has encouraged yet further, the inclination of American arms controllers to direct their attention almost exclusively to the nuclear Pearl Harbour genus of scenario.

Assured destruction is an incomplete doctrine; it confuses means with ends. Much of the arms control and strategic literature seems to suggest that the overwhelming purpose of a strategic posture is to guarantee the prompt demise of 60 million plus Russians. The conceptual limitations of this framework of thought begin to become all too apparent when one pauses to ask under what circumstances one would be prepared to execute all those Soviet hostages. Politically and morally sensitive replies suggest, to me at least, the profound folly of permitting one's strategic and arms control postures to be influenced significantly by classic assured destruction critera.

Technology has eroded and is eroding the attractiveness of assured destruction doctrine. However, that statement does not mean that either Superpower is unlikely to be able to guarantee the imposition of unacceptable damage at any time over the coming decade and as far beyond as one can foresee. What it does mean is that strategic options that were either impossible to implement or were likely to be extremely unproductive are now gaining in appeal. New technologies such as the Mark 12A re-entry vehicle, SINS, the Attack Assessment System, ICBM cold launching, AIRS, etc., will provide the United States with the ability not to reduce damage significantly by means of denial of access to civilian targets, but to execute limited counterforce strikes. Similarly, accuracy improvement combined with very small warheads (for example, the Pave Pepper Programme for Minuteman IV) will increase US ability to strike at very limited target systems, while imposing collateral damage several orders of magnitude less than that certain to be produced by former technologies.

If one grants the legitimacy and the determination of the two Superpowers to retain their assured destruction capabilities, defined in terms of a society-busting level of promised damage, there is nothing in the present mix of forces deployed, or technologies under development, that should promote any serious measure of alarm. If it were to be decided that the United States should reverse the trend, signalled first by President Nixon and later by Dr Schlesinger, towards the provision of a great flexibility for nuclear use (which, in principle at least, is very different indeed from the dedicated pursuit of a major hard-target killing capability), then certain technological implications follow. One difficulty is to know to what extent an assured destruction oriented administration would wish to provide for a very wide range of strategic targeting options. It would be extremely difficult to effect the determined pursuit of a capability for controlled response that was not at the same time to have the de-establishing consequences for the arms race that assured destruction devotees believe follow from war-fighting technologies. In essence, one would be seeking weapons good enough to strike (possibly) small targets precisely, but weapons not good enough to incline conservative Soviet military planners to believe that their hard-targets were prospectively in danger. One could seek to pacify exaggerated (though understandable, by this arms race logic) Soviet anxieties, but success would be unlikely. The eschewal of terminally guided MARV technology would provide an index of one's honourable MAD intentions, but suspicious Soviet analysts might be unimpressed.

A second difficulty in predicting the character of a future assured destruction oriented strategic posture is to know to what extent American political leaders would be sensitive to the possible political implications of a highly ambiguous Soviet posture. Assured destruction extremists hold that 'a deterrent is a deterrent', almost regardless of relative size or character.[37] McNamara could neglect the question of the political consequences of poor strategic appearances and of non-equivalent capabilities because his phase of dedication to assured destruction logic was characterised by a substantial, though rapidly disappearing, measure of American strategic superiority. Claims in 1967 and 1968 that the Soviet Union was bound on a strategic quest for a secure beyond doubt second strike capability, or for strategic parity in 'static' measures of strength, could not be refuted by any evidence. The proponent of an assured destruction orientation for the late 1970s and beyond must be aware of the fact he will be endorsing a considerable, unfavourable asymmetry of strategic options. The terms of SALT II do not promise to allow the United States to relax.

There is a distinction between an assured destruction devotee and a man who subscribes to a version of minimum deterrence in good part on economic grounds. Both share a number of common beliefs; for example, (a) that the threat of (massive or less massive) urban damage is the best deterrent to war; (b) that serious preparation and discussion relating to the tactics of war-waging render such a war rather more probable; and (c) that the hounds of total counterforce ambition lurk ready to assume control of any programme intended to provide for controlled nuclear response. Safety lies only in total abstention. However, they divide very sharply indeed on the question of the difficulty of sustaining a secure deterrent.

The minimum deterrer believes that nuclear war is so unattractive to prudent men that the vast size of the Superpower arsenals must reflect either the baleful influence of special interests or the influence of attitudes as yet uneducated to the requirements of a nuclear age. As McNamara made abundantly clear, the dedicated assured destruction adherent is willing to purchase enormous quantities of strategic insurance. Every major strategic programme now under way (barring those intended to augment hard-target kill prospects) is easily defensible in the logic of assured destruction. The B-1, the Trident SSBN and Trident I missile, AWACS and ASW, the MX follow-on ICBM programme, air and sea launched cruise missile programmes, and even MARV, may be held to contribute to the assuredness with which the United States threatens potential enemies with societal damage.

Assured destruction may be characterised as an automobile with optional extras. An eight cylinder vehicle will go from A to B, as will a four cylinder vehicle. However, the eight cylinder option will transport one with greater style and at greater cost, though possibly with greater safety. But in the eight cylinder vehicle one could well be tempted to drive faster, or, at the very least, with greater verve. The basic tenets of assured destruction are common to all models: populations must be assuredly vulnerable, while weapons systems must be assuredly invulnerable. Accepting this, a strategist can devise a whole range of variations. Among the variants of assured destruction, seven are analytically prominent.

First, there is the American posture as sanctioned by SALT I (as amended in July 1974), without the partial reorientation later effected through the Schlesinger shift. This posture is marked by the absence of any serious attempt at damage limitation, although token ABM deployment is endorsed by treaty (permitted deployment is restricted to one site). The targeting emphasis is upon relatively massive as opposed to small strikes. (Limited strategic options (LSOs) are not incompatible with an assured destruction orientation, in principle, but in practice assured destroyers tend to be profoundly sceptical of their feasibility). Second, as above, save for the token ABM deployment. Dedicated MAD analysts are unhappy with any ABM deployment because of the basis for expansion they believe it could provide. Third, hostage cities as above, with targeting emphasis again heavy and directed at urban areas. But heavy ABM defence of ICBM silos would be deployed. Such BMD would contribute to the confidence placed in assured destruction capabilities and would be unambiguously terminal.

The fourth variant is a minimum deterrent posture. With or without parallel Soviet action, and regardless of SALT II ceilings, offensive forces would be reduced sharply. Some arms controllers would anticipate a sympathetic parallel response from Soviet leaders. The Joint Chiefs of Staff would no doubt resign and there would be mutterings of possible impeachment proceedings from predictable sources in Congress. Hailed by equally predictable sources as a breakthrough to peace, and as a fracturing of the action—reaction linkage that allegedly drives the arms race, such a sharp unilateral de-escalatory move would be a dramatic policy example of the meaning of the adage that arms control begins at home. Soviet leaders would be suspicious but would probably conclude that one should not look a gift posture in the mouth and would draw the appropriate conclusions: that American political will had declined even more rapidly than they had expected. The consequences of an American shift to a minimum deterrent posture would be political rather than military. Extended deterrent linkages with Europe, Israel, and Japan would suffer a rapid decline in credibility. Attentive publics around the globe would conclude that the Soviet Century was beginning. The military detail of a minimum deterrent is difficult to specify. It could well be decided that 10 Trident submarines would be a formidable and sufficient force for American purposes. After all, the submarines could be on station even in US territorial waters and each submarine will carry twenty-four MIRVed (if not MARVed) missiles. Unfortunately, this American de-escalatory move would wonderfully concentrate the minds of Soviet ASW scientists and technologists. In my opinion, destruction would be inadequately assured. Even if the adverse military consequences of such a policy move are ignored, the political consequences should be expected to be disastrous.

Fifth, one may favour assured destruction with attention paid to strategic appearances. While eschewing the development of 'provocative' and 'de-stabilising' counterforce capable programmes, the United States would seek, as best it could, to match the Soviet strategic posture (save in its damage limiting orientation). The development by the Soviet Union of a substantial but limited (to one leg of the triad) counterforce option would be ignored on the grounds of its strategic irrelevance. This posture would be designed to pose an overwhelming threat to Soviet urban–industrial values, while it would rest upon the proposition that gross and militarily insignificant indices of relative strategic power may have some political import. The fine print of targeting would be a matter of little concern. A Soviet counterforce advantage would be deemed to be of no significance, since Soviet political leaders would never take the incalculable risks attendant upon a strike limited to US land-based missile forces. In any event, over a period of time this problem of counterforce non-equivalence could be solved by phasing out the ICBM silos, and/or (depending on appearances and vulnerability calculations) by phasing in a mobile land-based ICBM and an air launched ballistic and/or cruise missile, and by augmenting and diversifying the SSBM force.

As a consequence of pedagogic persistence, the Soviet Union might yet, in SALT III (SALT II now being a lost cause), be induced to accept a permanent offensive forces regime that would preclude destabilising qualitative improvements and would meet the American requirements over appearances. For reasons advanced earlier in this book (asymmetries of doctrine, weapon details and political motivation), it is highly unlikely that such a package could be negotiated. Silo-housed ICBMs can no longer be saved from obsolescence through SALT, but *the* problem for the 1990s – namely, the vulnerability of SSBNs – might usefully benefit from early prophylactic action in SALT III.

Sixth, assured destruction may be tempered with provisions for flexible retaliatory options. Shaken by the many cogent moral, military, and political arguments that have been levelled at MAD doctrine, some of the leading MAD bombers have turned to this variant of assured destruction, claiming that this is what they had always endorsed. The doctrine would place only the adversary's strategic forces (and presumably their command system) off targeting limits. In the words of Wolfgang Panofsky:

> With the exception of being denied a counterforce strike against the other side's hardened silos, the choice in number and kinds of targets – be they military or civilian – is governed only by the technical features of the command and control systems and the doctrine which governs its application.[38]

Therefore, the United States requires weapon systems in large numbers, diversified in their deployment characteristics, and accurate, but not too accurate. The non-hard-target counterforce flexible option position can be justifiably regarded as belonging to the assured destruction genus because it insists upon (a) the total vulnerability of societies; (b) the eschewal of active efforts to limit damage; and (c) it bears all the hallmarks of adherence to the mechanistic response model of arms race dynamics. In pursuit of a technical notion of stability Panofsky and others ignore the more salient problems of political stability. If the triads of each side are as secure in their diversity as Panofsky maintains, why should it matter whether or not hard-target killing counterforce options are pursued? More to the political point, does it matter if the Soviet Union continues to make progress towards achieving a counterforce option *vis-à-vis* land-based missiles, an option denied to the United States because of her dominant strategic doctrine?

Seventh, one might endorse assured destruction with light nation-wide ABM coverage. Fearful of third party catalytic action, of accidents, of small scale 'crazy state' initiatives, and as a small hedge against unforseeable future need, the United States could seek to revert to the postural logic of Sentinel and Safeguard Phase II. The ABM treaty would have to be either abandoned or rewritten, and domestic opinion would have to be re-educated. Since Congress was unwilling to fund even a very limited ABM deployment in defence of the National Command Authority (NCA), the scale of the necessary strategic persuasive task would have to be heroic indeed. Nevertheless, despite the 'building blocks for expansion to a thick system' possibilities of a thin area defence, such a deployment would be consistent with the letter (if not the spirit) of assured destruction doctrine. As was revealed in the protracted ABM debate, extant technologies are none too impressive for the task of city defence. However, updated versions of Spartan and Sprint would probably be good enough for the very limited tasks assigned to them under this posture. Whatever the limitations of existing technology, such a deployment would ensure the health of BMD research programmes, and could be valued as insurance against the day when the United States might wish seriously to evaluate the postural charms of a defensive emphasis.

The implications of a (post-Schlesinger) return to an assured destruction orientation are political rather than technical. (Technically, the United States could not credibly eschew a hard-target counterforce capability in the short term – the weapons would exist.) American self-denial of counterforce options would probably encourage the Soviet Union to bargain even more determinedly in SALT. The marked prospective counterforce asymmetry between the two sides should yield to the Soviet Union a favourable treaty in a SALT III. Agreements in Soviet, and indeed in most, perspectives should be just. That is to say, they should reflect the facts of and the prospects for the balance of power between the negotiating parties. It is unlikely that the Soviet leaders would accept the need for strategic postural sacrifice in the interests of a very technical American notion of strategic stability. One does not race in armaments in order to seek to remove them from a status of influence in international politics. Many arms controllers may harbour contrary expectations, but a United States sailing into the future on the wave of an assured destruction orientation may have to relearn, in the midst of an acute international crisis, that the Soviet Union had a strategic posture that lent credence to the arguments of those in Moscow who asserted that their country had obtained the means for escalation dominance.

The broad-fronted Soviet strategic modernisation programme, as permitted (and encouraged) by SALT II, is driven in rational actor perspective not so much by fear of American programmes as by the aspiration for political gain.[39] The respective and relative counterforce (and therefore possibly political) potentials of the two sides' missile forces are as calculable in Moscow as they are in Washington.

Counterforce

In good part as a consequence of laudable desires to restrict defence expenditure, to brake the velocity of the arms race, and to discourage unrealistic strategic aspirations, the mainstram of American strategists/arms controllers has set itself firmly against the deployment of hard-target counterforce-capable weapon system.[40] For a variety of reasons, many of which have been rehearsed earlier in this study, I am convinced that a counterforce orientation of strategic thought and the purchase of some counterforce options are highly desirable.

As with assured destruction, beyond a postural core logic counterforce doctrines (and postures) come in many different guises. Furthermore, adherents to some variant of counterforce philosophy need not eschew all interest in the assured destruction and defensive emphasis modes of reasoning. Save for the very unlikely circumstance in which an adversary has deployed a very thick ABM system around his urban areas but not around his missile silos, a good counterforce capability *should* also be a good assured destruction capability (presuming that a 'first strike only' posture is not acquired). Accurate missiles will be overdesigned for urban demolition, but they will certainly be capable of performing such a function. A really first class counterforce capability would, however, be incompatible with a condition of *mutual* assured destruction. Whether or not this is judged desirable is a matter determined by the distance down the road of counterforce theory that one is prepared to travel.

Defensive emphasis, as understood in this chapter and in the pertinent literature, is conceived to be an alternative to the logic both of assured destruction and of counterforce. However, an official determination to limit prospective damage by any and all means that could be developed would certainly imply a heavy investment in both counterforce-capable systems and in active and passive defence programmes. The more effective a counterforce strike is predicted to be, then the more attractive defensive programmes are likely to seem. The 'Higher-Than-Expected Threat' invoked by McNamara in his *Posture Statement* for FY 1968 was precisely such a synergistic combination of hard-target kill-capable MIRVs and nation-wide ABM defences.

Although counterforce strategy may have many postural referents, in the context of this study three counterforce postures (and postural aspirations) are discussed. First, one must identify 'flexible targeting options' *à la* Schlesinger shift of 1973–74. This is a posture intended to provide: an approximate equivalence of counterforce capability with the Soviet Union without, at the same time, providing any plausible prospect for the enforced disarmament of the Soviet Union; and a wider variety of SIOP and sub-SIOP options. Since a good total counterforce capability is deemed to be impossible, given the variety and character of strategic technologies (and tactics) deployed and deployable in the short to medium terms, the purchase of some counterforce capability ought not to provoke desperate reactions abroad.

Second, there is the very distant prospect of a major damage limitation or 'win the war' posture. This is really what McNamara endorsed in 1962–63 as a consequence of arms race 'accident'. This posture would be incompatible with assured destruction thinking, in that one would seek to remove the threat to one's urban–industrial values. Heinous though this postural aspiration may appear to many, rationales for it which do merit attention may be advanced. Whatever outcomes were predicted by war-games and operations analyses, no sane and reasonable politican could be expected to give the order for a final counterforce solution. The deterrent worth of such a posture should reside in the fact that the adversary ought to be most unwilling ever to begin to place the counterforce posturing power in a situation wherein sane and reasonable behaviour might be redefined in the light of the perceived impending costs of inactivity. A major damage limiting posture may be defensible on the grounds that its apparently dedicated pursuit should induce more reasonable behaviour abroad. It would be appreciated that there was no serious prospect of a totally effective counterforce capability ever being acquired. However, should war occur, such damage limitation as could be enforced would be useful, while the political consequences of an arms race canter or gallop should induce a redefinition of interests in Moscow.

Finally, the postural aspiration may be taken at its face value: a determination to pursue all avenues in the hope of attaining an exploitable, not too incredible, win the war posture. One difficulty attendant upon the attempted translation of military into political power is that one can never know, short of impossibly realistic field testing, just how good one's damage limiting capabilities really are.

Third, a counter-combatant strategic posture has been the subject of speculation. Eschewing the promotion of threats to the strategic forces of the adversary, targeting would be oriented towards the enemy in uniform. Bruce Russett has advanced this alternative as a result of his rejection (principally, though not exclusively, on moral grounds) of mainstream assured destruction reasoning, and of his acceptance of the validity of arms race and crisis stability theorems that suggest the baleful consequences of targeting strategic forces.[41] Russett suggests that counter-combatant strikes would deny any meaningful victory to an adversary. By targeting the non-strategic instruments of Soviet control, one would be posing the most awesome threat of all. The difficulties that would attend this posture are fairly obvious. For example, not all military units, nor KGB para-military units, are deployed in areas thinly populated by civilians. Also, such a posture would lack any very obvious benchmark of sufficiency.

There is a core logic pertaining to a counterforce posture which is common to most counterforce theorists. War is held to be possible. However unlikely war may seem, no one can be certain that it will not occur, possibly as the unintended consequence of a chain of events that were unanticipated. Given that some hypothetical wars are beyond deterrence, it is only responsible for the United States to be prepared to wage them. The availability of counterforce options, great and small, means that there is no strategic necessity for the massacre of politically innocent Soviet civilians to begin in round one. Both sides would share the strongest imaginable interest in preserving urban areas inviolate. Negotiated war termination is only practicable if both sides have values that remain at risk. Moreover, because it may be perceived (however fallaciously) as entailing smaller immediate risks than would a counter-city strategy, a counterforce strategy should increase the credibility of nuclear response. Counterforce options are more usable than countervalue options, a logical (though not necessarily political) fact that should serve not to make nuclear war more likely, but to help deter those acts that might be judged worthy of nuclear response.

The United States cannot eschew counterforce options, even if the Soviet Union should elect to do so. In practice, the Soviet Union has endorsed in its strategic programme and in fairly unambiguous declaratory form, the development of whatever counterforce capability, technological and budgetary traffic will bear. But, because of her *forward* defence commitments (particularly in Europe), it is the United States and not the Soviet Union that is in vital need of a nuclear strategy that provides for credible first use. A central nuclear war may comprise a series of limited strikes and not the *Götterdämmerung* of bilateral, near simultaneous spasms of much strategic fiction. If there is some value in this very tentative prediction, then the ability to inflict as much damage on, for example, Soviet strategic forces as they could on American strategic forces *could* be of profound military and political importance. Finally, so the argument goes, the arms race *may* be driven by American fears for the security of its strategic forces, but there is scant evidence to suggest that Soviet strategic programmes are, to any significant extent, sustained by fears of prospective vulnerability.

Counterforce adherents are able to reply to objections of a 'logic of the arms race' type in two ways. First, they can argue that, no matter how dedicated the pursuit of counterforce options may be, there is no danger that either side will ever be in a position wherein it would not be confident that it could impose a level of damage that would be deemed unacceptable. Second, it can be argued that even if there is some validity to the claim that Soviet strategic programmes are pursued because the vulnerability of particular components of the strategic forces is anticipated, there are other motives driving the arms race as well. Objections to a counterforce strategy should be appraised in the light of the factors discussed in Chapters 2–4.

Firm advocates of assured destruction and of counterforce postures are really addressing separate strategic problems. An assured destruction posture is intended to ensure that sufficient damage is promised so that no rational adversary will ever choose to initiate a nuclear war. Flexible targeting possibilities may be appended to the core of such a posture in order to make provisions for the dim possibility of some intrawar deterrence, but there is no doubt that assured destruction is really focussed upon prewar deterrence and arms race management.

Counterforce thinking, on the other hand, focusses primarily on the conduct of a war once deterrence has failed. The war-fighting orientation of many counterforce analyses is necessary, understandable, and yet unfortunate. At root, an enthusiastic adherent to counterforce reasoning is saying the following things: an assured destruction posture is not good enough for the deterrence of the range of threats that will be posed in the late 1970s and the 1980s, while only a counterforce strategy offers adequate deterrent effect, and usable hedges against the outside possibility that the deterrent effect provided is inadequate. In other words, the counterforce theorist maintains that a better war-fighting posture is a better deterrent. However, there is a significant distinction between the development of counterforce options designed to provide a rough, or at least adequate, equivalence of pre-attack capability for perceived equal security, and the development of an all-embracing total counterforce capability designed to provide a reasonable chance of winning a nuclear war. The former counterforce track is being followed by Schlesinger in his reorientation of American nuclear strategy. The political logic that underpins the Schlesinger shift may stretch the credulity of some assured destruction aficionados, but it hardly challenges their core beliefs.

After all, Soviet urban–industrial targets are not being removed from the American target list, while the United States has neither the ability nor the apparent intention to seek the ability to destroy every Soviet ICBM, long range bomber, and SSBN. Improvements in the hard-target kill capability of US ICBMs and SLBMs, duly orchestrated by more flexible targeting plans, should have two beneficial consequences. First, any limited disarming, punishing, or purely exemplary strikes by the Soviet Union *could* be met by responses in kind. An American president would not face the prospect of having to respond to a counterforce strike by means of countervalue execution. This, of course, is a somewhat extreme polarisation of the alternatives. Second, Soviet foreign policy behaviour should be disciplined by the appreciation that there was a rough asymmetry of strategic capabilities between the Superpowers.

Schlesinger's revision of the war plans is thus a profoundly defensive arms race move. Rather more pertinent than a charge of arms race de-stabilisation, or of an alleged greater willingness to conduct nuclear operations, is the danger that survival prospects may receive less attention than they merit. The new stress now placed on a flexibility of strategic use, a willingness to match limited Soviet strikes, and the need to limit collateral damage could serve to promote a certain legerdemain towards other strategic concerns.

Schlesinger rightly stated the general impossibility of attaining a forcible disarming capability, but this is true only to the extent that the problem of the survival of strategic forces continues to be taken very seriously. To stress the invulnerability that attends the triad structure of forces is correct today and probably for the next decade, but there is no such thing as an invulnerable weapon system, independent of considerations of time and adversary capability. The ABM treaty may stand as a monument to the dominant arms control credo (by standard Western interpretation), but it certainly made no worthwhile contribution to the survival prospects of American's ICBM silos. The ABM treaty really makes sense (for the United States) only in the context of oversimplified assured destruction reasoning. Specifically, token ABM deployment means that although, for example, more Minutemen will be destroyed in their silos, those Minutemen that do survive will have a guaranteed free ride to Soviet cities (other than Moscow). Alas, the scenario could be written somewhat differently. In the event of an all but annihilating Soviet assault on Minuteman–Titan, probably the last option that an

American president would wish to exercise would be the initiation of a civilian hostage 'exchange'. It is difficult to resist the conclusion that in SALT I the United States exchanged a good defence of its ICBM silos for a very poor Soviet urban defence system.

If one seeks sensibly to make provision for limited counterforce strikes, it is also essential that reasonable attention be paid to the survival prospects of those forces that are to be flexibly targeted. War-fighting forces need to have a utility that extends beyond their value for the conduct of pre-emptive first strike operations. Schlesinger's flexible options may look a little less impressive if, by the mid-1980s, the only leg of the triad likely to escape first strike destruction, and which is swift to target, is the SSBN force. SLBMs make far from optimal counterforce weapons. This judgement is particularly pertinent if one envisages a protracted war, as one must, given the drift of current official strategic logic. SSBNs face command and control problems that are not shared by land or air mobile systems, while the mobile character of the SLBM launch platform poses severe problems if one is concerned to ensure pinpoint re-entry vehicle accuracy. There is now a very strong case indeed for the United States to proceed with a programme to develop a land mobile ICBM. The accuracy problem of this (and other) mobile systems can be resolved by means of mid-course and terminal guidance correcting technologies. To improve the yield to weight ratio of Minuteman III through the introduction of the Mark 12A warhead and to improve missile accuracy will be of little value if the weapon is vulnerable to first strike destruction.

Despite their toying with flexible response notions, the adherents to assured destruction reasoning believe that stability resides in the promise of massive societal damage. Counterforce arguments are dangerous because, so it is alleged, they may mislead decision makers. The dangers of counterforce thinking, excluding arms race considerations, are twofold: firstly, truly imprudent politicians might be led (by Halperin's 'Clever Briefers') to believe that they had a 'win the war' strategy;[42] and secondly, the use of nuclear force is more likely if politicians believe that massive civilian casualties probably will not result.[43] Counterforce technologies are judged by many critics to be seen by their proponents as offering *de facto* inadequate technological panaceas. In fact, there are no panaceas available because the entire populations of states are now vulnerable to an apparently technologically irreversible superiority of the offence over the defence in strategic warfare. Therefore, so the argument goes, attempts to sell counterforce options are attempts to sell the idea of relatively safe nuclear wars. Moreover, the contemplation of the *how* of nuclear strike and counterstrike, and certainly the writing of plans induces unwarranted optimism (and bureaucratic parental affection) to the effect that theory and reality could be as one. There is a germ of truth in this stream of argument, but not much more. Profoundly revealing of a tacit theory that precludes much human control over the direction taken by, and the use to be made of, technology is the following argument advanced by Panofsky:

> Ill-bounded attempts to 'sanitize' nuclear war are a disservice to the maintenance of stability, as well as to efforts to reduce areas of risk.
>
> In essence, the critics of a primarily deterrent posture and the advocates of 'nuclear war fighting' assume that scientific progress will somehow alter the existing realities. I can see no technological basis for this assumpton. Specifically:
>
> No technological distinction exists or can be created between those nuclear weapons endangering the deterrent forces of the opponent in a first or pre-emptive strike (and thus decreasing stability) and weapons designed to attack the same forces by retaliation.[44]

Panofsky offers a popular caricature of the limited counterforce posture and of arguments that have begun to reshape American strategy. Surely there are no "advocates of 'nuclear war-fighting' ?" Nuclear war-fighting options should help to balance the Superpower strategic equation; possibily extend the geographical deterrenp writ of the strategic forces; help extend deterrence to war itself; and just possibly save lives by the tens of millions. To say that all nuclear use *need* not be massive nuclear use against urban–industrial targets is both a logical truth and a restatement of the revised assured destruction position regarding flexible retaliatory options.

Is stability immanent in certain weapon to weapon relationships, but not in others? To threaten a portion of the Soviet strategic forces, no more, is not necessarily destabilising. It depends upon one's strategic ideology. Brezhnev does not view the development of a MIRVed SS–18 as destabilising. Could one not argqe that to permit a limited and unmatched Soviet hard-target countarforce capability to develop is far more destabilising – in the political sense in which Soviet leaders may fairly be presumed to think – than is the slowly emerging American response to that predictable Soviet competence. Panofsky's contention that it is destabilising to threaten stategic forces may be granted, and then deliberately ignored. Part of the price to be paid for security may have to be an unstable weapons environment, by assured destruction definition. To cite putative arms race instabilities is not to foreclose discussion. Possible arms race consequences is nop a region of analysis fit to provide the sole criteria for the assessment of strategic programmes.

Perhaps the central difficulty encountered by critics of the Schlesinger shift is that the Soviet Union is guilty, on a truly massive scale, of nearly every sin of which Schlesinger himself is accused. In an arms race system, stability, by whatever definition, must be the product of bilateral effort (or accident). As the Soviet Union is proving profoundly reluctant to eschew the counterforce potential of her MIRV programmes, duly blessed to the level of 1,320 MIRV launchers by the terms of the Vladivostok accords, what would the assured destruction and 'strategic appearances are (fairly) unimportant' schools have the United States do? Perhaps, as Joseph Kruzel suggested in an article in *Orbis* (prior to Vladivostok), the United States should just accept whatever deal is negotiable. He indicated that the proclaimed and formally temporary nature of the offensive forces agreement of SALT I should be acceptable for the long term. Although much of Kruzel's article has been overtaken by events in the SALT II negotiations, his view of the strategic requirements of the United States is important in that it is indicative of the unwillingness of the arms control community to see Soviet arms race behaviour in any perspective save its own. The potential counterforce asymmetries between Soviet and American strategic forces suggest that the terms of the SALT I interim agreement (and the Vladivostok accords) are a vehicle for the freezing of the United States into a relative posture of politically meaningful strategic infariority. Kruzel, a former member of the SALT delegation, does not share this view:

> The (intarim) agreement is set to run for five years, and though several US officials have indicated that five years is as long as the United States could live with such limitations, statements like this should be seen as negotiating bravado. There are no strategic programmes under consideration that would force the Unite States to withdraw from the Interim Agreement, and learning to live with it should not present too great a problem.[45]

If only the Russians would behave as American arms controllers believe that they ought to behave.

In the present strategic and political contexts it is just possible that a tougher declaratory stance on the arms race by United States officials might induce a co-operative Soviet reaction. But the state of ASW research, the ABM treaty, and the all too obvious limitations of the current American inventory of ballistic missiles could be held to preclude the announcement of a determination to proceed towards a major damage limitation capability. The poor basis for such a posture provided by the present weapons inventory, plus the undeniable and predictable opposition of Congress and the media, would greatly diminish the credibility of such an announcement. The (candidate) macro response of the Schlesinger shift could grow into a serious bid for the recovery of strategic superiority, but this is far from certain at the moment.

Damage limiting options, which are not the options sought in American arms race programmes at present, would (and should) be sought in a defensive spirit. They would reflect an American judgement that the momentum of Soviet strategic forces improvements could betoken very unfriendly foreign policy intent. Therefore, as a hedge against the possibility of adventurous diplomacy in the years ahead, the United States would seek gradually to shift gears in order to recover the arms race ground lost in the years when the purer strains of assured destruction doctrine moved many official and congressional minds. The pursuit of a 'win the war' posture need reflect neither strategically atavistic thought, nor a confidence that the arms race could indeed be won in a militarily definitive sense. All that such postural pursuit need reflect would be a determination to induce reasonable, if ambitious, Soviet leaders to reconsider the cost effectiveness of the foreign policy that drives their arms programmes. Needless to say, a bid for a major damage limiting posture would be very expensive, could induce unduly self-confident American behaviour, and, if funded on a massive scale (for example, if the strategic forces budget were to be augmented by a factor of three or four), ought to begin to promote serious and probably healthy anxieties in Moscow concerning the adequacy of Soviet war-fighting capabilities. Soviet leaders would hardly be likely to revise their foreign and defence policy behaviour unless they were convinced that the alternative would become increasingly costly and dangerous.

This muscular variant of counterforce thinking is discussed here for two reasons. First, it retains some limited measure of popularity and, hence, cannot be ignored. Second, a mild version of it could have some policy relevance for the next decade. Conclusive evidence is missing, but it is reasonable to presume that the Soviet reluctance to make adequate concessions to moderate American security concerns in the SALT II forum (over such issues as verification and missile sub-limits) betrays a conviction that 'time is on our side'. The Schlesinger shift is, in part, intended to signal that both arms race actors can make good use of time. Americans must recognise the unwelcome possibility that expensive indices of strategic alarm may have to be provided before Soviet leaders will be convinced that no worthwhile gain is likely to be registered as a consequence of energetic arms racing. SALT agreements, of the variety concluded thus far, are no substitutes for a more robust strategic posture.

The counter-combatant variant of counterforce strategy is open to several criticisms. First, it could not meet the political requirements of a United States that had to co-exist with a Soviet strategic posture rapidly improving in its hard-target countarforce competence. Second, the strategy might prove to be infeasible. Even if the Soviet Union did not seek to deploy its armed forces in such a way as to maximise the difficulty of conducting hygienic nuclear strikes, the collateral civilian damage certain to be a consequence of counter-combatant strikes could well be so great that the principal rationale for the adoption of the strategy would prove to be chimerical. However, as additional evidence of the flight from assured destruction reasoning, the emergence of counter-combatant reasoning is to be welcomed. Whatever the practicality of the strategy, its academic proponents do share a profound moral distaste for the 'city busting' focus of the MAD bombers that is entirely laudable.

Bruce Russett's counter-combatant strategy is not to be seen as a serious contender for the American postural throne, but it is evidence of the ferment that now characterises strategic thought. Some of the items on Russett's target list have long held their places on the official American target list. Lukewarm tactical allies of Russett are not hard to locate. His analyses provide a devastating critique of assured destruction thinking which is welcomed by the proponents of hard-target counterforce options, while his explicit renunciation of the more thorough-going counterforce arguments is welcomed by assured destroyers as being supportive of one of the central tenets of their creed.

The arms race consequences of new counterforce technologies seem likely to be benign. In a political sense, the Schlesinger 'hedging' programme of counterforce options should serve to remind Soviet leaders that American science and industry (if not sustained political will), given time, money and official encouragement, is quite capable of setting at nought that degree of effort expended upon strategic forces after 1964 that transgresses against criteria for rough parity. Given that the Soviet Union is at present testing two new ABM systems, and is deploying the Backfire B and four new ICBM systems, it is difficult to see how she could 'react' to the Schlesinger shift for the next five to ten years.

In a technical sense, the development programmes pursued under the mantle of the Advanced Ballistic Re-entry System (ABRES) – for example, MARV and LABRV – and elsewhere should incline Soviet military planners to favour the deployment of their SS–X–16 mobile ICBM and could well promote an enhanced interest in SSBN deployment. but the momentum behind the Soviet strategic effort, and the doctrine that has informed it, is really impervious to American technical interdiction. The Soviet defence effort is moved by forces that far transcend the technical emulation or the offsetting of American weapon systems for strategically rational (by assured destruction criteria) purposes.[46] The advantages and disadvantages to the United States of deploying hard-target counterforce capable systems may be discussed with little fear that baleful arms race consequences will be set in train.

Defensive emphasis

With the lonely exception of the major damage limiting posture, every postural variant thus far discussed in this chapter accepts as a technological, if not political and strategic, fact that whole populations must remain at nuclear risk. All moderate counterforce proposals aspire to the limitation of potential damage by means of targeting restraint and close central control for the effecting of intrawar deterrence.

By contrast, the advocates of a defensive emphasis argue that a fundamental reorientation of defence spending and strategic thinking and planning, assisted by an appropriate arms control regime, could hold out the promise of a major damage denial capability. Defensive emphasisers tend to stress two over-riding objectives: the need to reduce probable casualties, should war occur, and the need to ensure that political advantage cannot be taken as a result of nuclear threats. It would be a mistake to equate sympathy for ABM deployment with adherence to defensive emphasis reasoning. The largest body of pro-ABM opinion was catalysed by the need to provide some active preferential defence for Minuteman silos.[47] Apart from the suspicion harboured by many that any ABM deployment, however respectable (in standard arms control terms) the strategic rationale, serves to keep hopes alive for destabilising city defences, it was difficult to fault hard-site defence options with the logic of assured destruction. Instead, recourse had to be made to the propositions that the weapon system in question would not work as claimed and as required; that ICBM silos did not need defending, in the short term at least; and that progress in SALT would be hindered. Conservative Russians would be obliged to presume that the ABM would work very well indeed and that site defence was the nose of the strategic camel of urban defences.

If the word 'emphasis' is downgraded in significance, it is clear that a variety of defensive options hovers around the postural core. The preferred strategic world of a dedicated defensive emphasiser would have the following features:

1 Offensive weapon systems would be much reduced in numbers and possibly in sophistication. MIRVed weapon systems would preferably be retro-fitted with single warheads. Such a development would reduce the scale of the threat; thereby facilitating the task of defence; and serve to reassure the adversary that one was not bidding for a credible first strike capability

(against ICBM silos). To qualify this logic, payload fractionation by MIRVing is an excellent means for the defeat of BMD (by exhaustion), but it is by no means always the optimal track to pursue in the quest for a good hard-target killer.

2 The above reduction in offensive systems would preferably be enshrined in the terms of an interstate treaty. A unilateral shift in strategic posture of such magnitude might be advisable, regardless of the behaviour of the arms race adversary, but the task of domestic salesmanship would be much facilitated by the fact that parallel action was required abroad.

3 Defensive survival technologies would receive at least as much financial support as would offensive technologies. Heavy urban–industrial ABM defence systems would be developed and deployed. Following a protracted hiatus, the United States would again look very hard indeed at integrated, three-tiered ABM possibilities (boost phase, mid-course, and terminal phase interceptions). Sea based and space based BMD system possibilities would be explored, as would the so called 'exotic' technologies. For the long term, the United States could well decide to fund a space based laser BMD system.

4 Heavy ABM deployment would serve to police an arms control regime that specified a much reduced deployment of offensive missiles. In the face of effective defences, anything short of cheating on a large (and therefore sure to be detected) scale should be of no strategic significance.

5 As strategically logical corollaries to BMD deployment, the United States would have to revive its continental air defence and civil defence programmes.

Taken together, the above developments would represent a fundamental shift in strategic posture. Whatever the logical attractions of defensive emphasis may be (and they are considerable), a number of strategists are prepared to endorse only very diluted features of the doctrine. For example, some strategists of all postural inclinations are willing to endorse the deployment of a thin urban ABM defence system for any number of the following reasons: as a hedge against accidental launchings; as insurance against small scale blackmail possibilities; as insurance against the ballistic behaviour of non-Superpowers; as a means of raising the required threshold for initial countervalue action; as a capability supportive of the flexible options of the new style counterforce thinking. This last point has yet to receive public analytical attention. In fighting a (possibly) fairly slow motion counterforce or counter-combatant war, errors of targeting judgement will probably be made. One way to help defuse the escalatory dangers that would attend the execution of limited counterforce options would be to be able to intercept any small scale ballistic missile strikes against urban–industrial targets (or against military targets that could not be struck without causing immense and unwanted collateral damage). Therefore, some BMD of urban areas would be a way of improving the prospect for the early and non-genocidal termination of a largely counterforce war.

Thick urban ABM defensive options have never been close to official adoption in the United States. General reasons for this may be inferred from the earlier discussion, in Chapters 2, 3 and 4, of arms race dynamics, the character of the American defence system, and the nature of the dominant American strategic ideology. To be specific, defensive emphasis has foundered on the rocks of alleged technological incompetence, a tendency towards ideological endorsement by American strategists of contemporary versions of Stanley Baldwin's maxim that 'the bomber will always get through.' In other words, the ascendancy of the offence over the defence is presumed to be eternal. Military history not being the strong suit of most American strategists, defensive emphasis has been compared with the alleged follies of the Maginot Line. Also, institutional interest in offensive technologies is enormous and no proponent of defensive emphasis can be sanguine about the possibility of effecting the arms control requirement of defensive emphasis for the eradication of MIRV deployment. A defensive emphasis, so the argument goes, must reduce to vanishing point the extended deterrent writ of American strategic forces (Franco-Polish analogies spring to mind here), while – one suspects – an insufficient number of influential people have been prepared to give it serious consideration. Defensive emphasis requires that one abandon the central tenet of the assured destruction ideology, namely, that populations must remain assuredly vulnerable. Finally, defensive emphasis is alleged to be fatally flawed by arms race consequences. In the most thorough-going (if not the most competent) of anti-ABM tracts, it was claimed that:

> We have demonstrated ... that to search for an effective ABM city-defense system against heavy attack is to chase a will-o'-the-wisp. The experience with smaller deployments is valueless because the goal is essentially unattainable. And the terrible logic of the arms race would force the other side to move to offset anything that began to look like a potential defense against a second strike.[48]

Despite the fact that defensive emphasis has scored no direct policy success, the impact of defensive emphasis thinking has been profound. Paradoxically, defensive emphasis doctrine has laid much of the intellectual groundwork for public acceptance of the Schlesinger shift to a more flexible strategic targeting philosophy. However unwilling individual officials and strategists have been to endorse thick ABM defences, part of the case developed in support of such a proposal has received widespread sympathy. Specifically, the proponents of defensive emphasis have developed their case in the sharpest possible counterpoint to a somewhat uncompromising portrayal of the logic of assured destruction. Indeed, the most prominent among them, Donald Brennan, coined the damaging acronym MAD in order to pillory the absurdities that he perceived in the logic of mutual assured destruction.

In a series of analyses, Brennan demonstrated the folly of MAD thinking.[49] In particular, he focussed on three areas of difficulty that beset the MAD bombers. First, despite all efforts and hopes, war could still occur. MAD *guarantees* that such an event would be an unlimited disaster. Second a defence establishment *ought* to seek to defend: it is not funded for the purpose of guaranteeing that over a hundred million Americans remain hostages. Third, the moral implications of MAD logic are quite indefensible. At the very least, says Brennan, MAD bombers and others 'should be looking for ways out of it (a MAD posture), not ways to enshrine it (as in SALT I).'[50]

The technological requirements for a truly dedicated defensive emphasis are onerous. However, a defensive emphasiser could argue that we should not permit the best to become the enemy of the good. Because no system could ever be totally impermeable, it does not follow that the logic of assured destruction, or even of counterforce, need be accepted, however reluctantly. Too often, the enemies of ABM deployment have denounced the defensive track for future strategic posture on the basis of the real and imagined shortcomings of existing technologies. Nonetheless, a system good enough for the preferential defence of Minuteman silos would be unlikely to be good enough to defend urban areas against a determined attack by a first class Superpower. It is for this reason that defensive emphasis requires the support of a congruent arms control regime that would reduce the threat significantly.

Opponents of the logic of defensive emphasis tend to neglect those features of the logic that meet the more salient of their objections. Defensive emphasisers maintain that no defence would ever be so good as to preclude large scale civilian damage. Hence no politician would launch nuclear war lightly. Also, a defensive emphasising country must ensure that it is always able to match the damage that an adversary could cause if he so chose. Even in a world of roughly balanced Superpower defensive emphases, any Soviet proclivity for adventuring (in Europe, for example) should be disciplined by the prospects of a nuclear war that would kill people by the millions. To take those foreign policy chances that carry a very high risk of a central nuclear response is to take a leap into the unknown. Whatever may be the precise character of strategic postures, they have not been tried in action. In short, defensive emphasis is sold as offering a better prospect for the limitation of casualties than do its postural competitors. It is not sold as offering nuclear wars without significant pain.

As an intellectual event in the history of modern strategic thought, defensive emphasis thinking is in the first rank of importance. As a contributor to the policy relevant dissatisfaction felt concerning assured destruction postures, it is also of major importance. But as a serious contender for postural adoption, it is of little significance. By way of illustration of the basis for this judgement, if illustration is required, given the contents of SALT I and prospectively of SALT II, the following words of Donald Brennan are significant:

> In consequence of both my work with Hudson Institute and my occasional consulting work for the government, I have been close enough to the analyses of American positions for the SALT to know what major alternatives and avenues have been considered and examined within the government. I should like to state flatly for the record that no serious consideration has been given to possible alternatives to a MAD posture.[51]

This contention is supported, inferentially at least, by John Newhouse in his study of SALT I.[52]

In terms of putative arms race interactive chains, there is good reason to believing that an urban defensive emphasis would be fairly innocent. American determination to save American lives by a major defensive denial strategy should induce no panic in Moscow. In the context of the placing of severe restraints on offensive developments and deployment, one could even argue that a defence–defence race should be welcomed. In the absence of the placing of severe restrictions on offensive improvement, it is possible that major defensive deployments would be seen by Soviet leaders as betokening the belated conversion of Americans to a sensible balanced and comprehensive war-fighting posture. It is not possible to pass confident judgement on the possible arms race consequences of a shift to defensive emphasis in the absence of firm assumptions concerning the scale and sophistication of offensive deployments. On past evidence, the Soviet Union has betrayed no particularly discernible degree of sensitivity to American urban defensive deployment programmes. The American ABM system effectively halted by the ABM treaty was intended primarily to defend missile silos.

Evaluating strategic postures

In terms of the relations between states, a strategic posture has three general functions: deterrent, defensive, and diplomatic. Unfortunately, at least for neatness of analysis, weapon development programmes do not provide an ever changing menu of items clearly and exclusively intended for one function or another. Adherents may be found to the rival propositions that 'a good deterrent precludes the need for a good defence', or 'the best deterrent is a good defence'. A classic dilemma over which strategic theologians have laboured long and hard, but to no conclusive effect, is that perceived between the defensive and the deterrent worth of strategic forces. Logically at least, the purchase of defensive (or war-fighting) options is deemed likely to be useful should war ever break out. But many analysts believe that the purchase of such options may also make the possibility of nuclear war marginally more likely.

The above somewhat unhelpful generalities should prepare readers for the observation that the kit of seven criteria for a good strategic posture offered earlier is really only of educational benefit. Were my criteria accepted in unamended form and computerised, a programme could not be devised to rank alternative postures in the order of their desirability. To cite but one illustration: criterion number 1 required that the posture be 'unmistakably deterring'. This criterion is not to be bypassed analytically, but what does it mean? The answer cannot help but be time, occasion, individual opponent, and strategic doctrine specific. Nonetheless, however variable the responsible answers may be, it is still desirable that a full range of potential postural characteristics be appreciated.

There are phases in every arms race when the natural and worthy bias of arms control enthusiasts in favour of self-restraint should be accorded no very substantial policy response. The analysis conducted in this book suggests that the great danger over the next decade resides not in the possibility that the United States will be too active in the arms race, but rather that she will not be active enough. Referring to the interactive pattern models of Chapter 4, the action–reaction merchants need to pay rather more attention to the inaction-reaction possibility. Bidding for a politically exploitable strategic lead, the less the United States does under the umbrella of the possible macro response of the Schlesinger shift, the more encouraged are Soviet leaders likely to be to maintain or to increase the momentum of their strategic programmes.

Therefore, *at this point in time,* the honourable causes of arms control and of political stability are best promoted by vigorous arms racing endeavour. This endeavour should embrace a search for lower CEPs and a determination to reduce the Soviet lead in throw-weight. Arms controllers should appreciate that there are no good time-independent strategic postures. My prescription is a prescription for the 1970s and 1980s. It does not betray a general attraction to very vigorous arms race behavior. However, as a general precept, I would endorse a posture that provided more, as opposed to fewer, strategic options and limited as opposed to massive nuclear strike plans, while recording my profound moral distaste for the large scale countervalue targeting requirement of the major variants of assured destruction thinking.

Notes

[1] For the classic statements on the nature and potential functions of arms control see Donald G. Brennan, 'Setting and Goals of Arms Control', in Brennan (ed.), *Arms Control, Disarmament, and National Security* (Braziller, New York 1961), pp. 19–42; and Thomas C. Schelling and Morton H. Halperin, *Strategy and Arms Control* (Twentieth Century Fund, New York 1961). For a wide-ranging examination of the state of arms control understanding and its relation to other policy issues see 'Arms, Defense Policy, and Arms Control', *Daedalus,* vol. 104, no. 3 (Summer 1975).

[2] For the view that the arms controller constitutes a happy blend of *Moralpolitik* and *Realpolitik* see Walter C. Clemens, Jr, *The Superpowers and Arms Control: From Cold War to Interdependence* (Lexington Books, Lexington, Mass. 1973), p. 90.

[3] Brennan, 'Setting and Goals of Arms Control', p. 40.

[4] Ibid., p. 20.

[5] I deal with the subject matter of this paragraph at length in my forthcoming book, *Strategic Studies and Public Policy,* particularly Chapter 5, 'Theory, Technology and Policy'.

[6] Van Cleave, 'Political and Negotiating Asymmetries: Insult in SALT I', pp. 13–14.

[7] In *Cold Dawn.*

[8] For thoroughgoing examples of the flurry of hostile commentaries, see Herbert Scoville, 'Flexible MADness?', *Foreign Policy,* no. 14 (Spring 1974), pp. 164–77; and Barry Carter, 'Nuclear Strategy and Nuclear Weapons', *Scientific American,* vol. 230, no. 5 (May 1974), pp. 20–31.

[9] See James R. Schlesinger, news conference of 10 January 1974 (mimeo); James R. Schlesinger, *Annual Defense Department Report, FY 1975* (US Government Printing Office, Washington D.C., 4 March 1974), pp. 49–78; US Congress, Senate Committee on Foreign Relations, Subcommittee on Arms Control, International Law and Organization, *US–USSR Strategic Policies, Hearing,* 93rd Congress, 2nd session (US Government Printing Office, Washington, D.C., 4 March 1974 [released 4 April 1974]); US Congress, Senate Committee on Foreign Relations, Subcommittee on Arms Control, International Law and Organization, *Briefing on Counterforce*

Attacks, Hearing, 93rd Congress, 2nd session (US Government Printing Office, Washington, D.C., 11 September 1974 [released 10 January 1975]); and James R. Schlesinger, *Annual Defense Department Report, FY 1976 and FY 197T* (US Government Printing Office, Washington D.C., 5 February 1975), pp. II–I–11.

[10] CEP (circular error probable) is an estimate of the radius of a circle within which 50 per cent of the re-entry vehicles are expected to land. Minuteman III has a CEP in the region of 1,000 feet: with the aid of AIRS the CEP could be reduced to 300–400 feet. AIRS is a single instrumentation package which co-locates, in one sphere, inertial navigation aids, thereby reducing cumulative sources of navigational error to only one source of error – and drastically cutting CEP. See *Strategic Survey, 1974,* pp. 46–50.

[11] See 'Nitze Delineates US–Soviet Differences', *Aviation Week and Space Technology,* vol. 102, no. 8 (24 February 1975), p. 63.

[12] Nixon's most explicit call for flexible targeting options was made in 1973 in *United States Foreign Policy for the 1970's: Shaping A Durable Peace,* a report to Congress, May 1973 (mimeo), pp. 180–2.

[13] Wohlstetter, 'Threats and Promises of Peace: Europe and America in the New Era', *Orbis,* vol. 17, no. 4 (Winter 1974), pp. 1107–44. Unlike all previous Secretaries of Defense, James Schlesinger was a well respected and senior strategic analyst long prior to his assumption of office, a man in no need of a crash course in strategic ideology.

[14] Van Cleave and Barnett, 'Strategic Adaptability', *Orbis,* vol. 18, no. 3 (Autumn 1974), pp. 655–76.

[15] Colin S. Gray, ' "The Second Wave": New Directions in Strategic Studies', *RUSI Journal,* vol. 118, no. 4 (December 1973), pp. 35–41; and *Strategic Studies and Public Policy,* Chapters 6–10.

[16] For example, see Jerome H. Kahan, 'Is U.S.–Soviet Nuclear Strategy Really Due for a Change?', *The Washington Post,* 23 April 1973; and Scoville, 'Flexible MADness', pp. 165–77.

[17] See, Colin S. Gray, 'Hawks and Doves: Values and Policy', *Journal of Political and Military Sociology* vol. 3, no. 1 (Spring 1975), pp. 85–94.

[18] See, for example, the arguments in Donald G. Brennan, 'The Case for Missile Defense', *Foreign Affairs,* vol. 47, no. 3 (April 1969), pp. 433–48.

[19] A recent and thorough overhaul of deterrence theory is Richard Rosecrance, *Strategic Deterrence Reconsidered,* Adelphi Papers, no. 116 (International Institute for Strategic Studies, London, Spring 1975).

[20] Dror, *Crazy States,* p. 26.

[21] Brodie, *War and Politics,* p. 378, note 3.

[22] But there is something in the allegation that NATO–Europe believes that its security is maximised by a 'planned insufficiency' of locally provided

forces. (Planned insufficiency is a term borrowed from *Defense Report, FY 1975*, p. 82.)

[23] Each side would have a counterforce, but not a useful damage limiting capability. Damage would be limited, if at all, by the functioning of intrawar deterrence. See *Defense Report, FY 1975*, pp. 36–7; and *Defense Report, FY 1976 and 197T*, pp. II–6–7.

[24] Background briefing on SALT, 25 November 1974 (mimeo), p. C-20.

[25] 'Fratricide' is a condition wherein a nuclear explosion creates so turbulent a local environment that other re-entry vehicles attacking the target in the proximity of which the explosion occurred are destroyed or deflected. See Nacht, 'The Vladivostok Accord and American Technological Options', p. 110.

[26] Unlike their Soviet equivalents, the American team of AWACS–F–15–SAM–D will be deployed for tactical and not for strategic air defence. OTH–B, if and when it is deployed, will provide long range warning of bomber attack, but the urgency of deploying this technology has diminished greatly, given the phasing out of strategic anti-bomber defences. See *Defense Report, FY 1976 and FY 197T*, pp. II–41–5.

[27] Wolfgang Panofsky, 'The Mutual-Hostage Relationship Between American and Russia', *Foreign Affairs*, vol. 52, no. 1 (October 1973), p. 110.

[28] Ibid., p. 112.

[29] See Donald G. Brennan, 'Some Fundamental Problems of Arms Control and National Security', *Orbis*, vol. 15, no. 1 (Spring, 1971), pp. 219–20.

[30] The ABM debate (this is a misnomer) produced new feuds and added fuel to old ones. For a plethora of examples of analytical infighting see 'Guidelines for the Practice of Operational Research', *Operations Research*, vol. 19, no. 5 (September 1971); and its sequel in *Operations Research*, vol. 20, no. 1 (January–February 1972), pp. 205–46. The analytical competence/integrity of the anti-ABM lobbyists was convincingly challenged. It is one thing to tell a man that he is in error; it is quite another to say, in however well-qualified and well-supported a manner, that he has sinned against the Hippocratic Oath of *homo strategicus*.

[31] Robert S. McNamara, *Statement on the Fiscal Year 1969–73 Defense Program and the 1969 Defense Budget*, 22 January 1968 (mimeo), p. 47.

[32] Robert S. McNamara, *Statement on the Fiscal Year 1968–72 Defense Program and 1968 Defense Budget*, 26 January 1967 (mimeo), p. 39.

[33] Testimony of Alain C. Enthoven in *Status of US Strategic Power*, p. 117.

[34] Ibid., pp. 117–18.

[35] A very good hostile life history of assured destruction reasoning in the 1960s is provided in Edward N. Luttwak, 'Nuclear Strategy: The New Debate', *Commentary* (April 1974), pp. 53–9.

[36] Panofsky, 'The Mutual-Hostage Relationship Between America and Russia', pp. 110, 118.

[37] See McGeorge Bundy, 'To Cap the Volcano', *Foreign Affairs,* vol. 48, no. 1 (October 1969), pp. 1–20.

[38] Panofsky, 'The Mutual-Hostage Relationship Between America and Russia', p. 115.

[39] A Soviet Union driven by the fear of American counterforce prowess would not be investing in the *silo-housed* SS–17, 18 and 19 ICBMs.

[40] See, for example, Kosta Tsipis, 'The Accuracy of Strategic Missiles', *Scientific American,* vol. 233, no. 1 (July 1975), pp. 14–23. This is a useful article but readers should be aware that Tsipis' numerous writings on the subject are fraught with persisting arithmetical errors, and with a somewhat eccentric choice in some of the major values assigned (for CEPs in particular).

[41] Bruce Russett, 'A Counter-combatant Deterrent? Feasibility, Morality and Arms Control', in Sam C. Sarkesian (ed.), *The Military–Industrial Complex: A Reassessment,* (SAGE, Beverly Hills, Calif. 1972), pp. 201–42; 'Short of Nuclear Madness', *Worldview,* vol. 15, no. 4 (April 1972), pp. 31–7; and 'Counter-Combatant Deterrence', *Survival,* vol. 16, no. 3 (May/June 1974), pp. 135–40.

[42] Morton Halperin, 'Clever Briefers, Myopic Analysts, and Crazy Leaders', paper prepared for the Aspen Arms Control Summer Study, June 1973, pp. 3–10; and Scoville, 'Flexible MADness', p. 172.

[43] Schlesinger has argued that a counterforce only attack on the United States should result in no more than 'five or six million' fatalities. *Briefing on Counterforce Attacks,* p. 12.

[44] Panofsky, 'The Mutual-Hostage Relationship Between America and Russia', pp. 117–18.

[45] Joseph Kruzel, 'SALT II: The Search for a Follow-On Agreement', *Orbis,* vol. 17, no. 2 (Summer 1973), p. 362.

[46] Note the illustrative examples of Soviet strategic initiatives in *Defense Report, FY 1975,* p. 29.

[47] See, for example, Albert Wohlstetter, 'The Case for Strategic Force Defense', in Johan J. Holst and William Schneider Jr. (eds), *Why ABM? Policy Issues in the Missile Defense Controversy* (Pergamon, New York 1969), pp. 119–42.

[48] Abram Chayes et al., 'Overview', in Abram Chayes and Jerome B. Wiesner (eds), *ABM, An Evaluation of the Decision to Deploy an Antiballistic Missile System* (Signet, New York 1969), p. 49. For fairly comprehensive

listing of the alleged inadequacies of ABM concepts see pp. 57–60. For the basic arguments against BMD see in particular Adams, *Ballistic Missile Defense,* pp. 100–1.

[49] Leaving aside Brennan's many congressional testimonies and the extensive list of Hudson Institute papers, the following brief selection is illustrative of the development of his thought: 'New Thoughts on Missile Defense', *Bulletin of the Atomic Scientists,* vol. 23, no. 6 (June 1967), pp. 10–15; Brennan and Johan J. Holst, *Ballistic Missile Defense; Two Views,* Adelphi Papers, no. 43 (Institute for Strategic Studies, London November 1967), pp. 1–23; 'The Case for Missile Defense'; and 'Strategic Forum: the SALT Agreements', *Survival,* vol. 14, no. 5 (September/October 1972), pp. 216–19.

[50] Brennan, 'When the SALT Hit the Fan'.

[51] Donald Brennan in *Strategic Arms Limitation Agreements,* p. 188.

[52] Newhouse claims that: 'The (SALT) Talks were launched ... from a mutual need to solemnize the parity principle – or, put differently, to establish an acceptance by each side of the other's ability to inflict unacceptable retribution in response to a nuclear attack.' *Cold Dawn,* p. 2.

6 Arms race and arms control

The identification of error is easier than the demonstration of truth. This study has sought to demonstrate that the arms race is essentially driven by the same international political forces necessarily perceived and reacted to domestically) that gave it birth. The importance of the qualification is a function of the level of analysis selected. If one wishes to consider the question 'why is MARV in the FY 1976 budget request?", then one must delve into the further recesses of weapon histories, bureaucratic politics, and organisational momentum. However, if one wishes to ask simply 'Why MARV?', one is drawn to a consideration of the factors that have evoked the Schlesinger shift, of which MARV warheads for the Trident I SLBM (the MK500 Evader) and eventually for the MX and Trident II (the terminally guided MARV) are but one feature. Much arms race analysis has tended to ignore a good part of the action because it has rested upon an unduly simple appreciation of the nature of the questions that could and should be asked of the data.

Much of the domestic process analysis that is becoming increasingly popular falls foul of an unappreciated circularity of logic. Having discovered that weapon laboratories will insist upon providing new weapon ideas, that bureaucrats play games, and that Air Force officers like to fly aircraft, there is a certain 'gee whizzery' about the new wave of arms race investigations. In fact, the discovery of such driving factors as bureaucratic politics, technological innovation, and organisational momentum is really the discovery of necessary truths that explain everything in detail, but nothing overall. All arms races require the activities of bureaucrats, hardware producers, and technologists — so what has been discovered? These sceptical comments do not imply any contempt for such studies. The excellent analyses of, say, Allison, Halperin and Sapolsky[1] both deepen our knowledge of the nuts and bolts of arms race decision making, and demonstrate the fatuity of many of the strategically rational models that have been alleged to fit arms race interactive history.

The most persistent source of error among Western arms race and arms control analysts has been of an ethnocentric character. Soviet arms race behaviour has persisted in betraying a very Soviet distinctiveness. This does not mean that Soviet motivations and doctrine are beyond our comprehension. What it does mean is that we should discard the last vestiges of the notion that there is a general strategic theoretical enlightenment towards which all arms race actors must necessarily strain. The pace of Soviet is deemed to be a function of the pace of Soviet technological development, the strength of bureaucratic interests, and the persuasiveness of American theorists. All that is certain is that American notions of strategic stability and its requirements will eventually be accepted in Moscow. Lest it be thought that the contentions of this paragraph are exaggerated, readers should reflect upon these words by Paul C. Warnke:

> In my view, the Soviets have always lagged behind the United States in their appreciation of the realities of nuclear logic. Since I feel that way and since they have now begun to move in a direction which I regard as being the desirable direction, *I don't think that we should substitute their judgement for our common sense* when it comes to the further accumulation of offensive nuclear weapons.
>
> We should accept, in fact, the reality that the ABM Treaty assures our deterrent for the years to come. We should not yield to the temptation to get back into a numbers race and, as far as any political disadvantage is concerned stemming from the appearance of mathematical superiority, *this can be prevented by a sound, rational explanation of our views to our own people, to our allies and to those who might be disposed to be hostile to us*. (Emphasis added.) [2]

There are several ways in which the phenomenon of American strategists hoping to educate ignorant Russians may be appreciated. There is nothing culpable in seeking to spread the popularity of ideas pertaining to strategic stability. An idea that could, if adopted officially, contribute usefully to the braking of the arms race should be propagated. What is culpable is for strategic thinkers to decline to recognise the facts of doctrinal divergence, of particular strategic interests and advantages, and of individual domestic circumstances. Ideas alone (even when they are congruent with available technologies) tend not to move public policy. Weapons and the strategic doctrine which rationalises and also directs weapons (in a proximate sense) are the instruments of politics. Technical strategic logic will not move Soviet decision makers unless political advantages beckon in the same direction. It is the task of skilful bureaucratic and strategic theoretical protagonists, East and West, to seek to convert their strategic beliefs into the *lingua franca* of political discussion, recognising, of course, that bureaucratic fora, East and West, are very different, as are the items of theoretical baggage inherited from, and partially inspired by, dissimilar national experiences.

One of the arguments advanced in Chapter 1 is worth repeating here: that the phenomenon known as the strategic arms race tends to isolate that which perhaps should not be isolated. In other words, arms race behaviour is really only normal Great Power behaviour somewhat accentuated. The 'somewhat' is perhaps not very great in magnitude. The so called Soviet–American arms race has attained its degree of public prominence for obvious, if potentially misleading, reasons. Specifically: there has never been a race between nuclear powers before; genocidal possibilities attend the race; very large sums of money, in absolute terms, are spent on nuclear arms (though nowhere near as much as some of the popular literature suggests, explicitly and implicitly); the two actors are politically and economically pre-eminent in world affairs; and, finally, one arms racing actor, the United States, has journalistic and analytical industries that thrive on arms race and defence problems. When journalists and analysts talk of the normalisation of Soviet–American relations, one wonders what they have in mind. What, if anything, apart from the destructiveness of the weapons involved and the geographical scope of the interaction, is unique about Soviet–American conflict relations? Clearly, political conflict between powers as great in capabilities (or power potential) as the Soviet Union and the United States is going to be on a grand scale. However, the abnormality of the character of Soviet–American relations, and of the dependent defence policy behaviour, is easily exaggerated.

To cite relational analogues is a perilous enterprise, since prior to World War II, despite occasional aberrational reductions in the number of great powers that played political games, the number of comparable actors always exceeded two. When one considers the arms relationships that characterised Anglo–American relations (from 1916 to the early 1930s), Anglo–French and Russian relations (1840s–1904), Franco–German relations, German–Russian relations, and American–Japanese (and British) relations, one begins to appreciate that in talking of an arms race one is perhaps discussing little more than typical Great Power behaviour. If this reasoning is persuasive, various implications may be discerned. Of relevance to this book is the implication that some of the more dedicated among the arms control fraternity may, from the best of motivations, be attempting the impossible. To attain and then to freeze a weapons plateau describable as being inherently stable would be to deny the very character of armaments as an index of necessarily competing Great Power relations.

The United States has been profoundly ill-equipped, intellectually and in terms of political institutions, to conduct protracted arms control negotiations with the Soviet Union. To Soviet leaders SALT has not provided a forum for the solution or partial solution of the problem mix of the arms race. To Soviet leaders the arms race has presented not problems, but rather opportunities. Strategic weaponry has constituted the elevator of Soviet international status. Soviet leaders have shown little evidence of concern for the braking of the arms race, or for the direction of arms race activity into channels considered benign in the well-disseminated literature of the American arms control community. This means neither that Soviet leaders are strategically illiterate, nor that they harbour first strike intentions. Rather it means that the Soviet Union is governed by men who approach strategic weaponry with the perspective of the requirements of political conflict, rather than with the perspective of Western strategic rationalism. Neither is right or wrong. Each is addressing very different problems. The Western arms controller asks, 'Which weapons, logically, should engender a strategic rebuttal?', while the Soviet political leader may be presumed to ask, 'What is the (offensive) political significance of this, as opposed to that, strategic posture?' At least until SALT was in progress, it was far from certain that the Politburo concerned itself with the detailed direction of the Soviet strategic programme.

Given a political competitive perspective on strategic armaments, it is scarcely surprising that this world view should be reflected in Soviet behaviour pertaining to SALT. Since, in the Soviet view at least, Soviet–American relations is a protracted (and, it is hoped, non-lethal) struggle for relative international political influence, and since the arms race is both a reflection of, and a form for that struggle, it would be strange indeed if Soviet leaders were prepared to adopt a technical arms control framework for the forging of their positions in SALT. This does does not mean that good SALT agreements are impossible (SALT I and the Vladivostok accords for SALT II were *not* good agreements). Rather it means only that it is an illusion to expect that grave strategic problems can be solved through SALT. Enlightened Russians, motivated by a strong desire to descend the futile arms race spiral, will not help solve the strategic problems of the United States through SALT. There is every reason to believe that the Russians in question do not view the arms race in this way. SALT, as with other international negotiating fora, is in the business of registering political facts.

Protracted arms control negotiations certainly help to create new political (and strategic) facts, but it is far from certain that those facts are conducive to the solution of arms race problems. Protracted negotiations evoke bargaining chip arguments in abundance, and they facilitate the promotion of weapon systems that might otherwise meet (in the United States, at least) with a very negative legislative response. Moreover, as Allison and Morris have stated:

> You can't have one agreement, unless you have three. The first two must be among the relevant parties within each government. Then the two governments can come to an agreement.[3]

The 'hedging' or compensation packages demanded by the armed forces of each arms controlling power may more than offset whatever arms race dampening effect is likely to be achieved as a consequence of the interstate agreement. A similar line of argument has been advanced by Feld and

Rathjens. They have argued that protracted arms control negotiations tend to promote unwarranted anxieties concerning the vulnerability of particular weapon systems.[4]

The above arguments, referring to the domestic bargain that must be struck before an arms control agreement is signed, and to the anxieties that arms control negotiations promote (and which may be exploited for bureaucratic benefit), tend to downgrade the importance of purposeful arms race behaviour. In line with the analyses of bureaucratic politics, I would suggest that a good strategic posture and a negotiable arms control package are constructed at home. The United States today is in an unenviable strategic position *vis-à-vis* likely movement in the strategic balance during the period of SALT II (1 October, 1977 – 31 December 1985). This is a direct product of the unbalanced asymmetries codified in the detente supportive terms of the SALT I treaty and interim agreement. These, in turn, reflected the more obvious facts of the dynamic strategic balance. It would be unjust to indict the negotiators of SALT I and SALT II for strategic and political sins, when really the culprits were the defence officials who sanctioned the American strategic posture which is the bedrock of the SALT agreements. However, this is not to say that the front and back channel negotiations of SALT I (and SALT II – to judge from the number of critical issues left for the detailed follow-on negotiations to the Vladivostik accords by Ford and Kissinger), were well conducted from the American point of view.

It could be profoundly misleading to consider arms control prospects in the light of an arms race perspective, unless one is prepared to consider the very strong probability that one of the negotiating parties is not interested in halting the arms race – *approached as an end in itself.*

The SALT II negotiations, which were in a state of total deadlock throughout 1973 and the spring and summer of 1974, were rescued by a 'conceptual breakthrough' effected by Kissinger and Brezhnev during the former's visit to Moscow late in September 1974, and by further mutual accommodations offered at the summit meeting in Vladivostok on 23 and 24 November that year. Kissinger claimed that the accords devised in Vladivostok as a framework for the detailed negotiation of a SALT II treaty on strategic offensive forces, would place a cap on the arms race for ten years.[5] Given the fact that both sides had been seeking earnestly to secure strategic advantage through SALT II, it is appropriate to enquire into the nature of the breakthrough that was effected. The basic agreement at Vladivostok was as follows: the Soviet Union agreed to the establishment of common specified aggregate ceilings for (a) strategic offensive delivery vehicles (2,400); and (b) MIRV-carrying ICBMs and SLBMs – contrary to her previous insistence that the numerical asymmetries of the interim agreement of SALT I were 'completed business'; she also agreed to exclude FBS and British and French strategic forces from the US ceiling(s), and dropped her insistence that the B–1 and Trident SSBN programmes be halted. In return, the United States ceased to demand restrictions upon, or sidepayments for, the growing Soviet advantage in missile throw-weight.[6]

In the course of 1975, apart from the considerable disquiet occasioned by the reports circulated concerning alleged Soviet 'violations' of SALT I,[7] it became apparent that the negotiating parties were far apart on such central matters as the verification of SALT II (defining the counting rules for MIRV launchers), and the question of what, precisely, was to be included within the agreed aggregate ceilings. But of far greater importance – for this book – than the details of disagreement in 1975 is the fact that SALT II does not address *the* critical question for the 1980s, namely, what should be done about the impending vulnerability of silo-housed ICBMs? SALT II permits such a high level of MIRV launchers that the qualitative arms race is bound to be accelerated over the next decade.

Opting for a negotiable, and really cosmetic, SALT II treaty, Kissinger deemed it a matter of *Realpolitik* to legitimise a Soviet MIRV launcher build-up from zero (in late 1974) to 1,320 by the end of 1985 – when SALT II is scheduled to expire. Expressed thus, the common aggregate is equitable enough. But Soviet MIRVs will be married to missiles enjoying an aggregate throw-weight advantage over the United States of close to 6:1 by 1985. Given that the SS–18 Mod. 1 (unMIRVed) and the SS–19 (MIRVed with up to six re-entry vehicles) have already attained CEPs of close to 0.25 n.m., Kissinger's 'cap on the arms race' renders it distinctly likely that the United States will be on the wrong side of a hard-target counterforce gap by the mid-1980s.[8] What this probable fact might mean for Soviet foreign policy behaviour no one can say. A measure of strategic superiority would be a novel condition for the Soviet Union.

SALT II will be defended as a detente promoting measure, as a confidence building measure (the upper limit of each side's building programme will be known), and as the best treaty available. In reply, a strategically educated public should respond to the effect that (a) agreements that are unsound on technical strategic grounds must damage detente in the medium term: there will be a domestic political backlash against a SALT II treaty that cannot fail to lead to acute anxieties over the vulnerability of the principal leg of the triad – the ICBM force; that (b) one cannot have confidence in a treaty that cannot be verified and which will probably exclude some Soviet intercontinental–capable bombers (Backfire B) and strategic cruise missiles; and that (c) the era of arms control by 'promissory note' must be ended. (A poor interim agreement in SALT I was defended on the ground that it was only temporary — a better SALT II would surely follow. SALT II is already being advertised as an imperfect agreement that will facilitate a far better SALT III.)

The only anxieties likely to be promoted in Moscow as a result of Schlesinger's reorientation of strategic American targeting plans and of his enthusiasm for the development of technologies intended to facilitate the execution of limited counterforce options lie in the realm of foreign policy ambitions likely to be thwarted. While it is most unlikely that the Schlesinger shift will accelerate the arms race, it is extremely probable that an eschewal by the United States of the counterforce and 'appearances matter' tracks will simply add to the putative relative Soviet advantage in war-fighting capabilities. The political consequences of strategic imbalance are unknown and unknowable. Should the Schlesinger logic not be sustained in the United States, then it may take an acute international crisis in the 1980s to remind Americans of the political meaning of strategic superiority. Even if that logic does continue to inform US defence policy makers, the depth and breadth of Soviet strategic programmes, conducted in the permissive environment of SALT II, could well produce a strategic non-equivalence that would take many years to correct.

Arms controllability is only one of the criteria of a good strategic posture. If a good posture is not negotiable, it does not follow that one must therefore accede to a bad posture that is negotiable. The record of SALT I, on ABM deployment particularly, shows how an overriding concern for the negotiability of a postural package may result in the severe neglect of national strategic requirements. To many Americans, including very senior officials, SALT I and the Vladivostok accords are political instruments in that they are deemed to comprise the continuing centrepiece of Superpower detente diplomacy. To the Soviet leadership, they are political both in that they symbolise detente, a policy line upon the success of which Brezhnev would seem to have staked his political life, and in that they facilitate the Soviet quest for politically usable strategic power. Military competition and detente diplomacy are not opposed conceptions in the Soviet political lexicon. An eventual collision between the tracks of detente and of vigorous international political competition might be avoided if well-meaning Americans could be induced to accept the new facts of a shift in the balance of Superpower political influence.

If this book may be said to yield a single prescription for the defence policy of the United States it is as follows: the path to equitable arms control agreements and to an eventual deceleration of the arms race now lies, paradoxically, in the direction of more energetic arms race behaviour. A good arms control agreement should reduce the likelihood that war will occur, should help to reduce the damage in any war that might occur, and should reduce the financial burden of defence preparation. SALT I and (prospectively) SALT II fail on all three counts. The United States must now accept the need for the earnest pursuit of a genuine equivalence in strategic capabilities.

Notes

[1] These are respectively: *Essence of Decision; Bureaucratic Politics and Foreign Policy;* and *The Polaris System Development.*

[2] Paul C. Warnke, in *Strategic Arms Limitation Agreements,* p. 181.

[3] Graham Allison and Fred Morris, 'What Determines Military Force Posture?', paper prepared for the Aspen Arms Control Summer Study, October 1973, p. 62.

[4] Feld and Rathjens, 'ASW, Arms Control and the Sea-Based Deterrent', pp. 143–5.

[5] Henry Kissinger, Press Conference in Vladivostok, 24 November 1974 (mimeo).

[6] On the course of the SALT II negotiations in 1974 see *Strategic Survey, 1974,* pp. 60–5.

[7] See Tad Szulc, 'Soviet Violations of the SALT Deal: Have We Been Had?', *The New Republic,* 7 June 1975, pp. 11–15; and Colin S. Gray, 'SALT I Aftermath: Have the Soviets Been Cheating?', *Air Force Magazine,* vol. 58, no. 11 (November 1975).

[8] See Gray, 'SALT II and the Strategic Balance'.

Selected Glossary

AIRS (Advanced Inertial Reference Sphere). A new guidance system designed, primarily, to reduce the gyroscopic drift which degrades missile accuracy. AIRS will be flight-tested for the first time in 1976 and is, at present, intended to be deployed with the MX ICBM. Whereas improvements in the current Minuteman III inertial guidance system should reduce CEP to 700 ft, AIRS is expected to effect a further reduction to 300–400 ft.

AWACS (Airborne Warning and Control System). A system comprising a 'look down' radar and a flying command post for the conduct of air defence operations. Bombers or cruise missiles attempting to penetrate at low levels will be distinguished from the 'ground clutter' that, thus far, has frustrated radar warning systems.

CEP (Circual Error Probable). The measure of missile accuracy – an estimate of the radius of a circle within which fifty per cent of re-entry vehicles are expected to land. All CEP figures are to be treated with scepticism.

Cold launch. A technique by which a missile is ejected from a silo or a launch tube on a submarine by means of low pressure gas. The first stage rocket motors are ignited once the missile is clear of the silo or has surfaced from a submarine. Cold launching means that internal silo shielding may be removed, thereby increasing the usable diameter of a silo by up to fifty per cent (i.e. much larger ICBMs may be launched from the same silos).

Collateral damage. Damage inflicted as a secondary effect of military action. This damage may be viewed as a bonus or as a minus – depending upon strategic doctrine. Some railway bridges over the Vistula happen to be located in Warsaw. In the event of war in Europe, those bridges are prime military targets, but Warsaw is not. Poles killed incidentally as a consequence of NATO strikes against those bridges constitute collateral damage.

Cruise missiles. Pilotless air-breathing vehicles capable of transonic speed and, if desired, a range in excess of 1,500 n.m. These missiles are much cheaper and smaller than are ICBMs or SLBMs. They are also capable of fulfilling a wide variety of tactical missions. First class air defence systems can, in principle, shoot them down, but they should prove highly effective when employed in large numbers and in conjunction with long range ballistic missiles and penetrating manned bombers.

Damage limitation. A strategy that seeks to deny the enemy access to population and industrial targets. The instruments of a damage limiting strategy include counterforce strikes, ABM and air defences, and civil defence.

EMT (Equivalent Megatonnage). A measure of the surface damage that could be wrought by a nuclear force, expressed in terms of 'one megaton equivalents'. Damage from a nuclear explosion diminishes from ground zero as a function of the cube root of the yield of the warhead. Hence, where N is the number of warheads, and Y their yields, the one megaton equivalent of a force may be calculated by the use of the formula $EMT = NY^{\frac{2}{3}}$.

Equal security. The concept advertised by Soviet spokesmen as their objective in arms control and other fora of detente politics.

Essential (strategic) equivalence. The concept proclaimed by Secretary of Defense Schlesinger as the US guiding light in SALT. Like equal security, essential equivalence defies precise definition.

FBS (Forward Based Systems). US nuclear–capable aircraft and missiles deployed in and around Europe. FBS is Soviet terminology and constitutues a hardy perennial on the Soviet-provided agenda for SALT negotiation. In Soviet eyes, any weapon system capable of striking at Soviet soil is a strategic system.

Finlandisation. A political condition wherein a government acquiesces in a tacit Soviet veto over its composition and its policies.

Fratricide. The phenomenon whereby nuclear explosions create such turbulent local conditions that other, in-coming, warheads are damaged, destroyed or are made to deviate from their intended trajectories.

GPS (Global Positioning System). A navigation system comprising twenty-four satellites that are to be 'parked' in synchronous equatorial orbits (that is at orbital speeds identical to the rotation of the earth), designed to provide – on demand – three-dimensional (longitude, latitude and altitude) position fixes for weapons and weapon platforms, to an accuracy of twenty feet. This US system should be fully operational by the mid–1980s.

Hard-target counterforce. A strategic doctrine and capabilities designed to destroy hard military targets (i.e. missile silos and command and control facilities).

Launch on warning (LOW); launch through attack (LTA). Firing tactics for fixed site weapon systems that cannot ride out an attack. LOW means firing on receipt of warning from the Satellite Early Warning System (SEWS), among others, while LTA would have the firing order withheld until some warheads had actually arrived. LTA does, of course, pose the reverse side of the fratricide problem. Namely, that ICBMs might be pinned down in their silos by nuclear effects.

MAD (Mutual Assured Destruction). A deterrent concept which holds that the touchstone of strategic adequacy is a bilateral ability to effect such destruction upon urban–industrial targets that neither side could survive as 'functioning Twentieth Century societies'. MAD is, of course, a pejorative acronym coined in order to pillory the assured destruction reasoning closely associated with Robert McNamara.

Mined cities. A telling debating point invented by Leo Szilard and deployed by Donald Brennan as a *reductio ad absurdum* of MAD reasoning. If MAD should be the strategic conceptual guiding lights in Moscow and Washington, then why not place nuclear weapons beneath the principal urban–industrial targets of each side? By this means MAD capabilities would be ensured.

MX ICBM. The follow-on system currently being studied by the US as a replacement for the 550 Minuteman IIIs in the late 1980s. MX would weigh close to 150,000 lbs (twice the weight of Minuteman III), might be deployed in a land-mobile version, and could well be fitted with terminally-guided MARVs.

PGMs (Precision Guided Munitions) or 'smart' weapons. Strategic and tactical weapon systems that are guided to their targets by means of TV optical, infra-red homing, or laser directed technologies (to cite only the current generation). PGMs are revolutionary in that they offer the prospect of single shot kill probabilities that are close to unity: if a target can be acquired, it can be killed. Whereas AIRS should ensure that a re-entry vehicle carried by an MX ICBM will land within 400 ft of a Soviet silo, precision (terminal) guidance should place that warhead within 30 ft.

Preferential defence. A tactic whereby ABMs would prefer some silos to others. ABM coverage of an ICBM farm would be highly selective. In effect, the enemy would be permitted a free ride to some silos, only to find that other silos were defended very heavily indeed. The enemy could not know in advance which silos would be defended, and in what strength, and which would not.

SAM (Surface to Air Missile)–upgrade. The process whereby high altitude SAM missiles and radars are developed to a level of sophistication capable of providing significant ABM capability. All high altitude SAMs have *some* ABM capability (including the US Nike-Hercules).

SIOP (Single Integrated Operations Plan). The US plan for the large-scale use of its strategic nuclear forces. Schlesinger's new provisions for very 'limited strategic options' are outside the scope of the SIOP – popular belief notwithstanding.

Stability. (a) Arms race. A condition wherein neither side is strongly motivated to improve existing weapon systems, introduce new ones, or increase existing quantitative force goals. (b) Crisis. A condition wherein neither side is seriously tempted to strike first as opposed to second, the first strike bonus being judged to be of trivial worth. (c) Weapon system. A condition wherein one deploys only those weapon systems that are (tautologically) deemed to be stabilising. (If one is a MAD bomber, then urban ABM defences and hard-target capable MIRVs are, by definition, destabilising).

Throw-weight (of a missile). The total weight of the re-entry vehicle(s) plus guidance unit which can be delivered over a particular range and in a stated trajectory.

Trident. Two SLBMs and a class of SSBNs — which gives rise to confusion. The Trident I SLBM should be operational early in 1979 and is scheduled to be fitted into ten new Trident SSBNs and retrofitted on the thirty-one Poseidon bearing SSBNs. Trident I will have a range slightly in excess of 4,000 n.m. and may carry the Mk 500 Evader MARV. Trident II, which can only be carried aboard large new Trident SSBNs, is a system which might be deployed in the late 1980s. This SLBM will have a range well in excess of 6,000 n.m. and should carry terminally-guided MARVs. The Trident SSBN will break with the tradition of sixteen SLBM launch tubes per boat and will, instead, be fitted with twenty-four.

War-fighting. An adjective applicable to any weapon system designed to engage the military forces of the enemy. This is often fallaciously opposed to the idea of deterrence. In principle, at least, a determination to deny is not at odds with an intention to deter.

Index

ABM systems: Soviet Union 24, 89, 92, 101, 104, 110, 115, 116, 118, 122, 123, 169
US: Nike–X 41; Sentinel 19, 35, 102, 117, 118, 124, 159; Safeguard 89, 92, 117, 159, 174; Site Defense 92; general 153, 156–7, 170–4
Action–reaction mechanism 5, 18–28, 44, 92, 96, 100, 102, 104, 105, 110, 118, 123, 125, 153, 157, 175
Adams, B. 102
Air defences, Soviet Union: Tallinn Line 23, 116, 119, 120; SAM-upgrade 81, 89, 116; general 85, 88, 89, 121, 146; in 1950s 114
US 88, 89, 114, 116, 118, 146–7, 171
AIRS (Advanced Inertial Reference Sphere) 87, 131, 132, 134, 154
Allison, G. 28, 51, 124, 181, 184
Arbatov, G. 65
'Armament tension dilemma' 15, 17
Arms control: as a political process 15, 128; domestic debate over 16; limits to 18; as a technical problem 59, 67–8, 131, 137; interdiction for 62; doctrine in the West 75; and a convergence of strategic doctrine 79; Soviet dissent from Western theories of 83; and cruise missiles 89; and rationality postulate 123; nature of 128–30; and land-mobile ICBMs 145; and parallel response 157; doctrine and the ABM Treaty 164; and a defensive emphasis 171; and restraint in the arms race 175; negative effect on arms race 184–5; by 'promissory note' 186–7; and strategic posture 187
Arms race: characteristics of 2, 125, 181; defined 3–4, 96; misleading uses of the term 8; and detente 17; and character of society 31–3; implications of James Kurth's theory 46–7; implications of MIC theories 52; political engine of 65, 99, 105, 142, 159–60, 181; contest between an air/sea power and a land power 71; scholarship and 77; domestic processes and 97–9; genesis of 106; US style in 116; over-reaction in 120–1; identifying actions and reactions 121; and damage limitation 150; and assured destruction doctrine 153; and vulnerability fears 163; theory, naivety in 181; distinctiveness of Soviet–American 183

Baldwin, S. 172
Barnett, R. 135
Berghahn, V.R. 32
'Bomber gap' 101, 107, 116
Bombers, Soviet Union: TU–4 Bull 112; TU–95 Bear 88, 107, 112; Mya–4 Bison 88, 107, 112; Backfire B 88, 169, 186
US: B–29 112; B–47 112; B–52 27, 88, 112, 116, 118; B–70 119, 120; B–1 44, 88, 112, 132, 134, 156, 186; FB–111A 44, 52, 90
Bradley Committee, Report of (30 January 1958) 114
Brennan, D. 129, 130, 173, 174
Brezhnev, L. 64, 65, 81, 109, 166, 185, 187
Brodie, B. 48, 52, 143
Bureaucratic politics paradigm 14, 18, 28–31, 37, 44, 45, 61, 100, 101, 181, 185

C–5A Galaxy 52
Canby, S. 90
Chinese People's Republic 72, 73, 74, 84, 117
Churchill, W. 111
Clausewitz, C. von 71
Command Data Buffer System 132, 145
Counter-combatant strategy 162, 168–9
Counterforce strategy: US fears of Soviet 87, 91, 134; US move towards 138; as a major alternative 138, 142; and assured destruction posture 152; and new technologies 154–5; partial 157–8; and the hard-target option 158–9; outlined 160–70; compatibility with other doctrines 160–1; and value of 'thin' urban area ABM defence 171; and promise of defensive emphasis 173
Cruise missiles, long range 89, 102, 132, 138, 146, 156, 186
Cuban Missile Crisis 109, 120
Czechoslovakia, 1968 64, 68

193

Defensive emphasis: as a major alternative 138; weakness in 144; compatibility with counterforce strategy 160–1; outlined 170–4; Maginot Line analogy 172; reason for opposition to 172; thinking, influence of 172–4; not a serious contender for official adoption 174
Detente 16–17, 136, 186, 187
Dror, Y. 59–60, 142
Dubcek, A. 64

Eigendynamik 6, 100–2, 110, 113–14, 125
Eisenhower, D. 38, 107, 108
EMT (equivalent megatonnage) 4, 36, 120, 152
Enthoven, A. 86, 151
'Essential strategic equivalence' 18, 75, 131
European balance of power system 70
'Extended deterrence' 86, 143, 157, 162–3

FBS (Forward Based Systems) 89–90, 134, 186
Feld, B. 184
Ford, G. 36, 81, 138, 185
Foster, J. S. 22
'Fratricide' 146

Gallagher, M. and Spielmann, K. 13, 30, 52–3, 61
Geopolitik 69
Global Positioning System (GPS) 87, 89, 132
Goldwater, B. 34
Great Powers, behaviour of 3, 7, 73, 104, 182–3
Greenwood, T. 115
Griffiths, F. 62
Guedalla, P. 19

Halperin, M. 28, 63, 102, 165, 181
'Heavy' ICBMs (SALT I definition) 23–4
Hegel, G.W.F. 130
Hoag, M. 135
Holst, J. 66
'Hostage Europe' 71
Howard, M. 32
Huntington, S.P. 8, 106

ICBMs, Soviet: SS–9 9, 91, 101, 117, 120; SS–11, 9, 90, 104, 120; SS–13 120; SS–X–16 90, 99, 118, 169; SS–17 9, 88, 91, 118, 132, 134; SS–18 88, 91, 96, 98, 101, 118, 132, 134, 166, 186; SS–19 9, 30, 87, 88, 91, 118, 124, 132, 134, 186
US: Atlas 113; Titan 113, 165; Minuteman 1 108; Minuteman 111 87, 92, 132, 142, 165; Minuteman, general references 117, 164–5, 170, 173; MX 132, 145–6, 156, 181
Intrawar deterrence 122, 139, 163, 170

Jervis, R. 105
Johnson, L.B. 35, 111
Joynt, C.B. 1

Kahn, H. 133
Kaldor, M. 46
Kaufmann, W. 135
Kennedy, J.F. 35, 105, 108
Khrushchev, N. 61, 64, 81, 105, 109
Kissinger, H. 91, 92, 134, 138, 185, 186
Knorr, K. 143
Kolkowizc, R. 59, 65, 67, 72, 83
Korean War 39, 52, 105, 106–7
Kruzel, J. 167
Kurth, J., on weapon system procurement 43–7, 51

Laird, M. 135
Launch on warning 132, 148
Lenin, V.I. 68
Liddell-Hart, B. 71
Limited strategic options (LSOs) 156–7, 187
Limited war theory 71–2, 86–7, 123

McNamara, R. 6, 19–20, 22, 35, 44, 76, 115, 116, 117, 122, 123, 124, 133, 136, 137, 140, 150, 151, 152, 153, 155, 156, 161
MAD (mutual assured destruction) 2, 20, 47, 59, 76–7, 85–6, 133, 135, 137, 138, 140, 144, 148, 149–60, 162, 163, 164, 165, 166, 168, 169, 172, 173, 176
Madariaga, S. de 48
MARV (manoeuvreable re-entry vehicle) 6, 122, 131–2, 134, 137, 155, 156, 157, 169, 181
M(B)FR (Mutual (and Balanced) Force Reductions) 15, 67
Marshall, A. 103, 135
Middle East in Soviet policy 70, 74
Military–Industrial Complex (MIC) 12, 18, 37, 43, 47–53, 75, 100
Minimum deterrence 140, 148, 156, 157

Mirror-image fallacy 13, 52, 58–9, 61, 87, 123, 181–2
MIRV (multiple independently targetable re-entry vehicle) 6, 19, 24, 35, 44, 53, 87, 91, 101, 103, 104, 109, 110, 112, 113–15, 116, 118, 119–20, 122, 137, 157, 161, 167, 170–1, 172, 185, 186
'Missile gap' 35, 100, 107, 116
Morris, F. 184
MRBMs and IRBMs: Soviet Union 89–90; US 113
MRV (multiple re-entry vehicle) 6, 104, 119

NATO 70, 90, 143–4, 147
Nerlich, U. 78
Neustadt, R. 45
Newhouse, J. 12–13, 59, 63, 80, 82, 131, 174
Nixon, R.M. 34, 135, 140, 155
NSC–68 106

October War (1973) 27, 64, 74
Orwell, G. 32
Overkill 152, 153

Panofsky, W. 146–7, 152, 158–9, 166
Parity 84, 109, 111, 120, 131, 152, 155, 169
Peace research 77
Pearl Harbour 66, 139, 154
Perry, R. 78
Pershing SRBM (short range ballistic missile) 25, 90
Precision guided munitions (PGMs) 145
Programme Evaluation and Review Technique (PERT) 140

Quester, G. 106

Ra'anan, U. 30
RAND Corporation, 'vulnerability studies' by 6
Rapoport, A. 32
Rathjens, G. 20, 21, 22, 118–19, 123, 185
Read, T. 143
Relative damage, as criterion for sufficiency 140–1, 173
Richardson, E. 135
Richardson, General R.C., on 'conceptual lead time' 40
Ruina, J. 42
Russett, B. 162, 169

SALT I: permissive character of 9, 134; and political confidence 16; unhappiness of arms control enthusiasts over 16–17; and the Soviet military 64; competence in 66; violations 81, 186; as evidence of Soviet doctrinal change 86; US counterforce fears and 91; unbalanced asymmetries of 98, 109, 165; and rationales for ABM 114–15; Soviet and US views of ABM Treaty contrasted 122–3; US posture and 156–7; and revision of MAD doctrine 159; and arms control doctrine 164; effect on strategic balance 167; and defensive emphasis 174; and negotiability 187
SALT II: Soviet aspirations following 9, 160; and end of the arms race 21; competence in 66; Soviet counterforce capability and 87, 91, 134; and the issue of Backfire B 88; and cruise missiles 89, 146; throw-weight issue and 91, 132; and strategic projections 98; Soviets building on advantages of SALT I 109, 134, 185; Soviet behaviour during 134, 142, 168, 187; conceptual base for 134; irrelevance of 138, 186; implications for US arms race effort 156; and SALT III 158; and defensive emphasis 174; course of negotiations on 185–6; and detente 186; danger of political backlash against 186
SALT negotiations: and detente 15; dependence upon NPT (Nuclear Non-Proliferation Treaty) 17; public attention to 134; and diplomatic utility of weapons 59–60; bureaucratic games and 63; and political struggle 68; and deterrence theory 75–6; MIRV as bargaining chip in 115; US approach to 131; and inadequacy of arms control doctrine 137; and a technological plateau 137; as a hindrance to defence policy 138; as a permanent seminar 141; and Soviet decision-making 184
Sapolsky, H. 181
Schlesinger, J. 7, 18, 72, 78, 87, 109, 131, 132, 133, 134, 135, 140, 141, 149, 155, 159, 164, 165, 167, 169, 187
'Schlesinger shift', in strategic doctrine 131–5, 140, 143, 144, 149, 156, 161, 164, 166–7, 167–8, 169, 172, 175, 181, 187
'Security gap' (1968) 34
SIOP (Single Integrated Operations Plan) 7, 133, 153, 161
SLBMs, Soviet Union 88
US: Polaris 108, 113; Poseidon 26; Tri-

dent 44, 132, 146, 156, 181
Smith, K. Wayne 86
Smith, Perry McCoy 31
Soviet Navy 117
Soviet Union: threat to Western Europe 3, 9, 90, 143–4; strategic behaviour of 9, 97; attitude to arms racing 15–16, 81, 160, 183–4; arms race goals 18; as a 'strategic man' 29, 30, 76, 110; domestic utility to of arms race 32; arms race performance 45, 121; MIC in 49; domestic forces and arms race behaviour 61–5; missile build-up 64, 83, 85, 105, 109; as a continental power 69–75; determinants of size of armed forces 72; foreign policy goals of 73–4; view of 'stability' 84; motives for MIRVing 113; 'promoted' by Western critics 136; and prospects for SALT III 159; probable view of a US defensive emphasis 174; attitude to SALT 184
Spielmann, K. *see* Gallagher, M.
SSBNs (nuclear powered ballistic missile-firing submarines), Soviet Union: Yankee 60, 88, 104, 112, 133; Delta 60, 88
   US: Polaris 60, 88, Trident 26, 132, 134, 156, 157, 186
Stability 20, 47, 60, 75, 80, 84, 86, 136, 137, 141, 148, 157, 158, 159, 162, 166, 170, 175, 182
Stalin, J. 67, 70, 71, 82
Steinberg, J. 33
Steiner, B. 17
Stellar Inertial Navigation System (SINS) 134, 154
Stone, J. 81
Strategic balance 5, 18, 109, 120, 133, 141–2, 155
Strategic doctrine: functions of 77–9; arms race consequences of asymmetries in 81; Soviet and American contrasted 85; American shift to flexible response 108; of sufficiency in mid-1950s 118; of sufficiency for Soviet Union 120; satisfaction with 136; labels for 149–50; divergence in 182
Strategic posture: defined 138; criteria for a 'good' 139; Soviet and American criteria differ 141; tasks assigned to 143; lead time for changing 144; and SALT 168, 185; three functions of 174–5
Sufficiency, different approaches to 140–1

Tactical nuclear weapons 41–2, 90, 144–5
TERCOM (Terrain Contour Matching System) 89
Threat, functions of 23, 48, 100, 101, 108, 124
Throw-weight 91, 113, 131, 132, 175, 186
Tolstoy, L. 71
Trans-Siberian railway 133
Trenchard, Lord, on strategic bombardment 40

US: spending on strategic forces 4–5; strategic thought 20, 80; control of research activity in 41; missile build-up, 1961–7 58, 105, 118; as arms race leader 60, 82, 112; strategic studies in 67, 130–1; as an insular power 69–75; and Soviet strategic ambitions 111; arms race behaviour of 122; and counterforce doctrine 138; could (and should) race much harder 142–3, 168, 187–8; arms controllers' Pearl Harbour focus 154; poor bargain in SALT I 165; ill-equipped to negotiate arms control with Soviet Union 183–4

Van Cleave, W.R. 66, 135
Vietnam War 52, 71, 137
Vladivostok accords 9, 17, 21, 64, 76, 87, 88, 91, 109, 132, 134, 167, 184, 185, 187

Warnke, P.C. 182
Washington Naval Arms Limitation Treaty (1922) 17–18
West Germany, Soviet anxiety concerning 84
Wiesner, J. 40
Wohlstetter, A. 4, 120, 135
Wolfe, T. 79–80

York, H. 6, 40, 72
Young, E., and 'ripening plum' syndrome 38

The Author

Dr Colin Gray has lectured in Politics at Lancaster University and Political Science at York University, Toronto, and worked for The Canadian Institute of International Affairs. In 1972–73 he was Visiting Associate Professor in Political Science at the University of British Columbia; the following year he was Ford Fellow in the Department of War Studies, King's College, London. He was Assistant Director of the International Institute for Strategic Studies, 1974–75. He has also acted as consultant to the Rand Corporation and to the Hudson Institute, New York, where he is now working.

Other SAXON HOUSE Studies

Hopwood, A. G.	*An accounting system and managerial behaviour*
Black, I. G., et al	*Advanced urban transport*
Pollock, N. C.	*Animals, environment and man in Africa*
McLean, A. T.	*Business and accounting in Europe*
Rogers, S. J., B. H. Davey	*The common agricultural policy and Britain*
Hermet, G.	*The communists in Spain*
Klingen, J. S.	*Company strategy*
Chrzanowski, I.	*Concentration and centralisation of capital in shipping*
Bailey, R. V., J. Young (eds)	*Contemporary social problems in Britain*
Mack, J. A.	*The crime industry*
Sjølund, A.	*Daycare institutions and children's development*
Lewis, C.	*Demand analysis and inventory control*
Jambrek, P.	*Development and social change in Yugoslavia*
Macmillan, J.	*Deviant drivers*
Richards, M. G., M. E. Ben-Akiva	*A disaggregate travel demand model*
Teff, H.	*Drugs, society and the law*
Snickers, F. et al (eds)	*Dynamic allocation of urban space*
Ellison, A. P., E. M. Stafford	*The dynamics of the civil aviation industry*
Birnbaum, K. E.	*East and West Germany*
Masnata, A.	*East-West economic co-operation*
Ghosh, D.	*The economics of building societies*
Richardson, H. W.	*The economics of urban size*
Starkie, D. N., D. M. Johnson	*The economic value of peace and quiet*
John, I. G. (ed.)	*EEC policy towards Eastern Europe*
More, W. S. (ed.)	*Emotions and adult learning*
Grassman, S.	*Exchange reserves and the financial structure of foreign trade*
Thompson, M. S.	*Evaluation for decision in social programmes*
von Geusau, F.A.M.A. (ed.)	*The external relations of the European Community*
Bergmann, T.	*Farm policies in socialist countries*
Ash, J. C. K., D. J. Smyth	*Forecasting the U.K. economy*
Blank, S.	*Government and industry in Britain*
Buttler, F. A.	*Growth pole theory and economic development*
Richardson, H. W., et al	*Housing and urban spatial structure*
van Duijn, J. J.	*An interregional model of economic fluctuations*
Brittain, J. M., S. A. Roberts (eds)	*Inventory of information resources in the social sciences*
Fukuda, H.	*Japan and world trade*
Jackson, M. P.	*Labour relations on the docks*
Stephenson, I. S.	*The law relating to agriculture*
Hess, H.	*Mafia and Mafiosi*
Vodopivec, K.	*Maladjusted youth*
Hovell, P. J., et al	*The management of urban public transport*
Funnell, B. M., R. D. Hey (eds)	*The management of water resources in England and Wales*
Martin, M. J. C.	*Management science and urban problems*
Rhenman, E.	*Managing the community hospital*
Giddings, P. J.	*Marketing boards and ministers*
Klaassen, L. H., P. Drewe	*Migration policy in Europe*
Chapman, C. B.	*Modular decision analysis*

Hodges, M.	*Multinational corporations and national governments*
Liggins, D.	*National economic planning in France*
Friedly, P. H.	*National policy responses to urban growth*
Madelin, H.	*Oil and politics*
Tilford, R. (ed.)	*The Ostpolitik and political change in Germany*
Friedrichs, J., H. Ludtke	*Participant observation*
Fitzmaurice, J.	*The party groups in the European parliament*
Brown, J., G. Howes (eds)	*The police and the community*
Lang, R. W.	*The politics of drugs*
Denton, F. T., B. G. Spencer	*Population and the economy*
Dickinson, J. P. (ed.)	*Portfolio analysis*
Wilson, D. J.	*Power and party bureaucracy in Britain*
Wabe, J. S.	*Problems in manpower forecasting*
Willis, K. G.	*Problems in migration analysis*
Farnsworth, R. A.	*Productivity and law*
Shepherd, R. J.	*Public opinion and European integration*
Richardson, H. W.	*Regional development policy and planning in Spain*
Sant, M. (ed.)	*Regional policy and planning for Europe*
Thorpe, D. (ed.)	*Research into retailing and distribution*
Dickinson, J. P.	*Risk and uncertainty in accounting and finance*
Hey, R. D., T. D. Davies (eds)	*Science, technology and environmental management*
Britton, D. K., B. Hill	*Size and efficiency in farming*
Buchholz, E., et al	*Socialist criminology*
Paterson, W. E.	*The SPD and European integration*
Blohm, H., K. Steinbuch (eds)	*Technological forecasting in practice*
Piepe, A., et al	*Television and the working class*
Goodhardt, G. J., et al	*The television audience*
May, T. C.	*Trade unions and pressure group politics*
Labini, P. S.	*Trade unions, inflation and productivity*
Casadio, G. P.	*Transatlantic trade*
Whitehead, C. M. E.	*The U.K. housing market*
Balfour, C.	*Unions and the law*